# ST PATRICK'S LETTERS

*A Study of their Theological Dimension*

*by*

## DANIEL CONNEELY
(Society of St Columban)

Edited and Presented by **Patrick Bastable**

*together with*

Thomas Finan, Maurice Hogan, Thomas Norris and Pádraig Ó Fiannachta
of St Patrick's College, Maynooth.

An Sagart 1993

Published by An Sagart, St Patrick's College, Maynooth.

The Committee which has edited and presented DANIEL CONNEELY'S work is as follows:

PATRICK BASTABLE, Society of St Columban, M.A., Ph.D., M.Psych.Sc., formerly Lecturer in Philosophy, University College Dublin.

THOMAS FINAN, M.A. B.D., Elève Titulaire de l'Ecole des Haute Études, Professor of Ancient Classics, St Patrick's College, Maynooth.

MAURICE HOGAN, Society of St Columban, M.A., S.T.L., L.S.S., Ph.D., Lecturer in Sacred Scripture, St Patrick's College, Maynooth.

THOMAS NORRIS, B.Ph., D.D., Lecturer in Dogmatic Theology, St Patrick's College, Maynooth.

PÁDRAIG Ó FIANNACHTA, M.A., M.R.I.A., formerly Professor of Modern Irish, St Patrick's College, Maynooth.

ISBN 1 870684 31 1

Typeset and Printed by Leinster Leader Ltd., Main Street, Naas.

Critical Apparatus Typeset by General Typesetting Ltd. (Tel: 01-2842269) and Make-up by Paul Bray Studio (Tel: 01-2894860).

# CONTENTS

Appendices

*Indices*

# Foreword

*by*

CARDINAL CAHAL B. DALY

This volume is a work of *pietas*, in the sense of that Latin word which cannot be translated by any single word in English, but which includes in its meaning such qualities as "dutifulness", "grateful and affectionate dispositions towards someone", "desire to carry out the wishes of a beloved and respected person". In all these senses of the term, this is a work of *pietas*: *pietas* of the late Patrick Bastable towards the original author, his brother Columban, the late Daniel Conneely; *pietas* of a group of Maynooth scholars towards both of these great Columbans; *pietas* of all of these towards St Patrick. It is fitting that Maynooth should have contributed so powerfully towards the final shape of the volume; for Maynooth College proudly bears the name of Patrick, and Maynooth was the cradle of the Maynooth Mission to China, which became the Society of St Columban. Both Maynooth College and the Society of St Columban have continued in modern times the great evangelising work of St Patrick, nourished by the same faith-life as that which made Patrick one of the greatest missionary bishops in the whole history of the Church. It is fitting also that the volume should appear at this time, when we are preparing to celebrate the Bicentenary of the College; and that it should be published by AN SAGART, so long associated with the College. It would be the wish of the scholars who collaborated in the final production that the volume might be seen as part of the celebration of the Bicentenary and might serve as an introduction to a new century of renewed theological and spiritual vitality and new missionary dynamism in the College.

The volume supplies a new dimension to Patrician studies, a dimension missing from many earlier studies, however excellent and irreplaceable these have been. Many learned studies of St Patrick and his writings have not highlighted that which was most formative of Patrick the Christian man and most determinative of his whole life's work, namely his life for and with and in Christ. Patrick was, above and before all else, a Christ-filled and a Christ-empowered man. His letter, the *Confession*, is primarily a paean of praise of the "glory of the grace" of Christ, which made him what he was. The authors encapsulate a whole new vision of the *Confession* in one phrase, when they give it the title: *"Confession of Grace"*. The comparison which they make between Patrick's text and the

*Confessions* of St Augustine is very apt. This aspect of the volume gives it a special relevance and actuality at this time in the national and religious experience of Ireland, a time of rapid social change, when the Christian faith and values which have shaped our identity are under constant challenge. A return to St Patrick, as he is freshly presented in these pages, can be a guide for us through these times and can help us to know who we are as a people and to remain true to ourselves and to the faith-life which has made us what we are, and which has given us our characteristic place in history.

One of the conclusions established by this volume is that Patrick's description of himself as "most unlettered" reflects his humility rather than the objective truth. Patrick emerges from these pages as a "Christian of great competence, a person of intellectual stature, an apostle of faith-life as the Fathers of the Church understood it". His deep and intimate familiarity with Holy Scripture is documented in full detail. His hitherto unsuspected familiarity with the great Fathers of the Church is documented by patient verification of Patrick's quotations from or allusions to the great Patristic authors. References to at least twenty of the Church Fathers are traced in Patrick's two writings. Most prominent among these are St Augustine and St Hilary of Poitiers. Patrick's immersion both in Scripture and in the Fathers is illustrated in this study by evidence of how deeply Pauline St Patrick was in his joyful wonder at the mystery of the amazing grace of Christ, and how deeply Augustinian in his theological understanding of the power and work of grace in the Christian's life.

Like the great Fathers whose thoughts and words he reflects, Patrick was concerned with faith as life in Christ, rather than with intellectual exploration of theories about Christ. His purpose was to share with others that life in Christ which was for him his real life. He stands among those whom we might call the great "autobiographers of grace". His aim was to share his personal experience of grace, his purpose was pastoral, missionary, spiritual. The *Confession* can be read as a forerunner to those great contemporary calls to evangelisation which we find in the Vatican Council's *Ad Gentes* and in Pope Paul VI's *Evangelii Nuntiandi* and in the summons of the Church to a new evangelisation which we find in Pope John Paul II's *Redemptoris Missio*. If the volume serves to deepen faith-life in all its readers and to intensify their desire to share that faith-life with "those who are near and those who are far off", then Father Conneely and Father Bastable will know that their labour in the Lord has not been in vain.

17 March 1993

# Acknowledgements

Bieler's critical edition of the text of St Patrick's Letters is reproduced with the permission of the Controller, Stationery Office, Dublin. A grateful acknowledgment is due to the Board of Trinity College Dublin for permission to reproduce the opening lines of St Patrick's *Confessio* (The *Book of Armagh*, TCD MS 52, fol.22R) on the cover.

In the process of bringing this book to its final form various people have been of invaluable assistance to the Committee. We are most grateful to them: Ms Elizabeth Geraghty, M.Phil., University College Dublin, helped the general editor, Fr Patrick Bastable, in the early stages of the construction of the apparatus from Fr Daniel Conneely's own notebooks; Mrs Phyl Dunne has been of unconditional help to Fr Bastable with the patient task of typing, photocopying, and binding the various drafts required at the different stages of the work; Fr Donald McIlraith, L.S.S., S.T.D., of the Society of St Columban, has helped with the biblical apparatus; the make-up of the whole critical apparatus has been carried out by Mr Paul Bray, a task demanding immense patience and dedication; Mr Stan Hickey of Leinster Leader Ltd. has generously provided the necessary technical assistance; Ms Marie-Thérèse Flanagan, M.A., D.Phil, of the Department of Modern History, The Queen's University of Belfast, has been most helpful with her critical advice and timely suggestions.

We want to acknowledge our particular indebtedness to Mr Aidan Breen, Ph.D., Trinity College, a biblical and patristic scholar, and presently Newman Scholar at University College, Dublin, for compiling the biblical, patristic and conciliar indices, and for a final check of the whole critical apparatus.

After the death of Fr Patrick Bastable, Ms Teresa Iglesias, M.A., D.Phil, of the Department of Philosophy, University College Dublin, colleague and friend, offered helpful advice and tireless assistance to bring the work to its conclusion. We are deeply grateful to her.

Grants for the publication have been gratefully received from the Maynooth Scholastic Trust and the National University of Ireland.

# Preface

St Patrick's letters are the two earliest documents in Ireland's literary heritage which are preserved in the form in which they were originally written. Together they would fill about twenty-four typed pages. They are written in Latin. Both letters are *pastoral* letters.

This is a theological study of the text of St Patrick's pastoral letters. In essence it is a sustained effort to fill an important gap in the work of Ludwig Bieler, the Austrian philologist and palaeographer who, coming to Ireland in December 1939, decided to devote his life to the study of St Patrick. Bieler's great achievement was to produce, from manuscript sources in Ireland, England and the Continent, a critical text of St Patrick's two pastoral letters in Latin, the *Confession* and the *Letter excommunicating Coroticus*. Father Daniel Conneely realised that Bieler's work is incomplete unless scholarship enables us to study the letters in their textual connections with Scripture, with magisterial pronouncements of the Church in contemporary controversies, and with the writings of the Fathers (St Patrick lived at the close of the Golden Age of Patristic literature).[1] In effect, this would result in having alongside Bieler's text, a threefold apparatus (Scriptural, Ecclesiastical and Patristic) enabling us to discern the full theological meaning of the text and to assess it properly.

The author, Fr Daniel Conneely died in 1986 and his work is presented now by a Committee as a whole, which includes two Patristic scholars, Fr Thomas Finan, and Fr Thomas Norris who undertook the most painstaking work of verifying the Patristic links; a Scripture scholar, Fr Maurice Hogan – present members of the staff of St Patrick's College, Maynooth, and Fr Pádraig Ó Fiannachta, formerly Professor of Modern Irish at Maynooth. The general editor, Fr Patrick Bastable, is a Columban colleague of Fr Daniel Conneely and a member of the staff of University College, Dublin.*

The division of labour was as follows: the Patristic and Magisterium sections of the threefold Apparatus is Fr Norris' work, that of the Scripture section is Fr Hogan's. Fr Bastable and Fr Finan made some amendations to Fr Conneely's translation into English of the two pastoral letters. The translation into Irish is the work of Fr Ó Fiannachta. With regard to the Commentary Section: the topics of literary genre and latinity of St Patrick were the responsibility of Fr Finan; Chapter One to a great extent wrote itself from the records of Fr Conneely; Chapter Two was drafted by Fr Norris, Fr Finan and Fr Hogan; Chapters Three and Four by Fr Bastable who was responsible also for the Preface and Appendix.

1. The text will use the convention of *Patrician* as the adjective corresponding to Patrick, and *Patristic* as the adjective corresponding to *Pater*, Father of the Church.

Fr John McAreavey, Professor of Canon Law at St Patrick's College, Maynooth, wrote the "Note on excommunication in the Early Church".

The book falls naturally into three parts. Firstly, Bieler's critical text is presented and, aligned with it, all the textual links there are with Scripture, with writings of the Church Fathers and with decrees of the Ecclesiastical Magisterium. This is the research work of Fr Conneely in its very substance: he wrote persistently of his research as simply "doing the homework" necessary and sufficient so that today anyone could read the pastoral letters with the spiritual pleasure and benefit of understanding all that was really in them.

Part Two of the book consists of new translations of the two pastoral letters. It is *theologically sensitive*, developed as it is from Fr Conneely's research work on the text.

The final part of the book consists of commentaries. Firstly, there is a chapter analysing the rich pastoral theology that is in the two letters. Then there is a chapter developing the concrete significance of the threefold apparatus: the scriptural consciousness of St Patrick and the particular period of the Patristic ethos in which he was educated for the priesthood and wrote his pastorals; also the literary genre of the letters. A third chapter is devoted to an all-important question: since St Patrick's pastorals belong to the Patristic era as distinct from our modern era of theology, how are the two eras properly differentiated? What does it mean to be writing pastorally in the 400s? One cannot read the text perceptively and discerningly without going into this question. The commentaries close with a final, fourth chapter evaluating St Patrick as a pastoral theologian of his time. Fr Conneely always maintained that such an evaluation should be made and that St Patrick, despite the big interruption in his formal education, would emerge as a person of intellectual stature. (This chapter includes a discussion of the latinity of St Patrick.)

The work has a particularly interesting and human history. It was begun in 1961 when Fr Conneely edited a special Patrician Centenary Year issue of the missionary magazine, the *Far East*, and from then until his death, over twenty-five years later, he spent all his leisure time on it.

To his surprise, Fr Conneely found that scholars were not sensitive to the theological gap he had noted in Patrician research. They had been either historians or philologists, finecombing the documents for any light they could yield on the life of St Patrick, on fifth century Ireland and on latinity as such. There was no recognised authority for the theological aspect and there was a prejudice that, while the author of the *Confession* and the *Letter* was a vibrant personality, he was not, in intellect or education, a person of any stature.

One must admire the judgment of Fr Conneely here and the generosity with which he undertook the task of compiling, himself, the threefold apparatus. The Patristic section above all must have appeared a very daunting one. And, indeed, before his death when he had pruned his records very much and disposed of material that was not strictly necessary, he had evidence linking the text of the pastoral letters to over twenty Patristic authors, most importantly with St Augustine and St Hilary of Poitiers.

He hoped not only to communicate his research to scholars but (separately and later) to present, to ordinary people (including teachers and students) his new translation of the two pastoral letters with a commentary on their rich theological, missiological and spiritual content. Ordinary people would then see in the text, substantially, what was there to be easily seen in the fifth century. Also in St Patrick they would be given an experience of a Churchman of great competence, typically Patristic in many qualities of his thought and presentation.

This is the perspective that defines Fr Conneely's work. He was quite clear that he was not attempting, in any way or to any degree, to write a Life of Patrick. He knew that materials for a Life do not exist, since practically every aspect has a background of scholarly controversy, trying to disengage facts and accretions in traditions about his birth and death; whether his "life" is really singular or the fusion of the work of two people; about his captivity and escape, his education and life before appointment as a bishop; his missionary journeys and organisation of the Irish Church; about Slemish, Armagh, Downpatrick, Croagh Patrick, Lough Derg, Tara, Cashel, Saul; about his relics and shrines for them, about manuscripts that contain his writings and folklore that preserve memories of shamrock and serpent; about the Old Irish he spoke; about devotions and festivals honouring him in France, Italy, Spain and Germany. The scholarship required for biographical matters was not his concern. His work was continuously focused on the writings of St Patrick. Being two pastoral letters of a missionary bishop, their content was theological, missiological and spiritual. His work would be completed when that content was fully, properly and universally communicated.

Needless to say, Fr Conneely could not resist the temptation of drawing, privately, some conclusions about the life of St Patrick. The main one was that he was educated for the priesthood in Gaul. However, what comes from Fr Conneely's work is not biographical detail but a demonstration that, substantially, we can read the pastoral letters as if we lived in the fifth century, and that St Patrick emerges from our reading as a Churchman of great competence, a person of intellectual stature, and an apostle of faith-life as the Fathers of the Church understood it.

Patrick Bastable

*Note:* After submitting the typescript for publication, Fr Patrick Bastable died on 27 September 1992. While we are happy to present the finalised work, it is an occasion of sadness for us that Fr Bastable himself did not live to see the fruits of his own dedicated efforts over a period of six years.

The Committee wishes to draw attention in particular to the two distinct but complementary aspects of the work as a whole. The specialising scholar may tend to be more interested in the Latin text of St Patrick's writings and its critical apparatus than in the theological and spiritual commentary of the third part of the work. Conversely, the general reader may be more attracted to this third part than to the first.

Nevertheless, the overall intention of the work could not be fulfilled without these two complementary aspects. For the assertions made, or implied, about the stature of St Patrick – as a man, as a Churchman, as a theologian, as a missionary, and as a man of rich and intense spirituality – these can be substantiated only in and through the close study of his writings. The third part of the present work, therefore, cannot be sustained without the first.

It must be borne in mind that among the Fathers of the Church – the high company to which St Patrick belongs – there was an essential connection between knowledge and holiness, theology and spirituality, responsible thinking and the fertilising faith of a life lived in union with Christ. Consequently, they have no trace of our characteristic contemporary dichotomy between abstract theory and concrete individual life, a duality that threatens both theory and life with sterility. It is easy to see this wholeness in the writings of St Patrick, the existential bond between mind and spirit, head and heart. The present work attempts to develop that perception. It is a collaborative "first-fruits" offering from an attempt to see, through his writings, into the whole man that was – and is – St Patrick.

The Committee
17 March 1993

## Part I

# The Biblical, Patristic and Magisterial Apparatus to the Critical Latin Text of St Patrick's Pastoral Letters

1. Introduction

2. Apparatus

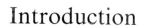

Introduction

# Introduction

As mentioned above, St Patrick's letters are the two earliest documents in Ireland's literary heritage.They are preserved in Latin as they were originally written by him.

Firstly, there is his *Letter excommunicating Coroticus.* There is no manuscript authority for a title to this letter but "Letter excommunicating Coroticus" expresses its content and intent exactly. Coroticus was a Christian British chieftain whose soldiers had carried out a raid in Ireland, slaughtered some of Patrick's converts and sold others into slavery under heathen masters. The letter is often referred to as the "Letter against Coroticus". However its ecclesiastical significance lies, of course, not in its denunciation of Coroticus or in the grief of St Patrick over the fate of his newly baptized converts, but in the fact that it is a letter of excommunication.

*The Confession of Grace* is very generally accepted as being the later of the two documents. This conclusion is based on probabilities of course, but they are very weighty. The title, *Confession*, is indicated in chapter 61 by "Here then, one more time, let me briefly set down the theme of my confession", but even more strongly by the very last sentence of the letter: "And that is my confession before I die" (62). Although not found in the earliest manuscripts, the title, *Confession,* is considered authentic. Expanding it to *Confession of Grace* renders content and intent more explicit. "Confession" for Patrick means "acknowledgment" – acknowledgment of God's mercy and grace bestowed on him throughout the course of his life. There is a small amount of other writings whose attribution to St Patrick is discussed by scholars. They consist of:

(a) three short sayings in Latin, *Dicta Patricii* (Sayings of Patrick); only one of them, an extract from his *Letter excommunicating Coroticus* – "you have gone from this world to paradise" (ch. 17) with the addition of "thanks be to God" – is certainly his;

(b) fragments of a letter to the bishops of Mag Ai, and of another unidentified letter;

(c) two Latin documents purporting to be the decisions of councils of clergy in which Patrick participated, so that the resulting canons or rules would have been endorsed by him.

It is evident that none of these three items is both substantial in content and clearly personal to St Patrick.

To assess the two pastoral letters of St Patrick, theologically, one must read them with the assistance of a threefold apparatus, bringing them into relationship with Sacred Scripture, with the contemporary exercise of the Church's Magisterium in papal, conciliar and synodal decrees, and with the Patristic theology of his time also. The threefold apparatus may be broadly described as follows:

**1. The Biblical apparatus** identifies quotations and allusions made by Patrick from the Bible, but they are limited to such as give evidence of a definite version. It does not include what Bieler calls "echoes of biblical phraseology", however interesting and noteworthy these may be. It provides evidence for:

(a) The extent to which Patrick knew and used the Bible to articulate his own faith-life.

(b) The ideas which constituted his theology.

(c) The extent to which he may or may not have used biblical texts to make up for a deficiency in Latin composition.

The biblical apparatus is arranged according to the following principles:

(i) The biblical apparatus of Bieler is used as a basis. The reader is referred to his two volumes, *Libri Sancti Patricii Episcopi* for a more detailed discussion of biblical texts and versions. This is supplemented from Hanson's *Saint Patrick: Confession et Lettre à Coroticus* and *The Life and Writings of the Historical Saint Patrick*; White's *Libri Sancti Patricii: The Latin Writings of St Patrick*, and the Notebooks of Conneely, wherever it was judged that a biblical quotation or allusion seemed probable.

(ii) References to the Old Testament are from the Vulgate. The Hebrew numbering of the Psalms is given in brackets.

(iii) Biblical quotations and allusions not italicized in the Bieler critical text are italicized in the apparatus *before* the biblical references themselves.

(iv) References to direct biblical quotations are given in the apparatus; allusions judged to be probable are preceded by cf.

(v) Where there is more than one biblical reference in a single line of text, they are separated by // in the apparatus.

The following is a list of Books of the Bible in alphabetical order of abbreviations:

| | | | |
|---|---|---|---|
| Ac | Acts | Lk | Luke |
| Am | Amos | Lm | Lamentations |
| Ba | Baruch | Lv | Leviticus |
| 1 Ch | 1 Chronicles | 1 M | 1 Maccabees |
| 1 Ch | 2 Chronicles | 2 M | 2 Maccabees |
| 1 Co | 1 Corinthians | Mi | Micah |
| 2 Co | 2 Corinthians | Mk | Mark |
| Col | Colossians | Ml | Malachi |
| Dn | Daniel | Mt | Matthew |
| Dt | Deuteronomy | Na | Nahum |
| Ep | Ephesians | Nb | Numbers |
| Est | Esther | Ne | Nehemiah |
| Ex | Exodus | Ob | Obadiah |
| Ezk | Ezekiel | 1 P | Peter |
| Ezr | Ezra | 2 P | 2 Peter |
| Ga | Galatians | Ph | Philippians |
| Gn | Genesis | Phm | Philemon |
| Hab | Habakkuk | Pr | Proverbs |
| Heb | Hebrews | Ps | Psalms |
| Hg | Haggai | Qo | Ecclesiastes/Qoheleth |
| Ho | Hosea | Rm | Romans |
| Is | Isaiah | Rt | Ruth |
| Jb | Job | Rv | Revelation |
| Jdt | Judith | 1 S | 1 Samuel |
| Jg | Judges | 2 S | 2 Samuel |
| Jl | Joel | Sg | Songs of Songs |
| Jm | James | Si | Ecclesiasticus/Ben Sira |
| Jn | John | Tb | Tobit |
| 1 Jn | 1 John | 1 Th | 1 Thessalonians |
| 2 Jn | 2 John | 2 Th | 2 Thessalonians |
| 3 Jn | 3 John | 1 Tm | 1 Timothy |
| Jon | Jonah | 2 Tm | 2 Timothy |
| Jos | Joshua | Tt | Titus |
| Jr | Jeremiah | Ws | Wisdom |
| Jude | Jude | Zc | Zechariah |
| 1 K | 1 Kings | Zp | Zephaniah |
| 2 K | 2 Kings | | |

**2. The Patristic apparatus** like the Biblical one identifies quotations. Vaguer influences from the Fathers and echoes of their phraseology, although noteworthy in themselves, are not identified and included in it. Sometimes conceptual forms in the Patrician text can become decisive for the assertion or denial of a linguistic connection.

The range of Patristic authors in the apparatus is indeed large. There are the familiar names of Ambrose and Augustine, Hilary of Poitiers and Jerome, Prosper of Aquitaine and Cyprian of Carthage. However, less familiar names also figure prominently, such as Arnobius and Cassian, Chromatius of Aquileia and Phoebadius of Agen, Hilary, Eusebius of Vercelli and Gregory of Elvira, Victorinus of Pettau and Paulinus of Nola. More than twenty in all figure in the apparatus. Besides, Patrick's texts link with numerous works in certain Fathers. For instance, there are connections with more than twenty works of St Augustine, ten of St Ambrose and six of St Jerome.

**3. The Magisterial apparatus** links the text with authoritative teachings, i.e. with the Magisterium of the Church exercised in papal, conciliar and synodal decrees of that period. In the early ecumenical councils (Nicea in 325, Constantinople in 381, Ephesus in 431 and Chalcedon in 451), the universal magisterium was stressing, in doctrine, the revelation of God as being mysteriously triune in nature, the fact that Jesus is a divine person and not simply a God-bearing man, and that for our personal salvation (ultimate human well-being), we are dependent on divine grace.

# The Biblical, Patristic and Magisterial Apparatus to the Critical Latin Text of St Patrick's Pastoral Letters

# LIBRI EPISTOLARUM SANCTI PATRICII EPISCOPI.
## LIBER PRIMUS: CONFESSIO.

N. White

235, 2     1. Ego Patricius peccator rusticissimus et minimus omnium
fidelium et contemptibilissimus apud plurimos
patrem habui Calpornium diaconum filium quendam Potiti pres-
5  byteri, qui fuit uico †bannauem taburniae†; uillulam enim prope
habuit, ubi ego capturam dedi.
Annorum eram tunc fere sedecim. Deum enim uerum ignorabam et
Hiberione in captiuitate adductus sum cum tot milia hominum —
secundum merita nostra, quia *a Deo recessimus* et *praecepta eius non*
10 *custodiuimus* et sacerdotibus nostris non oboedientes fuimus, qui
<nos>nostram salutem admonebant: et Dominus *induxit super nos*
*iram*
*animationis suae et dispersit nos in gentibus* multis etiam *usque ad*
*ultimum terrae,* ubi nunc paruitas mea esse uidetur inter alienigenas,
2   2. et ibi *Dominus aperuit sensum incredulitatis meae,* ut uel

---

235: 2     *Patricius peccator* cf I Tm 1: 15-16
  2-3     *minimus omnium fidelium* cf Ep 3: 8-9, I Co 15: 8-10
    7     *Deum enim verum ignorabam* cf Ga 4: 8-9; I Th 4: 3-5; Tb 8: 5; 13: 4,7; Jb 18: 21;
        Ws 12: 27
235: 9     cf Is 59: 13 *Hier^{LXX}*; Dt 32: 15; Ba 3: 8
  9-10     cf Gn 26: 5; Ex 20:6; Dn 9: 4-6
 11-12     Is 42: 25; cf Ps 77(78): 49; 2 Ch 29: 10 (*LXX*)
   12     Jr 9: 16; Tb 13: 4
 12-13     Ac 13: 47
   14     cf Lk 24:45; Ba 1: 22; Heb 3: 12; Ac 16: 14

---

235, 9     *secundum merita nostra, quia...* **Ambrose,** In Ps 118, 4, 11 "Qui se accusat, etsi peccator
        est, justus esse incipit, quia nec sibi parcit, et Dei justitias confitetur"
   14     *Dominus aperuit sensum incredulitatis meae:* cf. **Augustine,** De Praedestinatione
        Sanctorum, 41 "Hoc donum (initium fidei) coelestis gratiae in illam purpurariam
        descenderat, cui, sicut Scriptura dicit in Actibus Apostolorum, Deus aperuerat sensum
        eius, et intendebat in ea quae a Paulo dicebantur (16:14). Sic enim vocabatur, ut
        crederet, Agit quippe Deus quod vult in cordibus hominum"; 40; 34.

15 sero rememorarem delicta mea et ut *conuerterem toto corde ad Dominum Deum meum,* qui *respexit humilitatem meam* et misertus est adolescentiae et ignorantiae meae et custodiuit me antequam

236, 1 scirem eum et antequam saperem uel distinguerem inter bonum et malum et muniuit me et consolatus est me ut pater filium.

**3** 3. Vnde autem tacere non possum, *neque expedit quidem,* tanta beneficia et tantam gratiam quam mihi Dominus praestare dignatus

---

| | |
|---|---|
| **15** | *rememorarem delicta mea* cf Ps 24(25): 16-18; 68(69): 6 |
| **15-16** | Jl 2: 12, 13 |
| **16** | Lk 1: 48; Ps 112(113): 5; 24(25): 16-18 |
| **16-17** | *et misertus est adolescentiae et ignorantiae meae* cf Ps 24(25): 7 |
| **17** | *custodiuit me* cf Ps 24(25): 20; 114(115): 6; 120(121): 7 |
| **235: 17-236: 1** | *antequam scirem* cf 1S 3: 7; Jn 8: 19 |
| **236: 1-2** | *uel distinguerim inter bonum et malum* cf 1K 3:9 ff; Gn. 3:5. |
| **2** | *et muniuit me* cf Ws 4: 17 |
| | *et consolatus est me* cf Ps 118(119): 76; Mt 5: 4 |
| **3** | 2 Co 12: 1 |

---

**14-15** *ut vel sero rememorarem delicta mea et ut converterem...* **Ambrose,** Explanatio in Ps 37, 2 "Plena enim est definitio paenitentiae commemoratio delictorum, ut unusquisque peccata sua velut quodam cotidiani sermonis castiget flagello et commissa sibi flagitia condemnet"; ibid, 31 "Refugit ergo propheta evangelico jam spiritu sapientiam istius mundi, qua non cognoscitur Deus; quae tegit sua vulnera, non revelat ad Dominum. Melior igitur insipientia, quae oculos habet ut videat ulcera sua, quam sapientia quae non habet", cf. in Ps 118, 5, 17; De Poenitentia, II, 38 "Et ideo subjiciamus nos Deo, et non subditi simus peccato, et delictorum nostrorum memoriam recensentes, tamquam opprobrium erubescamus... et tanta fiat conversio, ut qui Deum non agnoscebamus, ipsi eum jam aliis demonstremus"; ibid; 28, 40, 41, 53; Apologia Prophetae David, 1, 9, 48 "Sine intervallo aliquo recordatio et species ipsa mei me erroris inpugnat. Considera quomodo nos confundat, cum aliquid deliquimus, quomodo incurset oculos, quomodo in memoriam semper recurrat"; ibid., 47; Expositio Evangelii secundum Lucam, 5, 55 "(Paulus) vult nos delictorum meminisse nostrorum"; cf. **Cassian,** Collationes XX, 3, 4, 5, 6, 7; **Origen** In Ps 37, 1; **Jerome,** Ep. 22:30; **Paulinus of Nola,** Ep. 23, 7; 29, 3; **Augustine,** Contra Duas Epistolas Pelegianorum, I, 38; Confessions, X, 27; 37

**236, 2** *Consolatus est me ut pater filium:* **Chromatius of Aquileia,** Tractatus in Evangelium Matthaei 5, 5 "Hujusmodi ergo luctum Dominus perpetui gaudii consolatione compensat"; Sermo de Octo Beatitudinibus, 6; **Jerome,** Commentariorum in Esaiam 40:1-2 "Causaque consolationis, remissio peccatorum est"; ibid., 57:17; In Psalmos homiliae 93:19 "Doloris enim magnitudo fiebat materia consolationis"; cf **Ambrose, In Ps** 118, 17, 35; **Hilary of Poitiers,** Tractatus in Ps 125, passim.

**236, 3-4** *Unde autem tacere non possum... tanta beneficia et tantam gratiam quam mihi Dominus praestare dignatus est:* **Augustine,** De Gratia Christi et Peccato Originali, 31 "Istam quippe gratiam qua justificamur, id est, qua caritas Dei diffunditur in cordibus nostris per Spiritum Sanctum qui datus est nobis, in Pelagii et Caelestii scriptis, quaecumque legere potui, nusquam eos inveni, quemadmodum confitenda est, confiteri"; De Correptione et Gratia, 6 "Patimini me paululum, fratres mei, non adversum vos, quorum rectum est cor cum Deo, sed adversus eos qui terrena sapiunt, vel adversus ipsas humanas cogitationes, pro coelestis et divinae gratiae veritate certare"; Expositio Epistolae ad Galatas, Praefatio "Causa propter quam scribit Apostolus ad Galatas, haec est, ut intelligant gratiam Dei id secum agere ut sub lege jam non sint"; **Cyprian,** De Dominica Oratione 33 "Opera Dei revelare et confiteri honorificum est" (Tb 12:7 Vg); cf. **Augustine,** Retractationes, II, 32.

5 est *in terra captiuitatis meae;* quia haec est retributio nostra, ut post
correptionem uel agnitionem Dei *exaltare et confiteri mirabilia eius*
coram *omni natione quae est sub omni caelo.*

4 4. Quia non est alius Deus nec umquam fuit nec ante nec erit
post haec praeter Deum Patrem ingenitum, sine principio, a quo est
10 omne principium, omnia tenentem, ut didicimus; et huius filium

---

| | |
|---|---|
| **3-5** | *tanta ... est* cf I Ch 17: 16, 26 |
| **5** | 2 Ch 6: 37; Tb 13: 7 |
| | *quia haec est retributio nostra* cf Ps 115(116): 12; I Th 3:9 |
| **6** | *correptionem* cf Pr 1: 23, 28-30; 29: 15; Ws 1: 9; 3: 10; 16: 16; 2M 6: 12 ff |
| | *agnitionem Dei* cf Ho 4: 1; 6:6; Ep 1: 17; 4: 13; 2P 1: 2, 3,8 |
| | / / Is 25:1; Ps 88 (89): 6 |
| **7** | Ac 2: 5; Dn 9: 12 |
| **8-9** | cf Is 43: 10-11 |

---

**5-6** *haec est retributio nostra, ut post correptionem vel agnitionem Dei exaltare et confiteri mirabilia eius:* **Augustine,** De Correptione et Gratia, 7 "Quicumque Dei praecepta jam tibi nota non facis, et corripi non vis, etiam propterea corripiendus es, quia corripi non vis... Non vis tibi tu ipse ostendi, ut cum deformem te vides, reformatorem desideres, eique supplices, ne in illa remaneas foeditate. Tuum quippe vitium est quod malus es, et majus vitium corripi nolle quia malus es; quasi laudanda vel indifferenter habenda sint vitia, ut neque laudentur neque vituperentur"; cf. 8-10 passim

**8-9** *Quia non est alius Deus nec umquam fuit nec ante nec erit post haec praeter Deum:* **Hilary,** De Trinitate, IV, 33 "Est enim Unigenitus Deus; neque consortem Unigeniti nomen admittit (sicuti non recipit Innascibilis, in eo tantum quod est Innascibilis, participem). Est ergo unus ab uno. Neque praeter innascibilem Deum innascibilis Deus alius est, neque praeter Unigentum Deum unigenitus Deus quisquam est"; cf. ibid., 35-7; **Prosper of Aquitaine,** De Vocatione Omnium Gentium, I, 7; **Council of Sirmium,** 351 A.D., Anathema XXIII.

**9** *Deum Patrem ingenitum:* **Hilary,** De Trinitate, II, 6 "Ipse (Pater) ingenitus, aeternus, habens in se semper ut semper sit"; 18 "Est ingenitus, qui factus a nemine est"; 19 "... unus ingenitus est"; III passim, 12 times "ingenitus"; III, 18 "Innerrabilis est Pater in eo quod ingenitus est"; IV, 9 "Inter caetera enim addiderunt, solum se Patrem innascibilem cognosse"; V, 36 "...ad Patrem innascibilem Deum"; Fragmenta theologica Arriana 17, "Sine initio ingenitus, omnitenens Deus"; cf. **Phoebadius of Agen,** Contra Arianos, IX, XIV; **Ambrose,** De Incarnationis Dominicae Sacramento, 1, 89f; **Augustine,** De Trinitate, XV, 47.

**9** *Deum Patrem... sine principio:* **Hilary,** Tractatus super Ps 2:13 "Deus (Pater) origine caret"; De Trinitate, IV, 6 "Confitetur Patrem aeternum et ab origine liberum"; 35 "Eius igitur qui sine initio est, demonstrata est dignitas; et eius qui ex innascibili est, honor conservatus est"; II, 6 "Caeterum eius esse in sese est, non aliunde quod est sumens, sed id quod est, ex se adque in se obtinens"; cf. IV, 15; **Arnobius,** Conflictus de Deo Trino et Uno, I, xi "Unus est enim omnium Deus sine principio"; **Phoebadius,** Contra Arianos, XIII 'Pater', inquit, 'major est me' (Jn 14:28). Merito major, quia solus hic auctor sine auctore"; cf. II; XVI; **Gregory of Elvira,** De Fide, 23; 25; **Novatian,** De Trinitate, 31; **Council of Sirmium** 351 A.D., Anathema XXVI.

**9-10** *a quo (Deo Patre) est omne principium:* **Hilary,** Tractatus super Ps 91:4 "... licet per Filium omnia, tamen a Deo (Patre) omnia. Ipse est etenim caput ac principium universorum"; De Trinitate, II, I "Auctor unus est omnium: unus est enim Deus Pater, ex quo omnia"; IV, 6 "Novit enim (Ecclesia) unum Deum ex quo omnia; novit et unum Dominum Nostrum Jesum Christum per quem omnia; unum ex quo, et unum per quem; ab uno universorum originem, per unum cunctorum creationem"; cf. II 6; **(Eusebius of Vercelli), Pseudo-Vigilius Thapsus,** De Trinitate, V, 20; 26; **Paulinus of Nola,** Ep 21, 4.

Iesum Christum, quem cum Patre scilicet semper fuisse testamur,
ante originem saeculi spiritaliter apud Patrem <et> inenarrabiliter genitum ante omne principium, et per ipsum facta sunt uisibilia et
inuisibilia, hominem factum, morte deuicta in caelis ad Patrem

---

**13-14**    cf Jn 1: 3; Col 1: 16
**14-15**    cf Mk 16: 19

---

**10**       *(Patrem) omnia tenentem:* **Prosper,** Sententia 278 "Creatoris omnitenentis omnipotentia
             causa est subsistendi omni creaturae"; Epigram 39 "Deus omnipotens, simul
             omnitenensque potestas, Nil perdit proprium, nil capit occiduum"; Fragmenta theologica
             Arriana 17, "(Pater) omnitenens Deus"; cf. Confessio quae dicitur S. Prosperi, PL, 51,
             col. 610; **Hilary,** De Trinitate, 1, 6; IV, 9; Tractatus super Ps 63:9; **Eusebius of Vercelli,**
             De Trinitate, V, 51-8 passim; **Augustine,** De Genesi ad Litteram, IV, 12:22-3; Tractatus
             in Joannem, 106, 5; Confessions, VII, 11, XI, 13.
**10**       *ut didicimus:* **Ambrose,** De Fide, II, 85: three times "didicimus"; II, 34.
**10-11**    *et hujus filium Jesum Christum... testamur":* **Hilary,** De Trinitate, 1, 23 "... sine Deo
             Christo unum Deum confiteri inreligiositas sit; et confesso unigenito Deo Christo, non
             unum Deum praedicare perfidia sit"; IV, 41 "Deum enim Dei Filium abnegando, non
             tam Deum tamquam solitarium gloriae honore veneraberis, quam Patrem Filii
             inhonoratione contemnes"; VII, II "Innascibilis Pater numquam omnino sine Verbo est";
             cf. I, 17, 26, 38; III, 17.
**11**       *(Filium) quem cum Patre scilicet semper fuisse:* **Phoebadius,** Contra Arianos, XV (XIV) "Non
             solum exivit a Patre sed in Patre et est, et fuit semper"; **Hilary,** De Trinitate, IV, 5 "Cum
             enim vitiose a nobis asserant dici, Filium semper fuisse, necesse est, excludendo quod
             semper fuerit, nativitatem eius confiteantur ex tempore.... Respuere se autem id, quod
             semper Filius fuerit, ob eam causam affirmant, ne per id quod semper fuit, sine nativitate
             esse credatur: tamquam per id, quod semper fuisse dicitur, Innascibilis praedicetur"; IX,
             57 "Fides igitur nostra, etsi initium nativitatis non apprehendens, Unigenitum Deum
             semper profiteatur"; Tractatus in ps 63:10 "Jam si fidem haereticus destruet, Dei Filium
             semper fuisse cognoscet, nullo a Patre intervallo temporis separatum"; cf. De Trinitate,
             IV, 15; VIII, 5; 52; XII, 52; **Eusebius of Vercelli,** De Trinitate, VI, 21 "Maledictus qui
             non confitetur ante omne omnino principium vel initium semper fuisse Filium cum
             Patre"; III, 47 "Numquid... non Deus Dei Filius ante omne omnino principium semper
             cum Patre fuit?"; XI, 3 "Ariani dicunt non semper fuisse cum Patre aut apud Patrem
             Filium vel Spiritum Sanctum"; cf. V, 13, 15, 17, 19, 26; XI, 57; **Gregory of Elvira,** De
             Fide, 27 "Non ergo aliunde quam de Patre (Verbum), quia semper cum Patre"; cf.
             **Vigilius Thapsus,** Contra Arianos, III, 28.
**12**       *ante originem saeculi... genitum:* **Hilary,** De Trinitate, II, 22 "liberum a tempore, solutum
             a saeculis"; I, 34 "ita semper (Filium) fuisse, ut et natum praedicemus; ita vero natum
             esse, ut semper fuisse manifestemus"; cf. II, 12; 17; III, 3; 4; 16; IV, 10; 12; IX, 57;
             Tractatus super Ps 2:23; De Synodis, 26.
**12-13**    *spiritaliter apud Patrem... genitum:* cf. **Hilary,** De Trinitate, II, 19; III, 3; 4; 19 "Quaeris
             quomodo secundum Spiritum Filius natus sit"; IV, 2; 6; VI, 30 "Exisse enim ad
             incorporalis nativitatis rettulit nomen".
**12-13**    *«et» inenarrabiliter:* **Hilary,** De Trinitate, II, 12 "Superest de inenarrabili generatione Filii
             adhuc aliquid";
             **Eusebius,** De Trinitate, V, 25 "Inenarrabiliter natus fuerat (Filius) de Patre"; cf ibid., 31;
             VI, 12; VII, 27; IX, 37; **Hilary,** De Trinitate II, 10; III, 3; 17; 18; 20; VII, 22; **Ambrose,**
             De Fide, I, 67.

15 receptum, *et dedit illi omnem potestatem super omne nomen caelestium et terrestrium et infernorum ut omnis lingua confiteatur ei quia Dominus et Deus est Iesus Christus,* quem credimus et expectamus aduentum ipsius mox futurum, *iudex uiuorum atque mortuorum, qui reddet unicuique secundum facta sua;* et *effudit in nobis*
20 *habunde Spiritum Sanctum, donum* et *pignus* immortalitatis, qui facit

| | |
|---|---|
| **15-17** | Ph 2: 9-11; cf Mt 28: 18; Ep 1: 21; Jn 20: 28 |
| **17-18** | *expectamus aduentum* cf Tt 2: 13 |
| **18** | Ac 10: 42 |
| **19** | Rm 2: 6; Mt 16: 27 |
| **19-20** | Tt 3: 5-6 |
| **20** | Ac 2: 38; Ep 1: 14 |

**13**    *ante omne principium:* **Phoebadius,** Contra Arianos, XVII (XVI) "Dei enim Verbum, hoc est Dei Filius, ante omne principium"; **Hilary,** De Trinitate, II, 14 "(Verbum) jam sine principio est apud Deum, quod erat ante principium"; XII, 25 "Ante tempora aeterna natus est (Filius)"; cf. II, 17; XII, 26; 27; 30; 31; 52; 54; 56; Tractatus super Ps 51:10 "Unigenitus Deus, qui ante saecula natus est". **Eusebius,** De Trinitate, V, 2.

**13-14**    *per ipsum facta sunt visibilia et invisibilia:* **Hilary,** De Trinitate, IV, 6 "Novit enim (Ecclesia) unum Deum ex quo omnia; novit et unum Dominum Nostrum Jesum Christum per quem omnia; unum ex quo, et unum per quem; ab uno universorum originem, per unam cunctorum creationem"; **Eusebius,** De Trinitate, III, 47 "Numquid per hominem visibilia et invisibilia facta sunt, sicut magister gentium testatur (Col 1:15)."

**14-15**    *hominem factum, morte devicta in caelis ad Patrem receptum:* **Victorinus of Pettau,** Commentarius in Apocalypsim, 131 "Novum est Filium Dei hominem fieri; 103; 107-108, 122, 123. **Hilary,** De Trinitate, I, 11 "Verbum Deus caro factum est, ut per Deum Verbum carnem factum caro proficeret in Deum Verbum"; III, 16 "Filius nunc caro factus orabat, ut hoc Patri caro inciperet esse quod Verbum"; 7 "Ipse deinceps homo natus sit, mortem vicerit"; 15 "Dei Filius crucifigitur, sed in cruce hominis mortem Deus vincit"; X, 65 "in coelos receptus"; XI, 36 "post novissime devictam mortem"; Tractatus super Ps 138:19 "Nemo autem... poterit ambigere Deum atque hominem Dominum Nostrum Jesum Christum confiteri et hominem quidem in tempore, Deum vero semper et ante hominem et post hominem; utrumque vero, Deum scilicet atque hominem, tunc tantum cum in homine fuit"; cf. De Trinitate, XI, 40.

**15-17**    *"et dedit illi omnem potestatem super omne nomen.... Dominus et Deus Jesus Christus":* **Hilary,** De Trinitate, VII, 9 "Deum igitur DNJC his modis novimus, nomine, nativitate, natura, potestate, professione"; II, 20 "Deus qui a Deo natus est, non postea quam natus est, sed nascendo Deus extitit... Hinc, 'Omnia quae habet Pater, dedit Filio'"; Tractatus super Ps 65:13. "Unigenitus enim Dei Filius etsi regnavit semper, non tamen semper regnavit in corpore"; cf. Super Ps 2:33; 68:25; 138:5; 143:7; De Trinitate, II, 22; III, 3; VII, 16; 21, VIII, 35; **Gregory Illiberitanus,** De Fide, 88; **Eusebius,** De Trinitate, XI, 12-5.

**17-18**    *exspectamus adventum ipsius mox futurum:* **Hilary,** Contra Constantium, 1 "Christus expectetur, quia obtinuit Antichristus"; in Ps 56:10; De Trinitate, V, 17.

**20**    *Et effudit in nobis habunde Spiritum Sanctum, donum:* **Hilary,** Tractatus in Ps 14:7 "per revelationem ac donum Spiritus Sancti intellegens"; cf. in Ps 52:6; 56:6; De Trinitate, II, 1 "Baptizare jussit 'in nomine Patris et Filii et Spiritus Sancti', id est, in confessione et auctoris, et unigeniti, et doni. Auctor unus est omnium. Unus est enim Deus Pater, ex quo omnia; et unus Unigenitus DNJC, per quem omnia; et unus Spiritus, donum in omnibus"; II, 29 "Quandoquidem (Spiritus) donatur, accipitur, obtinetur; et qui confessioni Patris et Filii connexus est, non potest a confessione Patris et Filii separari"; cf. 33; 34; 35; **Victorinus of Pettau,** Commentarius in Apocalypsim, 119-120; 126; 135.

credentes et oboedientes ut sint *filii Dei* et *coheredes Christi:* quem
confitemur et adoramus unum Deum in trinitate sacri nominis.

5   5. Ipse enim dixit per prophetam: *Inuoca me in die tribulationis*
*tuae et liberabo te et magnificabis me.* Et iterum inquit: *Opera autem*
25 *Dei reuelare et confiteri honorificum est.*

237, 1 **6**   6. Tamen etsi in multis imperfectus sum opto *fratribus et cognatis*
meis scire qualitatem meam, ut possint perspicere uotum animae
meae.

**7**   7. Non ignoro *testimonium Domini mei,* qui in psalmo testatur:
5 *Perdes eos qui loquuntur mendacium.* Et iterum inquit: *Os quod*
*mentitur occidit animam.* Et idem Dominus in euangelio inquit:
   *Verbum otiosum quod locuti fuerint homines reddent pro eo rationem in*
*die iudicii.*

---

| | |
|---|---|
| **21** | Rm 8: 16-17 |
| **23-24** | Ps 49(50): 15 |
| **24-25** | Tb 12: 7 |
| **237: 1** | Lk 21: 16 |
| **5** | Ps 5: 7 |
| **5-6** | Ws 1: 11 |
| **7-8** | Mt 12: 36 |

---

**20-21**   *qui facit credentes et oboedientes ut sint filii Dei et coheredes Christi:* **Augustine,** De Dono
Perseverantiae, 67 "Qui (Deus) ergo fecit illum hominem (Christum), sine ullis eius
praecendentibus meritis, nullum quod ei dimitteretur, vel origine trahere, vel voluntate
perpetrare peccatum; ipse nullis eorum praecendentibus meritis facit credentes in eum";
De Praedestinatione Sanctorum, 6 "Ipse (Deus) igitur fidem gentium facit"; 34 "Quid est
quod ait Apostolus, 'Sicut elegit nos in ipso ante mundi constitutionem' (Ephes. 1, 4)?
Quod profecto si propterea dictum est, quia praescivit Deus credituros, non quia facturus
fuerat ipse credentes... Elegit ergo Deus fideles, sed ut sint, non quia iam erant"; cf. 3;
17-20; 43; Contra duas epistolas Pelagianorum, IV, 14, "Deus ostendit nullis se
hominum bonis meritis provocari, ut eos bonos faciat, id est obedientes mandatis suis";
cf. III, 2; Contra Julianum, V, 13 "Nullum eligit (Deus) dignum, sed eligendo efficit
dignum"; cf. IV, 41; **Prosper of Aquitaine,** Epistola ad Rufinum de Gratia et Libero
Arbitrio, 5; cf. **Augustine,** Tractatus in Joannem 86, 2; Expositio Epistolae ad Galatas,
38; **Council of Carthage** (418 A.D.), Canon 5.

---

**21-22**   *quem confitemur et adoramus unum Deum:* **Hilary,** De Synodis, 41 "Rerum nobis
absolutam intelligentiam ipsa illa nominis religiosa professio tribuit"; cf. De Trinitate, XI, 48.

---

**22b**   *in trinitate sacri nominis:* **Council of Toledo I** *(400 A.D.)* "Credimus in... hunc unum
*Deum et hanc unam esse divini nominis (divinae substantiae) Trinitatem",* in **DS** 188; cf.
Formula "Fides Damasi" Nuncupata, in **DS,** 71; **Ambrose,** De Fide, I, 1, 8 "Si ergo unus
Deus, unum nomen, potestas una est trinitatis. Denique ipse dicit, 'Ite, baptizate gentes in
nomine Patris, et Filii, et Spiritus Sancti', in nomine utique, non in nominibus"; De
Spiritu Sancto 2, 4 "...unus Deus, unus est Dominus, et Unus Spiritus. Et ideo unitas
honoris, quia unitas potestatis"; **Jerome,** Commentariorum in Mathaeum, 28:19
"Baptizantur autem in nomine Patris, et Filii, et spiritus Sancti, ut quorum est una
divinitas, sit una largitio: nomenque Trinitatis, unus Deus est"; **Hilary,** Tractatus super
Psalmos, Praefatio; 13; **Augustine,** Expositio Epistolae ad Galatas, 32; **Eusebius,** De
Trinitate, II, 1.

**8**  8. Vnde autem uehementer debueram *cum timore et tremore*
10 metuere hanc sententiam in die illa ubi nemo se poterit subtrahere
uel abscondere, sed omnes omnino *reddituri sumus rationem* etiam
minimorum peccatorum *ante tribunal Domini Christi.*

**9**  9. Quapropter olim cogitaui scribere, sed et usque nunc haesitaui;
timui enim ne *incederem in linguam* hominum, quia non didici
15 sicut et ceteri, qui optime itaque iura et sacras litteras utraque
pari modo combiberunt et sermones illorum ex infantia numquam
mutarunt, sed magis ad perfectum semper addiderunt. Nam *sermo*
*et loquela* nostra translata est in linguam alienam, sicut facile potest
probari ex saliua scripturae meae qualiter sum ego in sermonibus
20 instructus atque eruditus, quia, inquit, *sapiens per linguam*
*dinoscetur et sensus et scientia et doctrina ueritatis.*

**10**  10. Sed quid prodest excusatio *iuxta ueritatem,* praesertim cum
praesumptione, quatenus modo ipse adpeto in senectute mea quod
in iuuentute non comparaui? quod obstiterunt peccata mea ut
25 confirmarem quod ante perlegeram. Sed quis me credit etsi
dixero quod ante praefatus sum?

238, 1  Adolescens, immo paene puer inuerbis, capturam dedi, antequam
scirem quid adpetere uel quid uitare debueram.
Vnde ergo hodie erubesco et uehementer pertimeo denudare imperi-
tiam meam, quia desertis breuitate sermone explicare nequeo,
5 sicut enim spiritus gestit et animus, et sensus monstrat adfectus.

**11**  11. Sed si itaque datum mihi fuisset sicut et ceteris, uerumtamen non silerem *propter retributionem,* et si forte uidetur apud

---

| | |
|---|---|
| **9** | Ep 6: 5; Ph 2: 12; cf Tb 13: 6 |
| **10** | *in die illa* Mt 7: 22; 24: 36 |
| **10-11** | *ubi... abscondere* Si 16: 16; Rv 6: 15-16 |
| **11** | Rm 14: 12; Mt 12: 36 |
| **12** | Rm 14: 10; 2 Co 5: 10 |
| **14-15** | *didici... sacras litteras* 2 Tm 3: 14-15 |
| **17-18** | cf Jn 8: 43; Ps 18(19): 4 |
| **20-21** | Si 4: 29 |
| **22** | cf Ac 22: 3 |
| **238: 4** | *sermone explicare nequeo* Qo 1: 8 |
| **7** | Ps 118(119): 112; cf 115(116): 12 |

---

**238 1-2**  *antequam scirem quid adpetere vel quid vitare debueram:* **Council of Carthage** (418
A.D.), Canon 5 "Item, quisquis dixerit, eandem gratiam Dei per Jesum Christum
Dominum nostrum propter hoc tantum nos adiuvare ad non peccandum, quia per ipsam
nobis revelatur et aperitur intelligentia mandatorum, ut sciamus, quid adpetere, quid
vitare debeamus, non autem per illam nobis praestari, ut quod faciendum
cognoverimus, etiam facere diligamus anathema sit", in DS 226; **Augustine,** De Spiritu
et Littera, 4 "... ut sciat homo in operibus suis quid evitare et quid adpetere debeat";
**Prosper,** Liber Auctoritates, VII.

aliquantos me in hoc praeponere cum mea inscientia et *tardiori lingua,*
sed etiam scriptum est enim: *Linguae balbutientes uelociter discent loqui*
*pacem.*

10     Quanto magis nos adpetere debemus, qui sumus, inquit, *epistola*
*Christi in salutem usque ad ultimum terrae,* et si non deserta, sed
†ratum et fortissimum† *scripta in cordibus uestris non atramento sed*
*spiritu Dei uiui.* Et iterum Spiritus testatur *et rusticationem*
*ab Altissimo creatam.*

12 15     12. Vnde ego primus rusticus profuga indoctus scilicet, *qui*
*nescio in posterum prouidere,* sed illud scio certissime quia utique
*priusquam humiliarer* ego eram uelut lapis qui iacet in *luto profundo:*
et uenit *qui potens est* et in sua misericordia sustulit me et quidem
scilicet sursum adleuauit et collocauit me in summo pariete;

20     et inde fortiter debueram exclamare ad retribuendum quoque
aliquid Domino pro tantis beneficiis eius hic et in aeternum, quae
mens hominum aestimare non potest.

13     13. Vnde autem ammiramini itaque *magni et pusilli qui timetis Deum*

| | |
|---|---|
| **8** | Ex 4: 10 |
| **9** | Is 32: 4 *LXX* |
| **10-13** | 2 Co 3: 2-3; Ac 13: 47; cf Jr 31: 31-34 |
| **13-14** | Si 7: 16 |
| **15** | *indoctus* Pr 21: 24; Qo 2: 16; 2 P 3: 16 |
| **15-16** | Qo 4: 13 |
| **17** | Ps 118(119): 67; / / Ps 68(69): 15 |
| **18** | Lk 1: 49; Rm 4: 21; 1 Tm 6: 15 |
| **19** | *adleuauit* cf Ps 144(145): 14; *collocauit* cf Ps 112(113): 7-8 |
| **20-21** | cf Ps 115(116): 12 |
| **23** | Ps 113(114): 21; Rv 19: 5 |

**15**     *indoctus:* **Augustine,** Epistola 214, 7 "Si posset hoc ipsum sine adiutorio gratiae fieri per
liberum arbitrium, ut intelligeremus atque saperemus, non diceretur Deo, 'Da mihi
intellectum, ut discam mandata tua (Ps 118:125)'"; De Peccatorum Meritis et
Remissione, II, 5 "Cum jubet (Deus) discendo, 'Intellegite ergo, qui insipientes estis in
populo' (Ps 93, 8), nosque illi dicimus, 'Da mihi intellectum, ut discam mandata tua' (Ps
118:73), quid aliud dicimus quam, 'Da quod jubes?'", cf. De Gratia et Libero Arbitrio,
5; De Continentia, 8; **Jerome,** Dialogi adversus Pelagianos, I, 29; **Pelagius,** Ad
Demetriadem, 2 "Haec igitur prima sanctae et spiritalis vitae fundamenta jaciantur, ut
vires suas virgo agnoscat: quas demum bene exercere poterit, cum eas se habere
didicerit"; cf. Epistola ad Adulescentem 2; 3; Epistola ad Celantiam 13; 14; De Divina
Lege, 3; **Prosper,** Carmen de Ingratis, 395-9; Epistola ad Rufinum, 18.

**17**     *eram velut lapis qui jacet in luto profundo:* **Prosper,** Pro Augustino Responsiones (Gall), VI
"Quoniam priusquam a dominatione diaboli per Dei gratiam liberatur, in illo profundo
jacet in quod se sua libertate demersit".

**23**     *Unde autem ammiramini itaque magni et pusilli:* **Augustine,** De Peccatorum Meritis et
Remissione, I, 54. "Non sint ingrati homines gratiae Dei, pusilli cum magnis, a minore
usque ad maiorem. Totius Ecclesiae vox est, 'Erravi sicut ovis perdita' (Ps 118:176).
Omnium membrorum Christi vox est"; cf. II, 48; Contra Duas Epistolas Pelagianorum, I,
2 "Novi quippe haeretici, inimici gratiae Dei, quae datur pusillis et magnis per Iesum
Christum Dominum nostrum, etsi jam cavendi evidentius apertiore inprobatione
monstrantur; non tamen quiescunt scriptis suis minus cautorum vel minus eruditorum

et uos dominicati rethorici audite et scrutamini. Quis me stultum
25 excitauit de medio eorum qui uidentur esse sapientes et legis periti
et *potentes in sermone* et in omni re, et me quidem, detestabilis
239, 1 huius mundi, prae ceteris inspirauit si talis essem — dummodo autem —
ut *cum metu et reuerentia* et *sine querela* fideliter prodessem genti ad
quam *caritas Christi* transtulit et donauit me in uita mea, si dignus

| | |
|---|---|
| 26 | Lk 24: 19; cf Ac 7: 22; 18: 24 |
| 239: 2 | Heb 12: 28 / / Lk 1: 6; 1 Th 2: 10; 5: 23 |
| 3 | 2 Co 5: 14 |

corda temptare"; cf. I, 12; De Nuptiis et Concupiscentia, I, 22; II, 24; De Dono
Perseverantiae, 30; Epistola 166 ad Hieronymum, 27; Epistola 186 ad Paulinum, 3;
Epistola 191 ad Sixtum, 1; Sermo 115, 4; Contra Julianum, II, 34; V, 49; De Peccato
Originali, 26; 45.

**24**      *et uos dominicati rethorici audite et scrutamini":* **Pelagius,** Ad Demetriadem, 3
"Utrumque nos posse voluit optimus Creator, sed unum facere, bonum scilicet, quod et
imperavit: malique facultatem ad hoc tantum dedit, ut voluntatem eius ex nostra
voluntate faceremus"; 4 "Instruamur domestico magisterio animi: et mentis bona non
aliunde magis quaeque, quam ab ipsa mente discamus"; cf. 8; 9; **Augustine,** Opus
Imperfectum contra Julianum, I, 78 "Libertas arbitrii, qua a Deo emancipatus homo est,
in ammittendi peccati et abstinendi a peccato possibilitate consistit. Emancipatum
hominem dicis (Juliane) a Deo"; De Peccatorum Meritis et Remissione, II, 10; De
Perfectione Justitiae Hominis, 44; Epistola 186, 13; Sermo 155, 2.

**24-25**      *"Quis me stultum excitavit...?* **Augustine,** Contra Duas Epistolas Pelagianorum, I, 37 "Vos
(Pelagiani) autem in bono opere sic putatis adjuvari hominem gratia Dei, ut in excitanda
ejus ad ipsum bonum opus voluntate, nihil eam credatis operari. Quod satis ipsa tua
verba declarant. Cur enim non dixisti, hominem Dei gratia in bonum opus excitari, sicut
dixisti, 'in malum diaboli suggestionibus incitari'; sed aisti, 'in bono opere a Dei gratia
semper adjuvari?' tanquam sua voluntate, nulla Dei gratia bonum opus aggressus, in ipso
jam opere divinitus adjuvetur; pro meritis videlicet voluntatis bonae; ut reddatur debita
gratia, non donetur indebita: ac sic gratia jam non sit gratia (Rom 11: 6); sed sit illud
quod Pelagius in judicio Palaestino ficto corde damnavit, gratiam Dei secundum merita
nostra dari"; cf. 36-8 passim; De Gestis Pelagii, 30; Opus Imperfectum contra Julianum,
I, 48; Epistola 177, 5; Epistola 214 ad Valentinum, 7; Expositio Quarundam
Propositionum ex Epistola ad Romanos, 60-2; **Jerome,** Dialogi adversus Pelagianos, I,
29; **Prosper,** Carmen de Ingratis, 395-9.

**25**      *sapientes et legis periti:* **Jerome,** Dialogi adversus Pelagianos, I, 25 "Dicis, 'Sine peccato
esse non posse, nisi qui scientiam legis habuerit', per quod magnam partem
Christianorum excludis a justitia, et qui praedicator es inpeccantiae, omnes prope
peccatores esse pronuntias"; cf. 29; **Prosper,** Epistola ad Rufinum, 18 "Quicumque ergo
his virtutibus student atque inhaerent, non sua, sed superna sapientia illustrati sunt";
**Augustine,** De Dono Perseverantiae, 43 "Haec ergo dona Dei sunt, id est, ut de aliis
taceam, sapientia et continentia. Acquiescunt et isti: neque enim Pelagiani sunt"; Opus
Imperfectum contra Julianum, II, 13; VI, 36; **Pelagius,** De Divina Lege, 1-3 passim;
Epistola ad Adulescentem, 2; 3; Epistola ad Celantiam, 13; Epistola ad Demetriadem 2;
9

**239, 2**      *cum metu et reverentia:* **Hilary,** Tractatus in Ps 13:1 "cum reverentia et metu".

**2-3**      *ut... fideliter prodessem genti ad quam caritas Christi transtulit et donavit me in vita mea:*
**Augustine,** Retractationes, I, 23, "Iam evertitur heresis Pelagiana, quae vult non ex Deo
nobis, sed ex nobis esse caritatem, qua bene ac pie vivimus"; Ad Romanos, (52) 60
"Propterea ergo intelligendum est, opera bona per dilectionem fieri, dilectionem autem
esse in nobis per donum Spiritus Sancti, sicut idem Apostolus dicit (Rom 5, 5). Non ergo
quisquam gloriari debet ex operibus suis, quae per donum Dei habet, cum ipsa dilectio in
eo bonum operatur"; cf. 61; 62; Epistola 140; Confessions, X, 29.

fuero, denique ut cum humilitate et ueraciter deseruirem illis.

**14** 5   14. In mensura itaque fidei Trinitatis oportet distinguere, sine re-
prehensione periculi notum facere *donum Dei* et consolationem
aeternam,

sine timore fiducialiter Dei nomen ubique expandere, ut etiam *post
obitum meum* exaga<e> llias relinquere fratribus et filiis meis quos in
Domino ego baptizaui tot milia hominum —

**15** 10  (15) et non eram dignus neque talis ut hoc Dominus seruulo suo
concederet, post aerumnas et tantas moles, post captiuitatem, post
annos multos in gentem illam tantam gratiam mihi donaret; quod ego
aliquando in iuuentute mea numquam speraui neque cogitaui.

**16**     16. Sed postquam Hiberione deueneram — cotidie itaque pecora
15 pascebam et frequens in die orabam — magis ac magis accedebat
amor Dei et timor ipsius et fides augebatur et spiritus agebatur,
ut in die una usque ad centum orationes et in nocte prope similiter,
ut etiam in siluis et monte manebam, et ante lucem excitabar ad
orationem per niuem per gelu per pluuiam, et nihil mali sentiebam
20 neque ulla pigritia erat in me — sicut modo uideo, quia tunc spiritus in
me feruebat —

**17**  (17) et ibi scilicet quadam nocte in somno audiui uocem
dicentem mihi: 'Bene ieiunas cito iturus ad patriam tuam', et
iterum post paululum tempus audiui *responsum* dicentem mihi:

---

| | |
|---|---|
| 5 | *in mensura... fidei* Rm 12: 3: cf 12: 6 |
| 6 | Jn 4: 10 |
| | *consolationem aeternam* 2 Th 2: 16 |
| 7-8 | 2 P 1: 15 |
| 16 | *fides augebatur* Lk 17: 5 |
| | *spiritus agebatur* Rm 8: 14 |
| 20-21 | *spiritus in me, feruebat* Rm 12: 11; Ac 18: 25 |
| 22-23 | *audivi vocem dicentem mihi* Ac 9: 4; 11: 7; 26: 14 |
| 24 | Rm 11: 4 |

---

5    *In mensura itaque fidei Trinitatis:* see note at 236, 22b above.

6    *consolationem aeternam:* **Hilary,** Commentarius in Matthaeum, 4:5 "Lugentibus aeternae
consolationis solatia repromittit. Non orbitates aut contumelias aut damna maerentibus,
sed peccata vetera flentibus, et criminum quibus obsordescimus conscientia aerumnosis,
haec sedula in coelo consolatio praeparatur"; **Jerome,** Commentariorum in Esaiam, 40:
1-2 "Causaque consolationis, remissio peccatorum est"; cf. 57:17; **Ambrose,** Expositio in
Ps 118, 10, 34; **Chromatius,** Tractatus in Evangelium Matthaei 5:5; see note at 236:2
above.

7    *Dei nomen:* **Hilary,** De Trinitate, VII, 9 "Deum igitur Domini Nostri Jesu Christi his
modis novimus, nomine, nativitate, natura, potestate, professione"; De Synodis 41; 43-44;
see note at 236, 22b above.

15-6  *magis ac magis accedebat amor Dei:* **Augustine,** De Gratia et Libero Arbitrio, 37 "Unde
est in hominibus caritas Dei et proximi, nisi ex ipso Deo? Nam si non ex Deo, sed ex
hominibus, vicerunt Pelegiani: si autem ex Deo, vicimus Pelagianos"; cf. 38; 40;
Confessions, X, 29; Epistola 140 passim.

25 'Ecce nauis tua parata est' — et non erat prope, sed forte habebat
ducenta milia passus et ibi numquam fueram nec ibi notum
quemquam de hominibus habebam — et deinde postmodum conuer-
sus sum
240, 1 in fugam et intermisi hominem cum quo fueram sex annis et
ueni in uirtute Dei, qui uiam meam ad bonum dirigebat et nihil
metuebam donec perueni ad nauem illam,
18 (18) et illa die qua perueni profecta est nauis de loco suo, et
5 locutus sum ut haberem unde nauigare cum illis et gubernator
displicuit illi et acriter cum indignatione respondit: 'Nequaquam tu
nobiscum adpetes ire',
et cum haec audiissem separaui me ab illis ut uenirem ad tego-
riolum ubi hospitabam, et in itinere coepi orare et antequam
10 orationem consummarem audiui unum ex illis et fortiter exclama-
bat post me: 'Veni cito, quia uocant te homines isti', et statim ad illos
reuersus sum,
et coeperunt mihi dicere: 'Veni, quia ex fide recipimus te; fac
nobiscum amicitiam quo modo uolueris' — et in illa die itaque
reppuli
*sugere mammellas eorum* propter timorem Dei, sed uerumtamen
ab illis speraui uenire in *fidem Iesu Christi,* quia gentes erant — et
ob hoc obtinui cum illis, et protinus nauigauimus.
19 (19) et post triduum terram cepimus et uiginti octo dies per desertum
iter fecimus et cibus defuit illis et *fames inualuit super eos,*
20 et alio die coepit gubernator mihi dicere: Quid est, Christiane? tu
dicis deus tuus magnus et omnipotens est; quare ergo non potes
pro nobis orare? quia nos a fame periclitamur; difficile est
enim ut aliquem hominem umquam uideamus'. Ego enim confidenter
241, 1 dixi illis: *'Conuertimini* ex fide *ex toto corde ad Dominum Deum
meum, quia nihil est impossible illi,* ut hodie cibum mittat uobis in
uiam uestram usque dum satiamini, quia ubique habundat illi',
et adiuuante Deo ita factum est: ecce grex porcorum in uia
5 ante oculos nostros apparuit, et multos ex illis interfecerunt et ibi

---

| 240: 2 | *in uirtute Dei* 1 Co 2: 3-5; 2 Co 6: 7; 1 P 1: 5 |
|---|---|
| | *uiam meam ad bonum dirigebat* Tb 4: 20; Ps 5: 9; 1 Th 3: 11 |
| 15 | cf Is 60:16 (Vulg) |
| 16 | *in fidem Iesu Christi* cf Ga 3: 26 |
| 19 | cf Gn 12: 10 |
| 21 | *magnus et omnipotens est* cf Dt 10: 17 |
| 241: 1-2 | Jl 2: 12-13 |
| 2 | Lk 1: 37 (cf Gn 18:14); Mt 17: 19 |

---

**240, 5-10**  *gubernator displicuit illi et acriter cum indignatione... coepi orare et antequam orationem consummarem... reversus sum:* **Augustine,** Contra Duas Epistolas Pelagianorum, I, 38 "Utquid ista in oratione dicit (Esther) Deo, si non operatur Deus in cordibus hominum voluntatem?... Et convertit Deus, et transtulit indignationem eius (regis) in lenitatem".

duas noctes manserunt et bene refecti et canes eorum repleti
sunt, quia multi ex illis *defecerunt* et secus uiam *semiuiui relicti*
sunt,

et post hoc summas gratias egerunt Deo et ego honorificatus
10 sum sub oculis eorum, et ex hac die cibum habundanter habuerunt;
etiam *mel siluestre* inuenerunt et *mihi partem obtulerunt* et unus
ex illis dixit: *'Immolaticium est';* Deo gratias, exinde nihil
gustaui.

**20** 20. Eadem uero nocte eram dormiens et fortiter temptauit me
15 satanas, quod memor ero *quamdiu fuero in hoc corpore,* et cecidit
super me ueluti saxum ingens et nihil membrorum meorum prae-
ualens. Sed unde me uenit ignaro in spiritu ut Heliam uocarem?
Et inter haec uidi in caelum solem oriri et dum clamarem 'Helia, Helia'
uiribus meis, ecce splendor solis illius decidit super me et
20 statim discussit a me omnem grauitudinem, et credo quod a
Christo Domino meo subuentus sum et spiritus eius iam tunc
clamabat pro me et spero quod sic erit *in die pressurae* meae,
sicut in euangelio inquit: *In illa die,* Dominus testatur, *non*
242, 1 *uos estis qui loquimini, sed spiritus Patris uestri qui loquitur in*
*uobis.*

**21** 21. Et iterum post annos multos adhuc capturam dedi. Ea
nocte prima itaque mansi cum illis. *Responsum* autem *diuinum*
5 audiui dicentem mihi: 'Duobus mensibus eris cum illis'. Quod
ita factum est: nocte illa sexagesima *liberauit me Dominus de*
*manibus eorum.*

**22** 22. Etiam in itinere praeuidit nobis cibum et ignem et siccitatem
cotidie donec decimo die peruenimus homines. Sicut superius in-
10 sinuaui, uiginti et octo dies per desertum iter fecimus et ea nocte qua
peruenimus homines de cibo uero nihil habuimus.

**23** 23. Et iterum post paucos annos in Brittanniis eram cum paren-
tibus meis, qui me ut filium susceperunt et ex fide rogauerunt me ut
uel modo ego post tantas tribulationes quas ego pertuli nusquam ab
15 illis discederem,

---

| | |
|---|---|
| **7** | cf Mt 15: 32; / / Lk 10: 30 |
| **11** | Mt 3: 4; Mk 1: 6 / / Lk 24: 42 |
| **12** | cf 1 Co 10: 28 |
| **14-15** | *temptauit me satanas* Ac 5: 3; 1 Co 7: 5 |
| **15** | cf 2 P 1: 13 |
| **22** | cf Ps 49(50): 15 *(LXX)* |
| **241: 23-242:2** | Mt 10: 19-20 |
| **4** | Rm 11: 4 |
| **6-7** | Gn 37: 21 |

---

**241, 17**     *unde me venit ignaro in spiritu:* see note at 238, 24-5 above.

et ibi scilicet *uidi in uisu noctis* uirum uenientem quasi de
Hiberione, cui nomen Victoricus, cum epistolis innumerabilibus,
et dedit mihi unam ex his et legi principium epistolae continen-
tem 'Vox Hiberionacum', et cum recitabam principium epistolae
20 putabam ipso momento audire uocem ipsorum, qui erant iuxta
siluam Vocluti quae est prope mare occidentale, et sic exclamaue-
runt *quasi ex uno ore:* Rogamus te, [sancte] puer, ut uenias et adhuc
ambulas inter nos',
243, 1 et ualde *compunctus sum corde* et amplius non potui legere et sic
expertus sum. Deo gratias, quia post plurimos annos praestitit illis
Dominus secundum clamorem illorum.

**24**     24. Et alia nocte — *nescio, Deus scit,* utrum in me an iuxta me —
5 uerbis peritissime, quos ego audiui et non potui intellegere, nisi
ad postremum orationis sic effitiatus est: '*Qui dedit animam suam pro te,*
ipse est qui loquitur in te', et sic expertus sum gaudibun-
dus.

**25**     25. Et iterum uidi in me ipsum orantem et eram quasi intra
corpus meum et audiui super me, hoc est super *interiorem hominem,*
10 et ibi fortiter orabat gemitibus, et inter haec *stupebam et ammira-*
*bam et cogitabam* quis esset qui in me orabat, sed ad postremum
orationis sic effitiatus est ut sit Spiritus, et sic expertus sum et
recordatus sum apostolo dicente: *Spiritus adiuuat infirmitates orationis*
*nostrae: nam quod oremus sicut oportet nescimus: sed ipse Spiritus*
15 *postulat pro nobis gemitibus inenarrabilibus, quae uerbis exprimi non*
*possunt;* et iterum: *Dominus aduocatus noster postulat pro nobis.*

**26**     26. Et quando temptatus sum ab aliquantis senioribus meis, qui
uenerunt, et peccata mea, contra laboriosum episcopatum meum,

---

|        |                                                        |
|--------|--------------------------------------------------------|
| **16** | Dn 7:13; cf Jb 4:13                                    |
| **22** | Dn 3:51                                                 |
| **243: 1** | cf Ac 2: 37; Ps 108(109): 17                       |
| **4**  | 2 Co 12: 2-3                                            |
| **6**  | 1 Jn 3: 16                                              |
| **7**  | *ipse est qui loquitur in te* cf. 2 Co 13:3; Jn 4:26; 9:37; Mt 10:19 |
| **9**  | Rm 7:22; Ep 3:16                                        |
| **10-11** | Is 29: 9; Ac 2: 12; 8: 13                           |
|        | cf Dn 8: 27 *(VULG)*; Hab 1: 5 (Is 29: 9, 14); cf Lk 1: 29 |
| **13-16** | Rm 8: 26                                            |
| **16** | 1 Jn 2: 1; cf Rm 8: 27, 34                             |

---

**243, 6-9**     *Qui dedit animam... super interiorem hominem:* **Augustine**, Confessions, VII, 10 "Intravi et
vidi qualicumque oculo animae meae supra eundem oculum animae meae, supra
mentem meam lucem incommutabilem, non hanc vulgarem et conspicuam... sed aliud,
aliud valde ab istis omnibus. Nec ita erat supra mentem meam, sicut oleum super aquam
nec sicut caelum super terram, sed superior, quia ipsa fecit me, et ego inferior, quia
factus ab ea"; cf. X, 6-8.

utique illo die fortiter *impulsus sum ut caderem* hic et in aeternum;
20 sed Dominus pepercit proselito et peregrino propter nomen suum benigne

et ualde mihi subuenit in hac conculcatione. Quod in labe et in obprobrium non male deueni! Deum oro ut *non illis in peccatum reputetur.*

**27**   27. *Occasionem* post annos triginta *inuenerunt me aduersus* uerbum quod confessus fueram antequam essem diaconus. Propter

244, 1   anxietatem maesto animo insinuaui amicissimo meo quae in pueritia mea una die gesseram, immo in una hora, quia necdum praeualebam. *Nescio, Deus scit,* si habebam tunc annos quindecim, et Deum uiuum non credebam, neque ex infantia mea, sed in morte et in increduli-

5 tate mansi donec ualde castigatus sum *et in ueritate humiliatus sum a fame et nuditate,* et cotidie.

**28**   28. Contra, Hiberione non sponte pergebam, *donec* prope *deficiebam;* sed hoc potius bene mihi fuit, qui ex hoc emendatus sum a Domino, et aptauit me ut hodie essem quod aliquando longe a me

10 erat, ut ego curam haberem aut satagerem pro salute aliorum, quando autem tunc etiam de me ipso non cogitabam.

---

| | |
|---|---|
| **19** | Ps 117(118): 13 |
| **22** | Dt 23: 21; 24: 15; cf 1 Ch 21: 3; 2 Tm 4: 16 |
| **23** | Dn 6: 5 |
| **244: 3** | 2 Co 12: 2, 3 |
| **5** | *castigatus sum* cf Ps 117(118): 18; / / Ps 118(119): 75 |
| **6** | Dt 28: 48; 2 Co 11: 27 |
| **7** | Ps 17(18): 28; 70(71): 9 |
| **9** | *aptauit me* Heb 13: 21 |

---

**243, 24-244,2** *verbum quod confessus fueram antequam essem diaconus... necdum praevalebam:* cf. **Council of Elvira** (inter 300-3 A.D.?) Canons 30; 76; **Synod of Neocaesarea** (a.319?), Canon 9; **Council of Nicaea**, Canon 9; **Council of Valence** 374 A.D., Canon 4; **Jerome** In Epistolam ad Titum Commentarium. "Primum itaque sine crimine sit (Tit 1:6,7): quod puto alio verbo ad Timotheum 'irreprehensibilem' nominatum (I Tim 3:2): non quod eo tantum tempore quo ordinandus est sine ullo sit crimine, et praeteritas maculas nova conversatione diluerit: sed ex eo tempore quo in Christo renatus est, nulla peccati conscientia remordeatur. Quomodo enim potest praeses Ecclesiae auferre malum de medio eius, qui in delicto simili corruerit?" cf. **Augustine,** Contra duas epistolas Pelagianorum, I, 28; Tractatus in Joannem 41, 10; Epistola 145, 45; Confessions II, 3.

**8-9**   *ex hoc emendatus sum a Dominio:* **Hilary,** Tractatus in Ps 118, 9, 8 "Bona omnis passio, bonae omnes tribulationes, per quas justificationes Dei cognoscuntur: ut peccantes humilitate emendet"; **Ambrose,** Expositio in Ps 118, 9, 14 "Jure ergo tentationibus traditus est, quoniam delinquebat autem, quia Dei eloquium non tenebat. Verum inde ordinem emandationis invenit, unde culpa processerat"; **Jerome,** In Psalmos homiliae 93, 19 "Doloris enim magnitudo fiebat materia consolationis".

**9**   *aptavit:* **Prosper,** Carmen de Ingratis, II, 239-41. "Objectum est aliud ipsum dixisse magistrum: Quod meritis hominum tribuatur gratia Christi, Quantum quisque Dei donis se fecerit aptum"; cf. **Irenaeus,** Adversus Haereses, III, 17, 2.

**29**     29. Igitur in illo die quo *reprobatus sum* a memoratis supradictis
ad noctem illam *vidi in uisu noctis* scriptum erat contra faciem
meam sine honore, et inter haec audiui *responsum diuinum* dicen-
15  tem mihi: Male uidimus faciem designati nudato nomine, nec
sic praedixit: Male uidisti, sed: Male uidimus, quasi sibi se iunxisset,
sicut dixit: *Qui uos tangit quasi qui tangit pupillam oculi mei.*

**30**     30. Idcirco *gratias ago ei qui me* in omnibus *confortauit,* ut non me
impediret a profectione quam statueram et de mea quoque opera
20  quod a Christo Domino meo didiceram, sed magis ex eo *sensi in
me uirtutem* non paruam et fides mea probata est coram Deo et
hominibus.

**31**     31. Vnde autem *audenter dico* non me reprehendit conscientia
mea hic et in futurum: *teste Deo* habeo *quia non sum mentitus*
25  in sermonibus quos ego retuli uobis.

**32**     32. Sed magis doleo pro amicissimo meo cur hoc meruimus audire
tale responsum. Cui ego credidi etiam animam! Et comperi ab
aliquantis fratribus ante defensionem illam (quod ego non interfui
245, 1  nec in Brittanniis eram nec a me orie<ba>tur) ut et ille in mea absentia
pulsaret pro me; etiam mihi ipse ore suo dixerat: 'Ecce dandus es
tu ad gradum episcopatus', quod non eram dignus. Sed unde uenit
illi postmodum ut coram cunctis, bonis et malis, et me publice deho-
5  nestaret quod ante sponte et laetus indulserat, et Dominus, qui *maior
omnibus est?*

**33**     33. Satis dico. Sed tamen non debeo abscondere *donum Dei* quod
largitus est nobis in *terra captiuitatis meae,* quia tunc fortiter inquisiui
eum et ibi inueni illum et seruauit me ab omnibus iniquitatibus

---

| | |
|---|---|
| **12** | Ps 117(118): 22:39; cf 1 P 2: 7 |
| **13** | Dn 7: 13 |
| **14** | Rm 11: 4 |
| **17** | Zc 2: 8 |
| **18** | 1 Tm 1: 12; Ph 4: 13; cf 2 Tm 4: 17 |
| **20** | *a Christo Domino meo didiceram* cf Mt 11: 29; Jn 6: 45 |
| **20-21** | Lk 8: 46: Mk 5: 30 |
| **21-22** | *probata est coram Deo et hominibus* Si 25: 1; cf 1 P 1: 7 |
| **23-24** | Ac 2: 29 / / *non me reprehendit conscientia mea* cf Jb 27: 6 |
| **24** | 2 Co 1:23 / / Ga 1:20 |
| **28** | cf 2 Tm 4: 16 |
| **245:4-5** | dehonestaret Pr 25:8 |
| **5-6** | Jn 10: 29; cf 1 Jn 3: 20 |
| **7** | Jn 4: 10 |
| **8** | Tb 13: 7; 2 Ch 6: 37 |
| **9** | *seruauit me* Si 33: 1; 2 Tm 1: 12 |

10 (sic credo) *propter inhabitantem Spiritum* eius, qui *operatus est* usque
in hanc diem in me. *Audenter* rursus. Sed scit Deus, si mihi homo
hoc effatus fuisset, forsitan tacuissem propter *caritatem Christi.*

**34** 34. Vnde ergo indefessam gratiam ago Deo meo, qui me fidelem
seruauit *in die temptationis* meae, ita ut hodie confidenter offeram illi
15 sacrificium ut *hostiam uiuentem* animam meam Christo Domino meo,
qui me *seruauit ab omnibus angustiis meis,* ut et dicam: *Quis ego sum,
Domine,* uel quae est uocatio mea, qui mihi †tanta diuinitate
cooperasti†, ita ut hodie *in gentibus* constanter *exaltarem et magnificarem nomen tuum* ubicumque loco fuero, nec non in secundis
20 sed etiam in pressuris, ut quicquid mihi euenerit siue bonum siue
malum aequaliter debeo suscipere et Deo gratias semper agere, qui

| 10 | Rm 8: 11 / / 1 Co 12: 11; Ph 2: 13 |
| 11 | Ac 2: 29 |
| 12 | 2 Co 5: 14 |
| 14 | Ps 94(95): 9 |
| 15 | Rm 12:1 |
| 16 | Ps 33(34): 7; cf 33(34): 5 |
| 16-17 | Ex 3: 11; 2 S 7: 18 |
| 18 | Ps 45(46): 11 |
| 18-19 | Ps 33(34) 4; 45(46): 11; Si 33: 10; cf Is 25: 1 |
| 20-21 | *siue bonum siue malum... suscipere* cf Jb 2: 10 |

**245, 10-11** *(Deus) operatus est usque in hanc diem in me:* **Augustine,** De Moribus Ecclesiae
Catholicae, 23 "Nullo modo autem redintegrari possemus per Spiritum Sanctum, nisi et
ipse semper et integer et incommutabilis permaneret"; cf. 31; Contra duas epistolas
Pelagianorum, I, 36 "'Homines', inquit, 'Dei opus esse' defendimus: nec ex illius potentia
vel in malum vel in bonum invitum aliquem cogi; sed propria voluntate aut bonum
facere, aut malum: in bono vero opere a Dei gratia semper adjuvari, in malum vero
diaboli suggestionibus incitari"; De Correptione et Gratia, 2 "In bono... liber esse nullus
potest, nisi fuerit liberatus ab eo qui dixit, 'Si vos Filius liberaverit, tunc bene liberi estis'
(Jn 8:36). Nec ita ut, cum quisque fuerit a peccati dominatione liberatus, jam non
indigeat sui liberatoris auxilio"; cf. De Gratia et Libero Arbitrio, 33; 37; 38; 40.

**13** *Unde ergo indefessam gratiam ago Deo meo, qui me fidelem seruauit:* **Augustine,** De Gratia
Christi et Peccato Originali, 31 "Istam quippe gratiam qua justificamur, id est, qua
caritas Dei diffunditur in cordibus nostris per Spiritum Sanctum qui datus est nobis, in
Pelagii et Caelestii scriptis, quaecumque legere potui, nusquam eos inveni,
quemadmodum confitenda est, confiteri"; Expositio Epistolae ad Galatas, Praefatio;
24.

**17-18** *qui (Dominus) tanta diuinitate cooperasti:* **Augustine,** De Gratia et Libero Arbitrio, 33 "Ut
ergo velimus, sine nobis operatur; cum autem volumus, et sic volumus ut faciamus,
nobiscum cooperatur: tamen sine illo vel operante ut velimus, vel cooperante cum
volumus, ad bona pietatis opera nihil valemus"; cf. 27-33 passim; Expositio quarundam
Propositionum ex Epistola ad Romanos, 12(18) "Gratia vero efficit ut non tantum velimus
recte facere, sed etiam possimus; non viribus nostris, sed liberatoris auxilio".

**20-21** *Quicquid mihi evenerit sive bonum sive malum... et Deo gratias semper ago:* **Augustine,**
Retractationes, II, 32 "Confessionum mearum libri tredecim et de malis et de bonis meis
Deum laudant justum et bonum atque in eum excitant humanum intellectum et
affectum"; Sermo 67, 1 "(Confessio) non solius est peccatoris, sed etiam aliquando
laudatoris. Confitemur ergo, sive laudantes Deum, sive accusantes nos ipsos"; cf. De
Correptione et Gratia, 7; De Dono perseverantiae, 33; **Cyprian,** De Dominica Oratione,
27; see notes at 253:5-6 and 253:15 below.

mihi ostendit ut indubitabilem eum sine fine crederem et qui me
audierit ut ego inscius et *in nouissimis diebus* hoc opus tam pium et
tam mirificum auderem adgredere, ita ut imitarem quippiam illos
25 quos ante Dominus iam olim praedixerat praenuntiaturos euangelium
suum *in testimonium omnibus gentibus* ante *finem mundi,* quod ita
ergo uidimus itaque suppletum est: ecce testes sumus quia
euangelium praedicatum est usque ubi nemo ultra est.

**35** 246, 1   35. Longum est autem totum per singula enarrare laborem meum
uel per partes. Breuiter dicam qualiter piissimus Deus de seruitute
saepe liberauit et de periculis duodecim qua periclitata est anima
mea, praeter insidias multas et *quae uerbis exprimere non ualeo.* Nec
5 iniuriam legentibus faciam; sed Deum auctorem habeo, qui nouit
omnia etiam antequam fiant, ut me pauperculum pupillum ideo
tamen *responsum diuinum* creber admonere.

**36**   36. *Vnde mihi haec sapientia,* quae in me non erat, qui nec *nume-*
*rum dierum noueram* neque Deum sapiebam? Vnde mihi postmodum
10 donum tam magnum tam salubre Deum agnoscere uel diligere, sed
ut patriam et parentes amitterem?

**37**   37. Et munera multa mihi offerebantur cum fletu et lacrimis et
offendi illos, nec non contra uotum aliquantis de senioribus meis,
sed gubernante Deo nullo modo consensi neque adquieui illis — non
15 mea gratia, sed Deus qui uincit in me et resistit illis omnibus, ut
ego ueneram ad Hibernas gentes euangelium praedicare et ab incredulis contumelias perferre, ut *audirem obprobrium peregrinationis*
*meae,* et persecutiones multas *usque ad uincula* et ut darem
ingenuitatem meam pro utilitate aliorum et, si dignus fuero,

---

| | |
|---|---|
| **23** | Ac 2: 17 |
| **26** | Mt 24: 14 |
| **27** | *suppletum est* Jm 2: 23 |
| **246: 1** | *per singula enarrare* Ac 21: 19 |
| **246: 4** | cf Rm 8: 26 |
| **5-6** | *qui nouit omnia etiam antequam fiant* Dn 13: 42 |
| **6** | *me pauperculum* Is 66: 2 |
| **7** | Rm 11: 4 |
| **8** | Mt 13: 54 |
| **8-9** | Ps 38(39): 5; Jb 38: 21 |
| **17-18** | Si 29: 30 |
| **18** | 2 Tm 2: 9 |

---

**246, 8-9**   *sapientia, quae in me non erat... neque Deum sapiebam:* see note at 238, 25 above.
**14-15**   *non mea gratia, sed Deus qui vincit in me et resistit illis omnibus:* **Augustine,** De Gratia et
Libero Arbitrio, 33 "(Deus) sine nobis operatur"; Contra duas epistolas Pelagianorum, I,
42 "Sed et Pelagianis non immerito anathema dicimus qui tam sunt inimici gratiae Dei,
quae venit per Iesum Christum Dominum nostrum (Rom 7.25), ut eam dicant non gratis
sed secundum merita nostra dari, ac sic gratia iam non sit gratia"; cf. Expositio
quarundum propositionum ex Epistola ad Romanos, (52) 60; Retractationes, I, 23.

20 *promptus* sum ut etiam *animam meam* incunctanter et *libentissime* pro
  nomine eius et ibi opto *impendere* eam *usque ad mortem,* si Dominus
  mihi indulgeret,

**38** (38) quia ualde *debitor sum* Deo, qui mihi tantam gratiam donauit
  ut populi multi per me in Deum renascerentur et postmodum con-
25 summarentur et ut clerici ubique illis ordinarentur ad plebem
  nuper uenientem ad credulitatem, quam sumpsit Dominus *ab extremis*
  *terrae,* sicut olim promiserat per prophetas suos: *Ad te gentes uenient*
  *ab extremis terrae et dicent: sicut falsa comparauerunt patres nostri idola*
247, 1 *et non est in eis utilitas;* et iterum: *Posui te lumen in gentibus ut*
  *sis in salutem usque ad extremum terrae.*

**39** 39. Et ibi uolo *expectare promissum* ipsius, qui utique numquam
  fallit, sicut in euangelio pollicetur: *Venient ab oriente et occidente*
5 *et recumbent cum Abraam et Isaac et Iacob,*
  sicut credimus ab omni mundo uenturi sunt credentes.

**40** 40. Idcirco itaque oportet quidem bene et diligenter piscare, sicut
  Dominus praemonet et docet dicens: *Venite post me et faciam uos*
  *fieri piscatores hominum;* et iterum dicit per prophetas: *Ecce*
10 *mitto piscatores et uenatores multos, dicit Deus,* et cetera.
  Vnde autem ualde oportebat retia nostra tendere, ita ut *multi-*
  *tudo copiosa et turba* Deo caperetur et ubique essent clerici qui

---

| | |
|---|---|
| **20** | Rm 1:5 / / Jn 13: 37 |
| **20-21** | 2 Co 12: 15 / / Ph 2: 8, 30 |
| **21-22** | *si Dominus mihi indulgeret* cf Is 26: 15 |
| **23** | Rm 1: 4 |
| **26-27** | Jr 16: 19 |
| **27** | *sicut olim promiserat per prophetas suos* Rn 1: 2 |
| **27-247: 1** | Jr 16: 19 *(LXX)* |
| **247: 1-2** | Ac 13: 47 (Is 49: 6) |
| **3** | Ac 1: 4; 2P 3: 13; cf Rm 4: 20-21 |
| **4-5** | Mt 8: 11 |
| **8-9** | Mt 4: 19 (Mk 1: 17) |
| **9-10** | Jr 16: 16 |
| **11-12** | Lk 6: 17; cf Lk 5: 6 |

---

| | |
|---|---|
| **23** | *(Deus) qui mihi tantam gratiam donavit;* cf **Augustine**, De Spiritu et Littera, 40; Opus Imperfectum contra Julianum, III, 106; Ad Romanos, 60-2 passim. |
| **247, 3-4** | *Et ibi volo expectare promissum ipsius, qui utique numquam fallit:* **Augustine**, De Spiritu et Littera, 40 "Hoc enim Deus promittit quod ipse facit: non enim ipse promittit et alius facit, quod iam non est promittere, sed praedicere"; De Praedestinatione Sanctorum, 6 "Cavendum est, fratres dilecti a Deo, ne homo se extollat adversus Deum, cum se dicit facere quod promisit Deus... Ipse igitur fidem gentium facit, qui potens est facere quod promisit"; cf. 19-20; De Gratia Christi et Peccato Originali, 31 "Quod enim promittit Deus, non facimus nos per arbitrium seu naturam, sed facit ipse per gratiam" cf. De Correptione et Gratia, 35-6 passim; Epistola 194 ad Sixtum 36; **Prosper,** De Vocatione Omnium Gentium, 1, 9; 20; Pro Augustino Responsiones, VIII. |

baptizarent et exhortarent populum indigentem et desiderantem,
sicut Dominus inquit in euangelio, ammonet et docet dicens: *Euntes*
15 *ergo nunc docete omnes gentes baptizantes eas in nomine Patris et Filii*
*et Spiritus Sancti docentes eos obseruare omnia quaecumque mandaui*
*uobis: et ecce ego uobiscum sum omnibus diebus usque ad consumma-*
*tionem*
saeculi; et interum dicit: *Euntes ergo in mundum uniuersum praedi-*
*cate euangelium omni creaturae; qui crediderit et baptizatus fuerit*
20 *saluus erit; qui uero non crediderit condempnabitur;* et iterum:
*Praedicabitur hoc euangelium regni in uniuerso mundo in testimonium*
*omnibus gentibus et tunc ueniet finis;*
et item Dominus per prophetam praenuntiat inquit: *Et erit*
*in nouissimis diebus, dicit Dominus, effundam de spiritu meo super omnem*
25 *carnem et prophetabunt filii uestri et filiae uestrae et iuuenes uestri*
248, 1 *uisiones uidebunt et seniores uestri somnia somniabunt et quidem super*
*seruos meos et super ancillas meas in diebus illis effundam de spiritu meo*
*et prophetabunt;* et *in Osee dicit: Vocabo non plebem meam plebem*
*meam*
*et non misericordiam consecutam misericordiam consecutam et erit in*
5 *loco ubi dictum est: Non plebs mea uos, ibi uocabuntur filii Dei uiui.*
**41** 41. Vnde autem Hiberione qui numquam notitiam Dei habuerunt nisi idola et inmunda usque nunc semper coluerunt quomodo
*nuper facta est plebs Domini* et filii Dei nuncupantur, filii Scottorum
et filiae regulorum monachi et uirgines Christi esse uidentur?
**42** 10 42. Et etiam una benedicta Scotta genetiua nobilis pulcherrima
adulta erat, quam ego baptizaui; et post paucos dies una causa uenit
ad nos, insinuauit nobis responsum accepisse a nuntio Dei et
monuit eam ut esset uirgo Christi et ipsa Deo proximaret: Deo

---

| | |
|---|---|
| **14-18** | Mt 28: 19-20 |
| **18-20** | Mk 16: 15-16 |
| **21-22** | Mt 24: 14 |
| **23-248: 3** | Ac 2: 17-18 (Jl 2: 28-29) |
| **248:3-5** | Rm 9: 25-26; cf Ho 2: 23; 2: 1; 1: 10; 1 P 2: 10 |
| **6** | *notitiam Dei* cf Rm 1: 28; 2 Co 2: 14; Heb 10: 26 |
| **7** | *immunda... coluerunt* 2 K 17: 12 |
| **12** | *responsum accepisse a nuntio Dei* Ac 10: 22; cf Mt 2: 12; Lk 2: 26; 2 Ch 36: 15-16; Is 42: 19 |

---

| | |
|---|---|
| **13** | *populum indigentem et desiderantem:* **Augustine,** De Correptione et Gratia, 2 "et desiderare auxilium gratiae, initium gratiae est"; Tractatus in Joannem 26, 4 "Da amantem et sentit quod dico; da desiderantem, da esurientem"; cf. De Praedestinatione Sanctorum, 3; **Prosper,** De Vocatione omnium Gentium, 1, 8" ...nec ullo hanc [dignitatem] desiderio appetit, qui calorem ipsius desiderii non accepit a Deo, 9 "... ipsum desiderium salutis ex Dei inspiratione concipiunt"; Contra Collatorem, IV, I "... prima salus est, ut sibi incipiat displicere, et vetustatem suae debilitatis odisse; sequens vero est, ut et sanari desideret"; 2 "... qui dedit desiderium, praestet effectum"; cf. VI, XIX. |

gratias, sexta ab hac die optime et auidissime arripuit illud quod
15   etiam omnes uirgines Dei ita hoc faciunt — non sponte patrum
earum, sed et persecutiones patiuntur et improperia falsa a par-
entibus suis et nihilominus plus augetur numerus (et de genere nostro
qui ibi nati sunt nescimus numerum eorum) praeter uiduas et conti-
nentes.
20   Sed ex illis maxime laborant quae seruitio detinentur: usque
ad terrores et minas assidue perferunt; sed Dominus gratiam dedit
multis ex ancillis suis, nam etsi uetantur tamen fortiter imitantur.

**43**   43. Vnde autem etsi uoluero amittere illas et ut pergens in Brittanniis — et libentissime *paratus eram* quasi ad patriam et
25   parentes; non id solum sed etiam usque ad Gallias uisitare frates et
ut uiderem faciem sanctorum Domini mei: scit Deus quod ego ualde
optabam, sed *alligatus Spiritu,* qui mihi *protestatur* si hoc fecero, ut
futurum reum me esse designat et timeo perdere laborem quem
inchoaui, et non ego sed Christus Dominus, qui me imperauit ut

**249, 1**   uenirem esse cum illis residuum aetatis meae, *si Dominus
uoluerit* et custodierit me ab omni uia mala, ut non *peccem coram illo;*

**44**   (44) spero autem hoc debueram, sed memet ipsum non credo
*quamdiu fuero in hoc corpore mortis,* quia fortis est qui cotidie nititur
5   subuertere me a fide et praeposita castitate religionis non fictae usque
in finem uitae meae Christo Domino meo, sed *caro inimica* semper

---

| | |
|---|---|
| **14** | arripuit cf Mt 11:12 |
| **24** | Ps 118(119): 60 |
| **25** | *uisitare fratres* Ac 7: 23; 15: 36 |
| **26** | *ut uiderem faciem* Ac 20: 25, 38; Col 2: 2; 1 Th 3: 10 |
| **27** | Ac 20: 22 / / Ac 20: 23 |
| **249: 1-2** | Jm 4: 15 |
| **2** | *ab omni uia mala* Ps 118(119): 101 / / Lk 15: 18, 21 |
| **4** | 2 P 1: 13; Rm 7: 24 |
| **6** | cf Rm 8: 7 |

---

**249, 3-4**   *memet ipsum non credo quamdiu fuero in hoc corpore mortis:* **Augustine,** Contra
Julianum, II, 32 "In hoc bello (carnis et spiritus) et ipsam carnem adversariam gravem
dicit (Ambrosius), cujus utique natura sicut primitus condita est, nobiscum
concordissima permaneret, nisi primi hominis praevaricatione vitiata, suo nobiscum
languore confligeret"; 11 "Vides unde caro concupiscit adversus spiritum, vides unde sit
lex in membris repugnans legi mentis. Vides vertisse in naturam, animae carnisque
discordiam, et per has inimicitias nobis abundare miserias, nonnisi Dei misericordia
finiendas"; 25 "Obsessa mens hominis, et undique diaboli infestatione vallata, vix
occurrit singulis, vix resistit"; De Dono Perseverantiae, 14; 16.

**5-6**   *subvertere me a fide et praeposita castitate religionis non fictae usque in finem vitae meae
Christo Domino meo:* **Hilary,** Tractatus in Ps 14, 14 "In his quae promissa sunt Deo, non
est aliquando fallendum"; **Ambrose,** In Ps 39, 23 "Gravis populus est qui fidem Deo suo
servat"; De Sacramentis, I, 2, 8 "Tu qui fidem debes Christo, fidem serva"; cf. De Officiis, I
140; II, 144; III, 65; **Augustine,** Ad Romanos, 12(13); De Dono Perseverantiae, 33.

trahit ad mortem, id est ad inlecebras inlicitate perficiendas;
et *scio ex parte* quare uitam perfectam ego non egi sicut et ceteri
credentes, sed confiteor Domino meo, et non erubesco in conspectu
10 ipsius, *quia non mentior,* ex quo cognoui eum *a iuuentute mea* creuit
in me amor Dei et timor ipsius, *et usque nunc* fauente Domino *fidem
seruaui.*

**45** 45. Rideat autem et insultet qui uoluerit, ego non silebo neque
abscondo signa et mirabilia quae mihi a Domino monstrata sunt
15 ante multos annos quam fierent, quasi qui nouit omnia etiam *ante
tempora saecularia.*

**46** 46. Vnde autem debueram sine cessatione Deo gratias agere, qui
saepe indulsit insipientiae meae neglegentiae meae et de loco non
in uno quoque ut non mihi uehementer irasceretur, qui adiutor datus
20 sum et non cito adquieui secundum quod mihi ostensum fuerat et
sicut *Spiritus suggerebat,* et *misertus est* mihi Dominus *in milia
milium,* quia uidi in me quod *paratus eram,* sed quod mihi pro
his nesciebam de statu meo quid facerem, quia multi hanc legationem
prohibebant, etiam inter se ipso pos tergum meum narrabant et
25 dicebant: 'Iste quare se mittit in periculo inter hostes qui Deum
non nouerunt?' — non ut causa malitiae, sed non sapiebat illis, sicut
et ego ipse testor, intellegi propter rusticitatem meam — et non
cito agnoui gratiam quae tunc erat in me; nunc mihi sapit quod
ante debueram.

---

| | |
|---|---|
| **7** | *trahit ad mortem* cf Pr 24: 11 |
| **8** | cf 1 Co 13: 9 |
| **9** | *non erubesco* Ps 24(25): 1, 20 |
| **10** | Ga 1: 20 / / Ps 70(71): 5, 17; 87(88): 16 |
| **11-12** | 2 Tm 4: 17 |
| **14** | *signa et mirabilia* Dn 3: 99; 6: 27 |
| **15-16** | cf Ac 15: 18 (Is 45: 21); 2 Tm 1: 9; Tt 1: 2 |
| **17** | *sine cessatione Deo gratias agere* Ep 1: 16; 1 Tm 2: 13 |
| **18** | *insipientiae meae* cf Ps 68(69): 6 |
| **19** | *uehementer irasceretur* 2 K 17: 18; Lm 5: 22 |
| **19-20** | *qui adiutor datus sum* cf 1 Co 3: 9 |
| **21** | Jn 14: 26 |
| **21-22** | cf Ex 20: 6; Rv 5: 11; Dt 5: 10; 7: 9-10 |
| **22** | Ps 118(119): 60 |
| **25-26** | *qui Deum non nouerunt* 2 Th 1: 8 |
| **28** | *gratiam quae... erat in me* 1 Tm 4: 14 |

---

| | |
|---|---|
| **6-7** | *sed caro inimica semper trahit ad mortem:* **Augustine,** Ad Romanos, (12) 13 "Quattuor istos gradus hominis distinguamus: ante Legem, sub Lege, sub gratia, in pace. Ante Legem sequimur concupiscentiam carnis; sub Lege, trahimur ab ea; sub gratia, nec sequimur eam, nec trahimur ab ea; in pace, nulla est concupiscentia carnis"; cf. Retractationes, I, 23; Contra Julianum, II, 11, 13, 15, 25, 27. |
| **9-10** | **Augustine,** Confessions, IV, 16-31. |
| **10-11** | *crevit in me amor Dei:* see note at 239, 15-16 above. |

**47** 30     47. Nunc ergo simpliciter insinuaui fratribus et conseruis meis
qui mihi crediderunt propter quod *praedixi et praedico* ad roborandam
et confirmandam fidem uestram. Vtinam ut et uos imitemini maiora et
250, 1  potiora faciatis! Hoc erit gloria mea, quia *filius sapiens gloria
patris est.*

  **48**     48. Vos scitis et Deus qualiter inter uos conuersatus sum *a iuuentute mea* in fide ueritatis *et in sinceritate cordis.* Etiam ad gentes
   5 illas inter quas habito, ego fidem illis praestaui et praestabo. Deus
scit *neminem* illorum *circumueni,* nec cogito, propter Deum et
ecclesiam ipsius, ne *excitem* illis et nobis omnibus *persecutionem* et
ne per me blasphemaretur nomen Domini; quia scriptum est: *Vae
homini per quem nomen Domini blasphematur.*

**49** 10     49. Nam *etsi imperitus sum in omnibus* tamen conatus sum quippiam seruare me etiam et fratribus Christianis et uirginibus Christi
et mulieribus religiosis, quae mihi ultronea munuscula donabant et
super altare iactabant ex ornamentis suis et iterum reddebam illis
et aduersus me scandalizabantur cur hoc faciebam; sed ego prop-
 15 ter spem perennitatis, ut me in omnibus caute propterea conseruarem,
     ita ut<non>me in aliquo titulo infideli caperent uel ministerium
       seruitutis
meae nec etiam in minimo incredulis locum darem infamare siue
detractare.

  **50**     50. Forte autem quando baptizaui tot milia hominum sperauerim
 20 ab aliquo illorum uel dimidio scriptulae? *Dicite mihi et reddam
uobis.* Aut quando ordinauit ubique Dominus clericos per modicitatem
meam et ministerium gratis distribui illis, si poposci ab aliquo
illorum uel pretium uel *calciamenti* mei, *dicite aduersus me et reddam
uobis.*

**51** 25     Magis (51) ego *impendi pro* uobis ut me *caperent,* et inter uos et
     ubique

---

| | |
|---|---|
| **31** | 2 Co 13: 2 |
| **31-32** | *ad roborandam... uestram* cf Jb 4: 3-4 |
| **250:1-2** | Pr 10: 1; 15: 20; cf 17: 6; Si 3: 13 |
| **3** | *Vos scitis et Deus* cf Ac 20: 18; 1 Th 2: 10 |
| **3-4** | 1 S 12: 2; Ps 70(71): 17; 87(88): 16 |
| **4** | *in fide ueritatis* 2 Th 2: 14 / / 2 Co 1: 12; I Co 5:8 |
| **6** | 2 Co 7: 12 / / *propter Deum* 1 P 2: 13 |
| **7** | Ac 13: 50 |
| **8-9** | Mt 18: 7 / / Rm 2: 24 |
| **10** | 2 Co 11: 6 |
| **15** | *caute* cf Ep 5: 15 |
| **18** | *detractare* 1 P 2: 12 |
| **20-21** | cf 1 S 12: 3 *(Vet Lat)* |
| **23-24** | cf 1 S 12: 3 *(Vet Lat)* |
| **25** | 2 Co 12: 15 / / cf 2 Co 7: 2 |

pergebam causa uestra in multis periculis etiam usque ad exteras partes, ubi nemo ultra erat et ubi numquam aliquis peruenerat qui baptizaret aut clericos ordinaret aut populum consummaret: donante Domino diligenter et libentissime pro salute uestra omnia<...> generaui.

**52** 30   52. Interim praemia dabam regibus praeter quod dabam merce-
dem filiis ipsorum qui mecum ambulant, et nihilominus compre-
251, 1 henderunt me cum comitibus meis et illa die auidissime cupiebant
interficere me, sed tempus nondum uenerat, et omnia quaecumque
nobiscum inuenerunt rapuerunt illud et me ipsum ferro uinxerunt, et
quartodecimo die absoluit me Dominus de potestate eorum et quic-
5 quid nostrum fuit redditum et nobis propter Deum et *necessarios*
*amicos* quos ante praeuidimus.

**53**   53. Vos autem experti estis quantum ego erogaui illis qui iudica-
bant *per omnes regiones* quos ego frequentius uisitabam. Censeo enim
non minimum quam pretium quindecim hominum distribui illis, ita
10 ut me *fruamini* et ego *uobis* semper *fruar* in Deum. Non me paenitet
nec satis est mihi: adhuc *impendo et superimpendam;* potens est
Dominus ut det mihi postmodum ut meipsum *impendar pro animabus*
*uestris.*

**54**   54. Ecce *testem Deum inuoco in animam meam quia non mentior:*
15 neque ut sit *occasio adulationis* uel *auaritiae* scripserim uobis
neque ut honorem spero ab aliquo uestro; sufficit enim honor qui
nondum uidetur sed corde creditur; *fidelis* autem *qui promisit:*
*numquam mentitur.*

**55**   55. Sed uideo iam *in praesenti saeculo* me supra modum exaltatum
20 a Domino, et non eram dignus neque talis ut hoc mihi praestaret,
dum scio certissime quod mihi melius conuenit paupertas et calamitas
quam diuitiae et deliciae (sed et *Christus Dominus pauper fuit*
*pro nobis,* ego uero miser et infelix etsi opes uoluero iam

---

| | | |
|---|---|---|
| 251: 2 | *sed tempus nondum venerat* Jn 7: 6 | |
| 5 | *propter Deum* 1 P 2: 13 | |
| 5-6 | Ac 10: 24 | |
| 8 | cf Ne (2 Ezr) 11: 25; cf Gn 41: 34 | |
| 10 | cf Rm 15:24 | |
| 11-13 | 2 Co 12: 15 | |
| 14 | 2 Co 1: 23; Ga 1: 20 | |
| 15 | 1 Th 2: 5 | |
| 17 | *nondum uidetur* cf 2 Co 4: 18 | |
| | *sed corde creditur* Rm 10: 10 | |
| 17-18 | Heb 10: 23; Tt 1: 2 | |
| 19 | Ga 1: 4 | |
| 22-23 | 2 Co 8: 9 | |

---

251, 16-17   *sufficit enim honor qui nondum videtur sed corde creditur:* **Augustine,** Contra duas
epistolas Pelagianorum, I, 38 "Si ergo ad honorem gratiae pertinemus, non simus ingrati
tribuendo nobis quod accepimus. 'Quid enim habemus quod non accepimus?'
(I Cor 4: 7)."

non habeo, *neque me ipsum iudico),* quia cotidie spero aut inter-
25 nicionem aut circumueniri aut redigi in seruitutem siue occasio
cuiuslibet; *sed nihil horum uereor* propter promissa caelorum,
quia iactaui meipsum in manus Dei omnipotentis, qui ubique
dominatur, sicut propheta dicit: *Iacta cogitatum tuum in Deum et
ipse te enutriet.*

**56** 30    56. Ecce nunc *commendo animam meam fidelissimo Deo* meo, *pro*
252, 1 *quo legationem fungor* in ignobilitate mea, sed quia *personam non accipit*
et elegit me ad hoc officium ut *unus* essem *de suis minimis* minister.

**57**    57. Vnde autem *retribuam illi pro omnibus quae retribuit mihi.*
Sed quid dicam uel quid promittam Domino meo, quia nihil ualeo
5 nisi ipse mihi dederit? Sed *scrutator corda et renes* quia satis et nimis
cupio et *paratus eram* ut donaret mihi *bibere calicem* eius, sicut indulsit
et ceteris amantibus se.

**58**    58. Quapropter non contingat mihi a Deo meo ut numquam
amittam *plebem* suam *quam adquisiuit* in ultimis terrae. Oro Deum
10 ut det mihi perseuerantiam et dignetur ut reddam illi testem
fidelem usque ad transitum meum propter Deum meum,

**59**    (59) et si aliquid boni umquam imitatus sum propter Deum meum,
quem diligo, peto illi det mihi ut cum illis proselitis et captiuis

---

| | |
|---|---|
| **24** | 1 Co 4: 3 |
| **26** | Ac 20: 24 |
| **27-8** | *qui ubique dominatur* cf 1 Ch 29: 12; 2 Ch 20: 6; Dn 4: 14, 22 |
| **28-29** | Ps 54(55): 23 |
| **30** | 1 P 4: 19; cf Ps 30(31): 6; Lk 23: 46 |
| **30-252: 1** | Ep 6: 20; 2 Co 5: 20 |
| **1** | Dt 10: 17; Ga 2: 6 |
| **2** | *elegit me* Jn 15: 16 / / Mt 25: 40 |
| **3** | Ps 115(116): 12 |
| **5** | *nisi ipse mihi dederit* cf Ws 9: 17; 8: 21 / / Ps 7: 10; Rv 2: 23 |
| **6** | Ps 118(119): 60 / / Mt 20: 22 |
| **8** | *non contingat mihi* 1 M 13: 5 |
| **9** | Is 43: 21 *(LXX)* |

---

**251, 30** *pro quo legationem fungor:* **Augustine,** Opus Imperfectum contra Julianum, I, 12 "Pro
**252, 1** Christo legatione fungimur, et pro virili portione quantum valemus opis ad defensionem
catholicae religionis afferimus"; cf. Enarrationes in Ps 67, 32, n, 40; **Prosper,** Liber
Auctoritates, VIII.

**1-2** *(Deus) personam non accipit et elegit me ad hoc officium:* **Augustine,**Contra Julianum, V,
13 "Nullum eligit dignum, sed eligendo efficit dignum"; cf. Tractatus in Joannem 86, 2.

**252, 9-10** *Oro Deum ut det mihi perseverantiam:* **Augustine,** De Dono Perseverantiae, 33 "Unde
satis dilucide ostenditur, et inchoandi, et usque in finem perseverandi gratiam Dei non
secundum merita nostra dari"; 39 "Immo cum constet alia Deum, danda etiam non
orantibus, sicut initium fidei; alia nonnisi orantibus praeparasse, sicut usque in finem
perseverantiam: profecto qui ex seipso hanc se habere putat, non orat ut habeat"; cf. 36;
55; 56; De Correptione et Gratia, 10.

pro nomine suo effundam sanguinem meum, etsi ipsam etiam
caream

15 sepulturam aut miserissime cadauer per singula membra diuida-
tur canibus aut bestiis asperis aut *uolucres caeli comederent illud.*
Certissime reor, si mihi hoc incurrisset, lucratus sum animam cum
corpore meo, quia *sine ulla dubitatione* in die illa *resurgemus* in
claritate solis, hoc est *in gloria* Christi Iesu redemptoris nostri,

20 quasi *filii Dei* uiui et *coheredes Christi* et *conformes futuri imaginis*

21.22 *ipsius;* quoniam *ex ipso et per ipsum et in ipso* regnaturi
sumus.

**60** 60. Nam sol iste quem uidemus<ipso>iubente propter nos cotidie
oritur, sed numquam regnabit neque permanebit splendor eius, sed et

25 omnes qui adorant eum in poenam miseri male deuenient; nos autem,
qui credimus et adoramus solem uerum Christum, qui numquam

253, 1 interibit, neque *qui fecerit uoluntatem* ipsius, sed *manebit in aeter-*
*num quomodo et Christus manet in aeternum,* qui regnat cum
Deo Patre omnipotente et cum Spiritu Sancto ante saecula et nunc et
per omnia saecula saeculorum, Amen.

**61** 5 61. Ecce iterum iterumque breuiter exponam uerba confessionis
meae. *Testificor* in ueritate et in *exultatione cordis coram Deo et*
*sanctis angelis eius* quia numquam habui aliquam occasionem praeter
euangelium et promissa illius et umquam redirem ad gentem illam
unde prius uix euaseram.

---

| | |
|---|---|
| **14-16** | cf Dt 28: 26; Ps 78(79): 2-3 |
| **16** | Jr 7: 33; Ezk 29: 5; 1 K 14: 11; 16: 4; Lk 8: 5 |
| **18** | Rt 3: 13 |
| **18-19** | cf Ml 4: 2; 1 Co 15: 43; Ph 3: 20-21 |
| **20** | *filii Dei uiui* Rm 9: 26 (Ho 1: 10); Rm 8: 16 / / Rm 8: 17 |
| **20-21** | Rm 8: 29 |
| **21-22** | Rm 11: 36 |
| | *regnaturi sumus* cf Rm 5: 17; 1 Co 4: 8; 2 Tm 2: 12; Rv 22: 5 |
| **23-24** | *sol...* «ipso» *iubente propter nos... oritur* cf Mt 5: 45 |
| **24** | *neque permanebit splendor eius* cf Ps 71(72): 5 |
| **253: 1-2** | 1 Jn 2: 17; Ps 88(89): 37 |
| **4** | *per omnia saecula saeculorum. Amen* cf Rv 11: 15 |
| **6-7** | 2 Tm 4: 1 / / Ps 118(119): 111 / / 1 Tm 5: 21; |
| | cf Mt 16: 27; Mk 8: 38 |

---

| | |
|---|---|
| **253, 2-4** | *Christus manet... cum Deo Patre... et cum Spiritu Sancto":* see note at 236, 22b above. |
| **5-6** | *Ecce iterum iterumque exponam verba confessionis meae":* **Augustine,** Sermo 67, 1 "Confessio non solius est peccatoris, sed etiam aliquando laudatoris. Confitemur ergo, sive laudantes Deum sive accusantes nos ipsos"; cf. Retractationes, II, 32; De Dono Perseverantiae, 33; **Ambrose;** In Ps 118, 15, 30 "Docet nos immemores beneficiorum coelestium nequaquam esse debere, sed meditari jusificationes Domini". |
| **7-8** | *numquam habui aliquam occasionem praeter evangelium et promissa illius ut umquam redirem ad gentem illam:* **Augustine,** Contra Julianum, IV, 21 "Noveris itaque, non officiis, sed finibus a vitiis discernendas esse virtutes. Officium est autem quod faciendum est: finis vero propter quod faciendum est". |

**62** 10    62. Sed precor credentibus et timentibus Deum, quicumque dignatus fuerit inspicere uel recipere hanc scripturam quam Patricius peccator indoctus scilicet Hiberione conscripsit, ut nemo umquam dicat quod mea ignorantia, si aliquid pusillum egi uel demonstrauerim secundum Dei placitum, sed arbitramini et uerissime credatur
15 quod *donum Dei* fuisset. Et haec est confessio mea antequam moriar.

### LIBER SECVNDVS: <EPISTOLA AD MILITES COROTICI>

254, 1    1. Patricius peccator indoctus scilicet Hiberione constitutus episcopum me esse fateor. Certissime reor a Deo *accepi id quod sum.* Inter barbaras itaque gentes habito proselitus et profuga ob amorem Dei; testis est ille si ita est. Non quod optabam tam dure et tam

---

**15**      Jn 4: 10; Ep 2: 8
**254: 2**      1 Co 15: 10; cf 1 Co 4: 7

---

**10-15**    *Sed precor credentibus... verissime credatur quod donum Dei fuisset:* **Augustine,** Epistola 214, 4 "Omne datum optimum, et omne donum perfectum decursum est, descendens a Patre luminum; ne quisquam dicat meritis operum suorum, vel meritis fidei suae, sibi traditam Dei gratiam, et putetur verum esse quod illi haeretici dicunt, gratiam Dei secundum merita nostra dari"; De Dono Perseverantiae, 33 "Hoc nobis expedit et credere et dicere: hoc est pium, hoc verum, ut sit humilis et submissa confessio, et detur totum Deo"; **Prosper,** Epistola ad Augustinum, 7 "In istis Pelagianae pravitatis reliquiis non mediocris virulentiae fibra nutritur, si principium salutis male in homine conlocatur.

**12**    *indoctus:* see notes at 238, 15 and 24 above.

**15**    *Et haec est confessio mea antequam moriar:* see notes at 245, 13; 245, 20-21 and 253, 5-6 above.

**254, 1-2**    *Patricius peccator indoctus scilicet Hiberione constitutus episcopum me esse fateor:* cf. Epistola Milevitani Concilii ad Innocentem Papam (IN ep 27), "Quia te Dominus gratiae praecipuo munere Sede Apostolica collocavit"; Epistola Romanorum Prebyterorum ad Honorium Imperatorem (COL-AV 17), "Quem Deus jussit, elegimus".

**2**    *Certissime reor a Deo accepi id quod sum:* **Ambrose,** De Poenitentia, II, 73 "Ergo enim sciebam quod non eram dignus vocari episcopus, quoniam dederam me saeculo huic; sed gratia tua sum quod sum"; **Augustine,** Tractatus in Joannem 5, 1.

**3-4**    *proselitus et profuga ob amorem Dei:* **Augustine,** Ad Romanos, (52) 60 "Propterea ergo intelligendum est, opera bona per dilectionem fieri, dilectionem autem esse in nobis per donum Spiritus Sancti, sicut... dicit Apostolus (Rom 5, 5). Non ergo equisquam gloriari debet ex operibus suis, quae per donum Dei habet, cum ipsa dilectio in eo bonum operetur"; Opus Imperfectum contra Julianum, III, 106 "Tam multa dicis quibus nos adjuvat Deus, id est 'praecipiendo, bendicendo, sanctificando, coercendo, provocando, illuminando': et non dicis, Charitatem dando; cum dicat Joannes apostolus, Charitas ex Deo est' (1 Jn 4:7)".

5 aspere aliquid ex ore meo effundere; sed cogor zelo Dei, et ueritas
Christi excitauit, pro dilectione proximorum atque filiorum, pro
quibus *tradidi* patriam et parentes et *animam meam usque ad mortem.*
Si dignus sum, uiuo Deo meo docere gentes etsi contempnor
aliquibus.

2 10 2. Manu mea scripsi atque condidi uerba ista danda et tradenda,
militibus mittenda Corotici, non dico ciuibus meis neque ciuibus
sanctorum Romanorum sed ciuibus daemoniorum, ob mala opera
ipso-
rum. Ritu hostili in morte uiuunt, socii Scottorum atque Pictorum
†apostatarumque†. Sanguilentos sanguinare de sanguine innocen-
tium Christi-

15 anorum, quos ego in numero Deo genui atque in Christo confirmaui!

3 3. Postera die qua crismati neophyti in ueste candida — flagrabat
in fronte ipsorum dum crudeliter trucidati atque mactati gladio
supradictis — misi epistolam cum sancto presbytero quem ego ex infantia docui, cum clericis, ut nobis aliquid indulgerent de praeda uel

20 de captiuis baptizatis quos ceperunt: cachinnos fecerunt de illis.

4 4. Idcirco nescio quid magis lugeam: an qui interfecti uel quos
ceperunt uel quos grauiter zabulus inlaqueauit. Perenni poena
gehennam pariter cum ipso mancipabunt, quia utique *qui facit
peccatum seruus est* et *filius zabuli* nuncupatur.

5 255, 1 5. Quapropter resciat omnis homo timens Deum quod a me alieni
sunt et a Christo Deo meo, *pro quo legationem fungor,* patricida, fratri-
cida, *lupi rapaces deuorantes plebem Domini ut cibum panis,* sicut ait:

---

| | |
|---|---|
| **5** | cf 1 M 2: 54 |
| **7** | Ph 2: 30; cf Ac 15: 26; Jn 13: 37 |
| **23-24** | Jn 8: 34 |
| **24** | cf Jn 8: 44 |
| **255: 2** | Ep 6: 20 |
| **3** | Mt 7: 15; Ac 20: 29; Ps 13(14): 4; 52(53): 5 |

---

**5-6**     *cogor zelo Dei, et veritas Christi excitavit pro dilectione proximorum et filiorum:* **Augustine,**
Contra duas epistolas Pelagianorum, I, 37 "Cur enim non dixisti, hominem Dei gratia in
bonum opus excitari?"; De Gratia et Libero Arbitrio, 37 "Unde est in hominibus caritas
Dei et proximi, nisi ex ipso Deo? Nam si non ex Deo, sed ex hominibus, vicerunt
Pelagiani; si autem ex Deo, vicimus Pelagianos".

**255, 1-3**     *Quapropter resciat omnis homo timens Deum quod a me alieni sunt et a Christo Deo meo...
patricida, matricida":* **Council of Tours** (461 A.D.), Canon 7 "Homicidis penitus non
communicandum, donec per confessionem paenitentiae ipsorum crimina diluantur";
**Council of Vienne** (461-91 A.D.), Canon 1 "Itaque censuimus homicidas et falsos testes a
communione ecclesiastica submovendos, nisi paenitentiae satisfactione crimina admissa
diluerint"; **Council of Agde** (506 A.D.), Canon 37 = **Council of Vienne,** Canon 1.

**2**     *pro quo legatione fungor:* **Augustine,** Opus Imperfectum contra Julianum, I, 12 "Pro
Christo legatione fungimur, et pro virili portione quantum valemus opis ad defensionem
catholicae religionis afferimus: nec piget mandare litteris remedia, quae contra errorum
venena conficimus"; cf. Enarrationes in Ps 67: 32, n. 40; **Prosper,** Liber Auctoritates
VIII; see note Confession of Grace at 251, 30-252, 1.

*Iniqui dissipauerunt legem tuam, Domine,* quam in supremis tempori-
5 bus Hiberione optime benigne plantauerat atque instructa erat
fauente Deo.

6      6. Non usurpo. Partem habeo cum his *quos aduocauit et prae-
destinauit euangelium praedicare in persecutionibus non paruis usque
ad extremum terrae,* etsi inuidet inimicus per tyrannidem Corotici, qui
10 Deum non ueretur nec sacerdotes ipsius, quos elegit et indulsit illis
summam diuinam sublimam potestatem, *quos ligarent super terram
ligatos esse et in caelis.*

7      7. Vnde ergo quaeso plurimum, *sancti et humiles corde,* adulari
talibus non licet *nec cibum* nec potum *sumere* cum ipsis nec ele-
15 mosinas ipsorum recipi debeat donec crudeliter<per>paenitentiam
effusis lacrimis satis Deo faciant et liberent seruos Dei et ancillas
Christi baptizatas, pro quibus mortuus est et crucifixus.

8      8. *Dona iniquorum reprobat Altissimus. Qui offert sacrificium
ex substantia pauperum quasi qui uictimat filium in conspectu patris*
20 *sui. Diuitias,* inquit, *quas congregauit iniuste euomentur de uentre
eius, trahit illum angelus mortis, ira draconum mulcabitur, interficiet
illum lingua colubris, comedit autem eum ignis inextinguibilis.* Ideoque:
*Vae qui replent se quae non sunt sua,* uel: *Quid prodest homini
ut totum mundum lucretur et animae suae detrimentum patiatur?*

9 25   9. Longum est per singula discutere uel insinuare, per totam
legem carpere testimonia de tali cupiditate. Auaritia mortale
256, 1 crimen. *Non concupisces rem proximi tui. Non occides.* Homicida
non potest esse cum Christo. *Qui odit fratrem suum homicida* adscri-
bitur. Vel: *Qui non diligit fratrem suum in morte manet.* Quanto
magis reus est qui manus suas coinquinauit in sanguine filiorum
5 Dei, quos nuper *adquisiuit* in ultimis terrae per exhortationem
paruitatis nostrae?

---

| | |
|---|---|
| **4** | Ps 118(119): 126 |
| **7-8** | Rm 8: 30 |
| **8-9** | Ac 13: 47 (Is 49: 6) |
| **11-12** | Mt 16: 19; 18: 18 |
| **13** | Dn 3: 87 |
| **14** | 1 Co 5: 11 |
| **18-20** | Si 34: 23-24 |
| **20-22** | Jb 20: 15, 16, 26 |
| **23** | Hab 2: 6 |
| **23-24** | Mt 16: 26; Lk 9: 25 |
| **256: 1** | Ex 20: 17, 13; Dt 5: 21, 17; Rm 13: 9 |
| **2** | 1 Jn 3: 15 |
| **3** | 1 Jn 3: 14 |
| **5** | Is 43: 21 *(LXX)* |

---

| | |
|---|---|
| **3** | *devorantes plebem Domini:* **Hilary** Tractatus in Ps 52, 13 "Comedunt... qui sanctorum injuriis vivunt". |
| **256, 1-2** | *Homicida non potest esse cum Christo:* **Cyprian**, De Dominica Oratione, 24 "(Homicida) non potest esse cum Christo qui imitator Iudae maluit esse quam Christi". |

**10**　　10. Numquid sine Deo uel *secundum carnem* Hiberione ueni?
Quis me compulit? *Alligatus* sum *Spiritu* ut non uideam aliquem *de*
*cognatione mea.* Numquid a me piam misericordiam quod ago
10　ergo gentem illam qui me aliquando ceperunt et deuastauerunt
seruos et ancillas domus patris mei? Ingenuus fui *secundum*
*carnem;* decorione patre nascor. Vendidi enim nobilitatem
meam — non erubesco neque me paenitet — pro utilitate aliorum;
denique seruus sum in Christo genti exterae ob gloriam ineffabilem
15　*perennis uitae quae est in Christo Iesu Domino nostro.*

**11**　　11. Et si mei me non cognoscunt, *propheta in patria sua honorem*
*non habet.* Forte non sumus *ex uno ouili* neque *unum Deum*
*patrem* habemus, sicut ait: *Qui non est mecum contra me est, et qui*
*non congregat mecum spargit.* Non conuenit: *Vnus destruit, alter aedi-*
20　*ficat. Non quaero quae mea sunt.*

---

| | |
|---|---|
| **256: 7** | 2 Co 1: 17 |
| **8** | Ac 20: 22 |
| **8-9** | Gn 12: 1 |
| **11-12** | 2 Co 1: 17 |
| **15** | cf Rm 6: 23 |
| **16-17** | Jn 4: 44 |
| **17** | Jn 10: 16 |
| **17-18** | Ep 4: 6 |
| **18-19** | Mt 12: 30; cf Lk 11: 23 |
| **19-20** | Si 34: 28; cf Ga 2: 18 |
| **20** | 1 Co 13: 5; cf 2 Co 12: 14; Ph 2: 21 |

---

**256, 7-8**　　*Numquid sine Deo... Hiberione veni? Quis me compulit? Alligatus sum Spiritu:* **Augustine,**
De Spiritu et Littera, 5 "Nos autem dicimus humanam voluntatem sic divinitus adjuvari
ad faciendam justitiam, ut praeter quod creatus est homo cum libero arbitrio (voluntatis),
praeterque doctrinam qua ei praecipitur quemadmodum vivere debeat, accipiat Spiritum
Sanctum, quo fiat in animo eius delectatio dilectioque summi illius atque incommutabilis
boni quod Deus est"; cf. De Gratia Christi et Peccato Originali, 31; De Gratia et Libero
Arbitrio, 37; De Peccatorum Meritis et Remissione, II, 27; **Prosper,** Epistola ad Rufinum,
8-9.

**9-10**　　*Numquid a me piam misericordiam quod ago erga gentem illam?* **Augustine,** Opus
Imperfectum contra Julianum, II, 228 "pia oboedientia... donum Dei", Contra Julianum,
V, 35 "Prorsus qui sibi committuntur, et a semetipsis aguntur, non sunt boni, quia non
sunt filii Dei. 'Quotquot enim spiritu Dei aguntur, hi filii sunt Dei' (Rom 8:14). Puto
quod agnoscas (Juliane) in hac sententia dogma apostolicum, quo illud subvertitur
vestrum"; Epistola 130 ad Probam, 21 "Cum dicimus, 'Fiat voluntas tua...' nobis ab illo
precamur ipsam oboedientiam"; cf. De Continentia, 8; De Virginitate, 42-3; De Bono
Viduitatis, 20-2.

Non mea gratia sed Deus *qui dedit hanc sollicitudinem in*
*corde meo* ut unus essem de *uenatoribus siue piscatoribus* quos olim
Deus *in nouissimis diebus* ante praenuntiauit.

**12**      12. Inuidetur mihi. Quid faciam, Domine? Valde despicior.

25 Ecce oues tuae circa me laniantur atque depraedantur, et supradictis
latrunculis, iubente Corotico hostili mente. Longe est a caritate
Dei traditor Christianorum in manus Scottorum atque Pictorum.
*Lupi rapaces* deglutierunt gregem Domini, qui utique Hiberione cum
summa diligentia optime crescebat, et filii Scottorum et filiae

257, 1 regulorum monachi et uirgines Christi enumerare nequeo. Quam ob
rem *iniuria iustorum non  te placeat;* etiam *usque ad inferos non*
*placebit.*

**13**      13. Quis sanctorum non horreat iocundare uel conuiuium fruere
5 cum talibus? De spoliis defunctorum Christianorum repleuerunt
domos suas, de rapinis uiuunt. Nesciunt miseri uenenum
letale cibum porrigunt ad amicos et filios suos, sicut Eua non
intellexit quod utique mortem tradidit uiro suo. Sic sunt omnes
qui male agunt: *mortem* perennem poenam *operantur.*

**14** 10     14. Consuetudo Romanorum Gallorum Christianorum: mittunt
uiros sanctos idoneos ad Francos et ceteras gentes cum tot
milia solidorum ad redimendos captiuos baptizatos. Tu potius inter-
ficis et uendis illos genti exterae ignoranti Deum; quasi in lupanar

---

| | |
|---|---|
| **21-22** | 2 Co 8: 16 |
| **22** | cf Jr 16: 16 |
| **23** | Ac 2: 17 |
| **28** | Mt 7: 15; Ac 20: 29 |
| **257: 2-3** | Si 9: 17 *(VULG)* |
| **9** | 2 Co 7: 10 |

---

**21-3** *Non mea gratia sed Deus qui... ante praenuntiavit:* **Augustine,** De Spiritu et Littera, 40
"Hoc enim Deus promittit quod ipse facit: non enim ipse promittit et alius facit, quod
iam non erat promittere sed praedicere"; cf. De Correptione et Gratia, 35; 36; De Gratia
Christi et Peccato Originali, 31; Epistola 194 ad Sixtum, 36; De Gratia et Libero
Arbitrio, 37-40; De Praedestinatione Sanctorum, 6; 12-20; **Prosper,** Pro Augustion
Responsiones, VIII; De Vocatione omnium Gentium, I; IX; XX; see note in Confession of
Grace at 247, 3-4.

**26-7** *Longe est a caritate Dei traditor Christianorum in manus...:* **Augustine,** De Peccatorum
Meritis et Remissione, II, 27 "Tanto autem magis delectat opus bonum, quanto magis
diligitur Deus summum atque incommutabile bonum, et auctor qualiumcumque
bonorum omnium"; De Moribus Ecclesiae Catholicae, 18 "Si nulla res ab eius (Dei)
caritate nos separat, quid esse non solum melius, sed etiam certius hoc bono potest?";
21-22; De Gratia et Libero Arbitrio, 37.

**257, 4-5** *Quis sanctorum non horreat jocundare vel convivium fruere cum talibus?"* **Pope Innocent**
**I,** "Qua re Pelagium Caelestiumque, id est inventores vocum novarum, ... ecclesiastica
communione privari apostolici vigoris auctoritate censemus" (being in Epistola 182, 6 of
**Augustine**); cf. **Cyprian,** Epistola 67.

tradis *membra Christi.* Qualem spem habes in Deum, uel qui
15 te consentit aut qui te communicat uerbis adulationis? Deus
iudicabit. Scriptum est enim: *Non solum facientes mala sed etiam
consentientes damnandi sunt.*

**15** 15. Nescio *quid dicam* uel *quid loquar* amplius de defunctis
filiorum Dei, quos gladius supra modum dure tetigit. Scriptum est
20 enim: *Flete cum flentibus,* et iterum: *Si dolet unum membrum
condoleant omnia membra.* Quapropter ecclesia *plorat et plangit
filios* et filias *suas* quas adhuc gladius nondum interfecit, sed
prolongati et exportati in longa terrarum, ubi *peccatum* mani-
feste grauiter impudenter *abundat,* ibi uenundati ingenui
25 homines, Christiani in seruitute redacti sunt, praesertim indignissi-
morum pessimorum apostatarumque Pictorum.

**16** 16. Idcirco cum tristitia et maerore uociferabo: O speciosissimi
258, 1 atque amantissimi fratres et filii *quos in Christo genui* enumerare
nequeo, quid faciam uobis? Non sum dignus Deo neque hominibus

subuenire. *Praeualuit iniquitas iniquorum super nos.* Quasi *extranei
facti sumus.* Forte non credunt *unum baptismum* percepimus uel
5 *unum Deum patrem* habemus. Indignum est illis Hiberionaci
sumus. Sicut ait: *Nonne unum Deum habetis? Quid dereliquistis
unusquisque proximum suum?*

**17** 17. Idcirco doleo pro uobis, doleo, carissimi mihi; sed iterum

---

| 14 | cf 1 Co 6: 15 |
| 16-17 | Rm 1: 32 |
| 18 | cf Jn 12: 49 |
| 20 | Rm 12: 15 |
| 20-21 | 1 Co 12: 26 |
| 21-22 | cf Mt 2: 18 (Jr 31: 15) |
| 23-24 | cf Rm 5: 20 |
| 258: 1 | 1 Co 4: 15; cf Phm 10 |
| 3 | Ps 64(65): 4; cf Ezk 18:20; 33: 12 |
| 3-4 | Ps 68(69): 9 |
| 4 | Ep 4: 5 |
| 5 | Ep 4: 6 |
| 6-7 | Ml 2: 10 |

---

21  *Quapropter ecclesia plorat et plangit filios et filias suas:* **Ambrose,** De Poenitentia, II, 92
"Fleat pro te mater Ecclesia, et culpam tuam lacrimis lavet, videat te Christus
moerentem"; cf. 73; 91; Explanatio in Ps 37, 10 "Ipsa (ecclesia) pro te fleat, ipsa tua
peccata deploret, et fleat plurimum".

gaudeo intra meipsum: non gratis *laboraui* uel peregrinatio mea
10 *in uacuum* non fuit. Et contigit scelus tam horrendum
ineffabile, Deo gratias, creduli baptizati, de saeculo recessistis
ad paradisum. Cerno uos: migrare coepistis ubi *nox non erit*
*neque luctus neque mors amplius, sed exultabitis sicut uituli ex*
*uinculis resoluti et conculcabitis iniquos et erunt cinis sub pedibus*
15 *uestris.*

**18** 18. Vos ergo regnabitis cum apostolis et prophetis atque marty-
ribus. Aeterna regna capietis, sicut ipse testatur inquit: *Venient*
*ab oriente et occidente et recumbent cum Abraham et Isaac et Iacob in*
*regno caelorum. Foris canes et uenefici et homicidae,* et: *Mendacibus*
20 *periuris pars eorum in stagnum ignis aeterni.* Non inmerito ait
apostolus: *Vbi iustus uix saluus erit, peccator et impius transgressor*
*legis ubi se recognoscet?*

**19** 19. Vnde enim Coroticus cum suis sceleratissimis, rebellatores
Christi, ubi se uidebunt, qui mulierculas baptizatas praemia
25 distribuunt ob miserum regnum temporale, quod utique in momento
transeat? *Sicut nubes uel fumus, qui utique uento dispergitur,* ita
*peccatores* fraudulenti *a facie Domini peribunt; iusti autem epulentur*
*in magna constantia* cum Christo, *iudicabunt nationes et* regibus
iniquis *dominabuntur* in saecula saeculorum, Amen.

**20** 259, 1  20. *Testificor coram Deo et angelis suis* erit sicut
intimauit imperitiae meae. Non mea uerba sed Dei et apostolorum
atque prophetarum quod ego Latinum exposui, qui numquam enim
mentiti sunt. *Qui crediderit saluus erit, qui uero non crediderit con-*
5 *dempnabitur, Deus locutus est.*

**21** 21. Quaeso plurimum ut quicumque famulus Dei promptus
fuerit ut sit gerulus litterarum harum, ut nequaquam subtrahatur
uel abscondatur
a nemine, sed magis potius legatur coram cunctis plebibus et prae-

---

| | |
|---|---|
| **9-10** | Ph 2: 16 |
| **12-13** | Rv 22: 5; 21: 4 |
| **13-15** | Ml 4: 2-3 |
| **17-19** | Mt 8: 11 |
| **19** | Rv 22: 15 |
| **19-20** | Rv 21: 8; Ml 3: 5; 1 Tm 1: 10 |
| **21-22** | 1 P 4: 18 (Pr 11: 31) |
| **26-29** | cf Ws 5: 15; Ps 67(68): 3-4; 36(37): 20; Ws 5: 1; 3: 8 |
| **29** | *in saecula saculorum* Rv 20: 10 |
| **259: 1** | 2 Tm 4: 1; 1 Tm 5: 21; cf Mt 16: 27; Mk 8: 38 |
| **4-5** | Mk 16: 15-16 |
| **5** | Ps 59(60): 8; 107(108): 8 |

---

**259, 9-13**  *Quod si Deus inspirat illos... ita ut vel sero paeniteant... et sani efficiantur hic et in aeternum:*
see note in Confession of Grace at 235, 14-5.

sente ipso Corotico. Quod si Deus inspirat illos *ut quandoque Deo*
10  *resipiscant,* ita ut uel sero paeniteant quod tam impie gesserunt —
homicida erga fratres Domini — et liberent captiuas baptizatas
quas ante ceperunt, ita ut mereantur Deo uiuere et sani efficiantur
hic et in aeternum! Pax Patri et Filio et Spiritui Sancto, Amen.

---

**9-10**       cf 2 Tm 2: 25-26

## Part II

# Translation into English and Irish of the
## *Confession of Grace* and the
## *Letter Excommunicating Coroticus*

1. Translation into English of the two letters

2. Translation into Irish of the two letters

Translation into English of the two letters

# St Patrick's *Confession of Grace*

1. I am Patrick, a sinner, unlettered, the least of all the faithful, and held in contempt by a great many people. I am the son of Calpornius, a deacon, son of Potitus, a priest. My father lived at the village of Bannavem Taburniae, for he had an estate nearby, where I was taken captive.

I was then about sixteen years old. I did not know the true God, and for this reason I was led in captivity to Ireland, with so many thousands of people. It was in accordance with our deserts, because we had forsaken God and did not keep His commandments, and were not obedient to our bishops who used to admonish us for our salvation. God brought to bear upon us the wrath of His anger and scattered us among many peoples, even to the uttermost part of the earth, where now, in my lowliness, I dwell among strangers.

2. And there the Lord opened my unbelieving mind, so that even at that late hour I should remember my sins and turn with all my heart to the Lord my God, who looked upon my abjection, and had mercy on my youth and ignorance, and watched over me before I knew Him, and before I came to be wise, or to discern between good and evil; and He kept me safe and comforted me as a father would his son.

3. And that, then, is why I cannot remain silent, nor is it expedient that I should, about such great favours and so great a grace as the Lord deigned to bestow on me in the land of my captivity. Because this is the return we can make after God corrects us and brings us to know Him: to exalt and praise His wonderful deeds before every nation under the whole heaven.

4. Because there is no other God, nor was there ever before, nor will there be hereafter, except God the Father, unbegotten, without beginning, from whom is all beginning, containing all things, as we have been taught; and His Son Jesus Christ, whom we declare to have been always with the Father; before the beginning of the world begotten of the Father after the manner of Spirit, inexpressibly, before all beginning; and through Him were made all things visible and invisible.

He was made man, and having conquered death He was received in heaven into the presence of the Father. And He gave Him all power above every name in heaven, on earth, and under the earth; and let every tongue confess to Him that Jesus Christ is Lord and God, in whom we believe in and whose coming we look for soon, to be judge of the living and the dead, and to render to everyone according to his deeds.

And He poured out the Holy Spirit upon us abundantly, as gift, and pledge of immortality, who makes believers and listeners in order that they shall be sons of God and fellow heirs with Christ. Him we confess and adore, One God in the Trinity of the Sacred Name.

5. For the Lord himself said through the prophet: *Call upon me in the day of your trouble; and I will deliver you, and you shall glorify me.* And again He says: *It is honourable to reveal and confess the works of God.*

6. Notwithstanding that I am in many things imperfect I want my brethren and kinsmen to know what sort of man I am, so that they may be able to perceive the desire of my soul.

7. I am not ignorant of the testimony of my Lord, who declares in the Psalm: *You will destroy those who speak falsely.* He says again: *A lying mouth destroys the soul.* And the same Lord says in the Gospel: *On the day of judgement men will render account for every careless word they utter.*

8. I have every ground, then, in fear and trembling to dread this sentence on that day when no-one shall be able to withdraw or hide himself, but when we shall all, without exception, render account of even the smallest sins before the judgement seat of Christ the Lord.

9. For those reasons I long ago thought of writing, but I have hesitated until now for fear of what critics should say. Because I was not a student as others were, who thus thoroughly drank in the law and the holy Scriptures, the two in equal measure, and never changed their language from childhood but rather were always engaged in perfecting it. Whereas I have had to change my language and speak that of a foreign people, as may easily be proved from the flavour of my writing, which shows how poorly I am instructed and how little skilled in expressing myself. As Scripture says: *Through the way he expresses himself shall the wise man be discerned, and his understanding, and knowledge and instruction in truth.*

10. But what will an excuse avail me (even when it is in accordance with the truth), especially when the excuse is accompanied by presumption? Here am I in my old age seeking something I did not acquire when I was young: my sins prevented me from mastering what I had read through in only a perfunctory way. But who will believe me even if I repeat what I have said? As an adolescent, indeed as almost a speechless boy, I was taken captive before I knew what I should seek and what I should

avoid. And so today I am ashamed and greatly afraid to expose my ignorance, because to people trained in self-expression I am unable to express myself briefly, as my spirit and mind long to do, in such a manner that what I say will reveal my feelings.

11. But if what was given to others had been given to me I certainly would not have remained silent, because of my duty to return thanks, as I was saying; and if, perhaps, in doing so now I may appear to some to be pushing myself forward with my lack of knowledge and my difficulty in expressing myself, Scripture also says: *The tongues of stammerers will quickly learn to speak peace.* How much more ought we seek to speak who are, says Scripture, *a letter of Christ bearing salvation to the uttermost parts of the earth*; and, if not an elegantly written letter, yet a letter firmly and powerfully written on your hearts, not with ink, but with the Spirit of the living God. And the Spirit further testifies: *Even rusticity was created by the Most High.*

12. Wherefore although I was at first an unlettered exile, truly ignorant, who knew not how to provide for the life hereafter, I know this for a certainty: that assuredly before I was humbled I was like a stone lying in deep mire; and that He who is mighty came and in His mercy lifted me up; and, more than that, truly raised me aloft and placed me on top of the wall. It is therefore my bounden duty to cry out aloud in order to make some return to the Lord for such great favours of His here and in eternity, favours which it is beyond the mind of man to measure.

13. Wherefore, wonder you at this, you great and small who fear God; and you, lordly and clever men of letters, listen, and examine closely what I am about to say. Who was it that roused me, a fool, from the midst of those who are wise, and learned in the law, and skilled in speaking and in general affairs; and in preference to others inspired me, me whom this world rejected, to be such a man, (if only I were!), as in awe and reverence and without cause of complaint would faithfully work for the good of the people to whom the love of Christ brought me and made a gift of me for the duration of my life (if I should be worthy of it); to be, in a word, a man who would humbly and sincerely serve them to the end?

14. In proportion, then, to the faith which I have received from the Trinity, it is my duty to make this choice: without thought of the risk of censure I incur, to make known the gift of God and His everlasting consolation; fearlessly and confidently to spread God's Name everywhere; so that even after my death I may leave a legacy to my brethren and sons whom I have baptized in the Lord – so many thousands of people.

15. And I was not worthy, nor such a sort that the Lord should grant this to His little servant; that after my so numerous hardships and troubles, after my captivity, after many years had gone by, He should bestow on me so great a grace in favour of that people – a thing that once, in my youth, I never expected nor thought of.

16. But after I came to Ireland I was daily herding flocks – and I used to pray many times a day – more and more the love of God and the fear of Him came to me, and my faith was increased, and my spirit was moved so that in one day I would pray as many as a hundred times, and in the night nearly as often, even while I was staying in the woods and on the mountain; and before daylight I used to be stirred to prayer, in snow, in frost, in rain; and I felt no ill effects from it, nor was there any slug-gishness in me, such as now I see there is, because then the spirit was fervent in me.

17. And there, as it happens, one night in my sleep I heard a voice say to me: "It is good that you fast, you who are soon to go to your own country". And after a little while again I heard a voice say to me: "Look, your ship is ready". It was not nearby, but was at a distance of perhaps two hundred miles; and I had never been there, nor did I know anybody there. Shortly after that I took to flight, left the man with whom I had been for six years, and journeyed by the power of God, who directed my way unto my good, and I feared nothing until I reached that ship.

18. And on the day I arrived the ship left its anchorage and I spoke to the crew that I might have the possibility of sailing with them, but the captain was displeased and answered sharply in anger: "On no account are you to try to go with us"; and when I heard that I withdrew from them to go to the little hut where I was staying, and on the way I began to pray, and before I had finished my prayer I heard one of them who was shouting loudly after me: "Come quickly, for these people are calling you"; and immediately I went back to them and they began to say to me: "Come, for we take you on trust; make friends with us in any way you wish"; and that day, accordingly, I refused to suck their breasts through fear of God, but rather hoped that some of them would come to faith in Jesus Christ, for they were heathens; and thus I had my way with them, and straight away we set sail.

19. And after three days we reached land, and for twenty-eight days we journeyed through deserted country, and food failed them and hunger overcame them, and one day the captain said to me: "How now, Christian? You say your God is great and all-powerful; why then can't you

pray for us? For we are in danger of starving; it will go hard with us ever to see a human being again". I said confidently to them: "Turn sincerely with all your heart to the Lord my God, because nothing is impossible to Him, so that today He may send you food in your way until you are satisfied, because He has abundance everywhere". And with the help of God it so came to pass: lo, a herd of pigs appeared on the way before our eyes, and they slaughtered many of them, and there they stayed for two nights, and they were well restored and their bodies were refreshed, for many of them had collapsed and had been left half dead by the wayside. And after this they gave full thanks to God, and I became honourable in their eyes; and from that day they had food in abundance; they even came upon wild honey, and they offered me a share of it, and one of them said: "It is a sacrificial offering". Thanks be to God, I tasted none of it.

20. That very same night I was sleeping when Satan mightily put me to the test – I shall remember it as long as I am in this body. He fell upon me like a huge rock, and I could not move a limb. But whence did it occur to me, ignorant in spirit, to call upon Helias? And while this was happening I saw the sun rise in the heavens, and as I was crying out: "Helias, Helias", with all my strength, lo, the splendour of that sun fell on me and promptly shook all heaviness from me; and I believe that I was aided by Christ my Lord, and that His Spirit was even then crying out on my behalf; and I hope that it will be so in the day of my distress, as He says in the Gospel: *In that day,* the Lord testifies, *it is not you who speak, but the Spirit of your Father speaking through you.*

21. And again, many years later, I was once more taken captive. When I was with them, accordingly, for that first night I heard a divine voice telling me: "For two months you will be with them". And that was what actually came to pass: on the sixtieth night the Lord delivered me from their hands.

22. Even on the journey He provided us daily with food and fire and dry quarters, until on the tenth day we reached human habitation. As I related above, for twenty-eight days we journeyed through deserted country, and on that night in which we reached human beings we had, in fact, no food left.

23. And once more, after a few years I was in Britain with my family, who received me as a son, and sincerely begged of me that at least now, after all the many troubles I had endured, I should not leave them to go anywhere. And there, truly, I saw in a vision of the night, a man coming as it were from Ireland, whose name was Victoricus, with countless

letters, and he gave me one of them, and I read the beginning of the letter, which ran: "The Voice of the Irish"; and as I was reading the beginning of the letter aloud I thought I heard at that very moment the voice of those who lived beside the wood of Voclut, which is near the Western sea, and thus they cried out as with one voice: "We beg you, holy youth, to come and walk once more among us". And I was greatly troubled in heart and could read no further, and so I awoke. Thanks be to God that after many years the Lord granted them according to their cry.

24. And on another night – I do not know, God knows, whether it was in myself or beside myself – very distinctly, in words which I heard but could not understand except at the end of the prayer, He thus declared Himself: "He who gave His life for you, He it is who is speaking in you"; and at that I awoke rejoicing.

25. And another time I saw Him praying within me, and I was as it were within my body, and I heard [One] above me, that is to say, above my inner man; and there He was praying earnestly, with sighs; and as this was happening I was in amazement and wonder and puzzlement about who it was that was praying within me. But at the end of the prayer He declared that He was the Spirit; and at that I awoke, and I recalled what the apostle had said: *The Spirit helps the weaknesses of our prayer; for we do not know how to pray as we ought; but the Spirit himself pleads for us with sighs unutterable that cannot be put into words.* And again: *The Lord our Advocate pleads for us.*

26. And when I was tested by some of my seniors, who came and cast up my sins as unfitting me for my laborious episcopate, assuredly on that day I was sorely tried, to the point where I could have fallen here and forever; but the Lord graciously spared the alien and stranger for His Name's sake; and He came powerfully to my aid when I was being walked upon, so that I did not fall unhappily into discredit and disgrace. I pray God that it be not accounted to them as a sin.

27. They found occasion for their charge against me – after thirty-years – in a deed I had confessed before I became a deacon. In my anxiety I confided to my best friend, my mind full of sorrow, what I had done one day in my boyhood, indeed in one hour, because I was not yet in control of myself. I know not, God knows, if I was then fifteen years old; and I did not believe in the living God, nor had I believed in Him from childhood, but remained in death and unbelief until I was severely chastised and truly humbled by hunger and nakedness – and that, daily.

28. In contrast, I was not setting out for Ireland until I was approaching my declining years, but this was in fact to my advantage, for in the interval I was corrected by the Lord, and so fitted by Him that today I should be what once was far beyond me: that I should be concerned or active myself about the salvation of others, at a time when I was taking no thought even for myself.

29. And so, on the day when I was rejected by the above-mentioned persons − that night I saw a vision in the night, I looked [and] before my face was a writing that stripped me of my honour. And as I looked at it I heard a divine voice say to me: "We have seen with disapproval the face of so-and-so" (designated by name). Nor did He say: "*You* have seen with disapproval", but: "*We* have seen with disapproval", as if He had associated Himself with me. As He said in Scripture: *He who touches you is as one who touches the apple of my eye.*

30. That is why I give thanks to Him who in all things gave me strength, so that He did not hinder me from the journey I had decided on, nor from that work of mine which I had learned from Christ my Lord, but rather did I feel in myself no little power from Him, and my fidelity was approved before God and men.

31. Wherefore I say boldly that my conscience does not reproach me now, and will not hereafter: I have God as my witness that I have not lied in the words I have reported to you.

32. Rather do I grieve for my best friend, that he should have given cause for our hearing such a statement from the Lord. A man to whom I had entrusted my very soul! And I had learned from some of the brethren before that gathering at which my defence came up − I was not present at it, nor was I in Britain, nor did the matter originate from me − that he too would argue for me in my absence; even to myself he had said with his own mouth: "Look, you must be raised to the episcopate" − of which I was not worthy. But why did it occur to him afterwards that before everybody, good and bad, he should put me even publicly to shame [for a deed] for which he had earlier freely and gladly granted me pardon − as did the Lord, who is greater than all?

33. I have said enough. I must not, however, hide the gift of God which He bestowed on me in the land of my captivity, because then I earnestly sought Him and there I found Him, and He preserved me from all iniquities (so I believe) through His indwelling Spirit, who has worked to this day within me. I am speaking boldly again. But God knows that

if a mere man had declared this to me I should perhaps have remained silent, for the love of Christ.

34. Wherefore I give unwearying thanks to my God, who kept me faithful in the day of my trial, in such wise that today I may confidently offer Him my life in sacrifice, as a living victim to Christ my Lord. [I give unwearying thanks to my God] who delivered me from all my troubles, so that I can even say: "Who am I, Lord, or what is my calling?" – You who helped my work with such divine power that today among the nations I steadfastly exalt and glorify Your Name wherever I am; and that, not only when circumstances favour me, but also when I am afflicted; so that whatever happens to me, good or bad, I must accept with an even mind, and thank God always; God who showed me that I should believe Him endlessly to be trusted; and who so helped me that I, a man ignorant [of His designs], in the last days should dare to undertake this work so holy and so wonderful; in such fashion that I might in some degree imitate those whom the Lord already long ago foretold would announce His Gospel in witness to all nations before the world's end. And as we have seen it written, so we have seen it fulfilled: behold, we are the witnesses that the Gospel has been preached to the limit beyond which no-one dwells.

35. It would take too long to relate all my labours, one by one or even in part. Briefly let me say how the most gracious God often freed me from slavery, and from the twelve perils in which my life was at stake, in addition to many plots against me, and things I cannot express in words. Nor shall I bore my readers. But I have God as my witness, who knows all things even before they come to pass, how a divine voice often forewarned me, poor ignorant ward that I was.

36. Whence was this wisdom given to me, who had it not of myself, I who knew not the number of my days nor had any mind for God? Whence was I afterwards granted that gift so great, so salutary, to know God and also to love Him, even to the point where I should forsake my homeland and my family?

37. And many gifts were offered to me with weeping and tears, and I gave offence to the givers; and not [to them only, but also], against my wish, to some of my seniors. But under God's guidance, in no way did I consent or give in to them. It was not I but the grace of God, who overcame in me and resisted all those things, so that I came to the heathen Irish to preach the Gospel and to endure insults from unbelievers; to hear myself taunted for being a foreigner; [to experience] many persecutions

unto bonds; and to surrender my free-born status for the benefit of others. And if I shall be found worthy of it, I am ready to give even my life unhesitatingly and very gladly for His Name's sake; and there I desire to spend it until I die, if the Lord will grant me that.

38. Because I am exceedingly in debt to God, who granted me so great a grace that through me a multitudinous people should be reborn in God, and afterwards confirmed; and that clerics should everywhere be ordained for them – for a people newly coming to belief whom the Lord took from the uttermost parts of the earth, as long ago He had promised through His prophets: *To you the nations will come from the uttermost parts of the earth and say, Our fathers got for themselves worthless idols, and there is no profit in them.* And again: *I have set you to be a light for the Gentiles, that you may bring salvation to the uttermost parts of the earth.*

39. And there I wish to await His promise, who certainly never deceives, as He promises in the Gospel: *They will come from east and west and sit at table with Abraham and Isaac and Jacob,* just as we believe that from the whole world believers shall come.

40. For that reason, accordingly, it is indeed our duty to fish well and diligently, as the Lord fore-admonishes and teaches, saying: *Follow me, and I will make you fishers of men.* And again He says through the prophets: *Behold, I am sending fishers and many hunters, says God;* and so on. We were gravely bound, then, to spread our nets, so that a great multitude and throng should be caught for God, and that everywhere there should be clergy to baptize and exhort a needy and thirsting people, as the Lord in the Gospel admonishes and teaches, saying: *Go therefore now, make disciples of all nations, baptizing them in the name of the Father and of the Son and of the Holy Spirit, teaching them to observe all that I have commanded you; and lo, I am with you always, to the close of the age.* And again He says: *Go therefore into all the world and preach the Gospel to the whole creation. He who believes and is baptized will be saved; but he who does not believe will be condemned.* And again: *This Gospel of the kingdom will be preached throughout the whole world, as a testimony to all nations; and then the end will come.* And again the Lord announces beforehand through the prophet; *And in the last days it shall be, God declares, that I will pour out my Spirit upon all flesh, and your sons and your daughters shall prophesy, and your young men shall see visions, and your old men shall dream dreams; yea, and on my menservants and my maidservants in those days I will pour out my Spirit; and they shall prophesy.* And *in Hosea He says: Those who were not my people I will call "my people" and her who had not received mercy I will call "her who has received mercy".*

*And in the very place where it was said, "You are not my people", they will*
*be called "sons of the living God".*

41. Consequently, then, in Ireland, they who never had knowledge of God, but up till now always worshipped only idols and abominations – how they have lately been made a people of the Lord and are called
children of God; sons of the Scotti and daughters of their kings are seen
to be monks and virgins of Christ!

42. And there was even one blessed Scottic girl of noble birth,
very beautiful, full-grown, whom I baptized; she came to us a few days
afterwards for one reason only: to tell us she had received a message from
a messenger of God who instructed her to become a virgin of Christ and
to draw close to God. Thanks be to God, six days later she most laudably
and ardently laid hold of that life. [For] what all the virgins [do] they [the
Irish] likewise do; not with their parents' consent, rather do they suffer
both persecutions and false reproaches from their families; and nevertheless, their number ever increases [in fact from those of our own race
born there we do not know the number who have become virgins of
Christ], not counting the widows, and the married persons who practise
continence. But among them slave girls are in greatest trouble: they suffer
continually, even to the extent of terror and threats. But the Lord has
given grace to many of His handmaids, because even though they are for-
bidden they continue steadfast in their following of Him.

43. As a result, then, even if I should wish to leave them and
make a journey to Britain – and I would most dearly love to make that
journey, so as to see my homeland and family; not only that, but also [to
proceed] as far as Gaul to visit the brethren and see the face of the saints
of my Lord: God knows I greatly desired it – still I am bound by the
Spirit, who testifies to me that if I do this He will pronounce me guilty;
and I am afraid of losing the labour I began, and not I but Christ the Lord,
who ordered me to come and be with those people for the rest of my life
– if God wills it, and keeps me from every evil way, so that I sin not in
His sight.

44. This, indeed, it is my duty to hope for, but my own self I
do not trust as long as I am in this body of death. For he is strong who
daily strives to subvert me from fidelity, and from the chastity I have
undertaken, in devotion unfeigned to Christ my Lord, to the end of my
life. But the hostile flesh is always pulling us towards death, that is to say,
towards the unlawful satisfying of what it entices us to do. And I know
this in part because I have not always led a perfect life, as other believers

have. But I confess to my Lord, and I do not blush before Him, because I am not lying: from the time I came to know Him, from my early manhood, the love of God and the fear of Him have grown in me, and up till now, by the favour of the Lord, I have kept faith.

45. Let who will laugh and scorn: I shall not be silent, nor do I hide the signs and wonders which were shown to me by the Lord many years before they came to pass, by Him who knows all things even before the beginning of time.

46. That is why, then, it is my duty to give unceasing thanks to God, who often pardoned my lack of wisdom and my negligence; and who on more than one occasion held back from vehement anger with me, who had been chosen as His helper and yet was slow to act in accordance with what I had been shown and what the Spirit was prompting me. And the Lord had mercy on me thousands of times because I saw in myself that I was ready, but that I did not know how to direct myself in regard to the matter, for many were trying to forbid this mission of mine; among themselves they were even talking behind my back, and asking: 'Why is that fellow thrusting himself into danger among a hostile people who do not know God?' They said this not out of malice, but because it did not make sense to them, for the reason that, as I myself bear witness, I was uneducated. And I myself was slow to recognize the grace that was then in me; now I understand – what I ought to have understood earlier.

47. Now, then, I have given an honest account to my brethren and fellow servants, who have believed me because of what I have proclaimed and am proclaiming, in order to strengthen and confirm your faith. My desire is that you also strive after greater things, and do more excellent deeds. This will be my glory, because a wise son is the glory of his father.

48. You know, and God knows, how I have lived among you from my early years, in true faith and in sincerity of heart. Even in respect to those heathens among whom I dwell, I have kept my word with them, and will continue to keep it. God knows I have deceived none of them, nor do I have any intention of doing it, for the sake of God and of His Church, lest I should stir up persecution for them and for us all, and lest the Name of the Lord should be blasphemed through me; for it is written: *Woe to the man through whom the name of the Lord is blasphemed.*

49. For although I am very inexperienced, I have nevertheless tried in some measure to keep my reserve even from the Christian brethren

and the virgins of Christ and the religious women who used to make me little gifts spontaneously, and would cast something from their ornaments on to the altar. These I would return to them, and they would be annoyed with me for doing so. But I [did it] for the hope of eternal life: that for the sake of it I should in all things act with circumspection, in such a way that they should not accept me or the ministry of my service on any ground that did not pertain to the Faith; and so that I should give no opportunity to unbelievers, even in the least matter, to defame or disparage [me].

50. But when I baptized so many thousands of people, did I perhaps look for even half a screpall from any of them? Give me the evidence, and I will restore it to you. Or when the Lord ordained clerics everywhere through my insignificant person, and I shared the ministry with them for nothing, if I demanded from any of them so much as the price of even my shoe, testify against me and I shall restore it to you.

51. On the contrary, I paid out monies for your sake, that they might accept me; and I journeyed among you, and everywhere, in your interest, in many dangers, even to the remotest parts beyond which nobody lived, and whither no-one had ever come to baptize, or ordain clerics, or confirm the people; by gift of the Lord I did it all, with diligence and great joy, for the sake of your salvation.

52. And all that time I used to give presents to the kings, in addition to paying wages to their sons who travel with me; and nonetheless they seized me with my companions, and on that day they were keen and avid to kill me, but my time had not yet come; and everything they found with us they seized, and myself they bound in irons; and on the fourteenth day the Lord freed me from their power; and all our belongings were also restored to us, for the sake of God and the close friends with whom we had provided ourselves beforehand.

53. But you know yourselves how much I paid out to those who wielded authority throughout the districts I more frequently visited. For I estimate that I distributed to them not less than the price of fifteen men, so that you might have the benefit of my presence, and I might always have the joy of your presence before God. I do not regret it, nor do I count it enough: I am still spending, and will spend more; for the Lord has the power to give me the privilege later of being spent myself for your souls.

54. Behold, I call God to witness upon my soul that I am not lying: and it is not to provide an occasion for your flattering me or

ministering to my greed, that I have written to you. Nor is it that I am looking for honour from any of you. Enough for me that honour which is as yet not seen but which is believed in with the heart: *He who has promised is faithful; He never lies.*

55. But even in this present world I see myself exalted beyond measure by the Lord. And I was not worthy of it, nor was I of the sort that He should bestow it on me; for I know as a certainty that poverty and adversity are better suited to me than lucre and luxury. But Christ the Lord, too, was poor for our sake. And I, poor and needy as I am, even if I were to wish for wealth, I no longer have it; nor can I judge what my future is going to be; because daily I expect to be slaughtered, or defrauded, or reduced to slavery, or to any condition that time and surprise may bring. But I fear none of these things because of the promise of Heaven, for I have cast myself into the hands of Almighty God, who rules everywhere. As the prophet says: *Cast your care upon God, and He will sustain you.*

56. Behold then, I now commend my soul to my most faithful God, for whom I am an ambassador in my lowliness. But He is no accepter of persons, and for this office He chose me from among His least ones, that I should be one of His ministers.

57. Let me make return to the Lord then for all His bounty to me. But what shall I say, or what shall I promise to my Lord? – for I am unable to do anything unless He himself enables me. But let Him search my heart and my mind, for with desire I desire, and ready I would be, to drink of His chalice, as He granted it to many others who loved Him.

58. Wherefore may my God preserve me from ever losing His people, the people He has won for Himself in the furthest parts of the earth. I pray God that He may give me perseverance, and deign to keep me a faithful witness to Him until I die, for the sake of my God.

59. And if in my life I have ever achieved any good for the cause of my God whom I love, I ask Him to let me shed my blood with those who are exiles and captives for His name, even if I should go without burial itself, or should my wretched remains be divided, limb by limb, among dogs or wild beasts, or should birds of the air devour them. I hold it as certain, that if this should happen to me, I shall have gained my soul along with my body, because without any doubt we shall rise on that day in the glory of the Sun: that is to say, in the glory of Christ Jesus our Redeemer, as sons of the living God and fellow heirs with Christ and

destined to be conformed to His image: because it is from Him, and through Him, and in Him that we are to reign.

60. For that sun which we see [with our bodily eyes] rises daily at God's command for our sake; but it will never reign, nor will its splendour abide; but all who adore it will come, as unhappy men, unhappily to punishment. We, on the other hand, [are a people] who believe in the true Sun and adore Him, Christ, who will never perish. And neither will he who does His will; but he will abide for ever, as Christ abides for ever, He who with God the Almighty Father and with the Holy Spirit reigns before all ages, as now, and for ever and ever. Amen.

61. Here then, one more time, let me briefly set down the theme of my confession. I testify in the Truth, and in exultation of heart before God and His holy angels, that I never had any reason other than the Gospel and its promises for ever returning to that race from whom, in an earlier time, I had barely made good my escape from captivity.

62. And now, to all who believe and hold God in reverence, should one of them condescend to inspect and accept this writing put together in Ireland by Patrick, a mere unlettered sinner, this is my prayer: that if I have accomplished or brought to light any small part of God's purpose, none shall ever assert that the credit is due to my own uneducated self, but regard it rather as a true fact to be firmly believed that it was all the gift of God. And that is my confession before I die.

# St Patrick's
## *Letter Excommunicating Coroticus*

1. I, Patrick, a sinner and unlearned, resident in Ireland, declare myself to be a bishop. I believe with complete certainty that it is from God I received what I am. I dwell, then, among non-Roman peoples, a stranger and exile for the love of God; He is my witness that it is so. Not that I wished anything so harsh and so rough to come from my lips; but I am driven by zeal for God, and the truth of Christ has provoked me, for love of the neighbours and sons for whom I have given up homeland and family, and my life even unto death—should I be worthy of that. I live for my God, to teach the heathens, even if I am despised by some.

2. With my own hand I have composed and written these words, to be given, sent and delivered to the soldiers of Coroticus; I do not say, to my fellow citizens, or to fellow citizens of the holy Romans, but to fellow citizens of the demons, because of their evil deeds. In enemy fashion they live in death, allies of the Scotti and the apostate Picts. Blood-stained men bloodied in the blood of innocent Christians, whom I have begotten in countless numbers unto God, and have confirmed in Christ!

3. The day following that on which the white-robed neophytes had been anointed with chrism—it was still fragrant on their foreheads when they were cruelly butchered and put to the sword by those I have named—I sent a letter with a holy priest whom I had taught from his infancy, clerics accompanying him, to ask that they give us back some of the booty and of the baptized captives they had taken. They made a mockery of the messengers.

4. Hence I know not for which I should grieve the more: whether for those who have been slain, or those taken captive, or those whom the devil has grievously ensnared. Together with him they will be the slaves of hell in everlasting punishment, because he who commits sin is indeed a slave, and is called a son of the devil.

5. Consequently let every Godfearing person know that they are excommunicate from me, and from Christ my God for whom I am an ambassador. Parricides! Fratricides! Ravenous wolves gobbling up the people of the Lord like bread on the table! As Scripture says: *Lord, the wicked have destroyed your law*, which in these the last times He had successfully and graciously planted in Ireland, and which had grown up by the favour of the Lord.

6. I am no maker of false claims. I have a share with those whom He called and predestined to preach the Gospel amid no small persecutions unto the farthest part of the earth, even if the enemy gives vent to his malice through the tyranny of Coroticus, who has no reverence for God or for His bishops, whom He chose, and to whom He granted the highest, divine, sublime power, that those whom they should bind on earth would be bound also in Heaven.

7. This, then, you holy and humble of heart, is my most earnest plea to you: It is not lawful to pay court to such people, or to eat or drink with them; nor may their alms be accepted, until through rigorous penance, unto the shedding of tears, they render satisfaction to God, and free the menservants of God and the baptized maidservants of Christ, for whom He died and was crucified.

8. The Most High rejects the gifts of the wicked. The man who offers a sacrifice from the property of the poor is like one who slays a son in sacrifice before his father's eyes. *The riches,* says Scripture, *which he gathered unjustly shall be vomited up from his belly; the angel of death drags him away; with the fury of dragons he shall be beaten; the viper's tongue shall slay him; unquenchable fire shall devour him.* Therefore: *Woe to those who fill themselves with what is not their own.* And again: *What does it profit a man that he should gain the whole world and suffer the loss of his own soul?*

9. It would be tedious to examine every single text, or even to indicate them – to gather from the entire range of the Law the testimonies concerning such greed. Avarice is a deadly sin. *You shall not covet your neighbour's goods. You shall not kill.* A murderer cannot be with Christ. He who hates his brother is accounted a murderer. Or: *He who does not love his brother remains in death.* How much more is he guilty who has stained his hands with the blood of children of God, whom he recently acquired for Himself in the uttermost parts of the earth through the Gospel message from my own lowly person!

10. Was it without the inspiration of God, or on my own merely human initiative, that I came to Ireland? Who drove me to it? It is by the Spirit I am bound, to the extent of no longer seeing anyone of my own kindred. Is it from myself there springs the holy mercy I exercise towards that people who once took me captive and carried off the menservants and maidservants of my father's house? I am freeborn by descent: I am the son of a decurion. The fact is that for the benefit of others I sold my freeborn state – I am not ashamed of it, and I have no regrets;

in short, I am a slave in Christ to a foreign people for the sake of the inexpressible glory of the eternal life which is in Christ Jesus our Lord.

11. And if my own know me not, [it is true that] *a prophet has no honour in his own country.* Could it be that we are not from one sheepfold, and do not have one God for our Father? As Scripture says: *He who is not with me is against me, and he who does not gather with me scatters.* Is it not well said that *one man pulls down and another builds up?* I seek not my own interest. It was not I but God's grace that put this anxious concern into my heart, to be one of the hunters and fishers whom long ago God foretold He would send in the last days.

12. I am looked on with malice. What am I to do, Lord? I am greatly despised. Behold, your sheep are butchered and ravaged around me, by all that band of robbers under orders from the evil-minded Coroticus. Far from the love of God is he who betrays Christians into the hands of Scotti and Picts. Ravenous wolves have gobbled up the flock of the Lord, which in Ireland under excellent care was really flourishing – [so well that] the sons of the Scotti and the daughters of their kings who have become monks and virgins of Christ are beyond my power to number. Take no pleasure then in the wrong done to the just; even unto hell it shall be unacceptable.

13. Which of the saints would not shrink in horror from making merry with such persons, or enjoying a banquet in their company? They have filled their houses with the spoils of dead Christians; they live on plunder. They know not, the wretches, that they are offering deadly poison as food to their friends and children, as Eve did not understand that it was really death she was handing to her husband. Such are all who do evil: they wreak death as their eternal punishment.

14. The following is the custom of the Christians of Roman Gaul: they send chosen and holy men to the Franks and other heathen peoples with so many thousands of *solidi* to ransom baptized captives. But your way is to slay them, or sell them to a foreign nation that knows not God; you hand over the members of Christ as it were to a brothel. What sort of hope have you in God, you or anybody who approves of you, or communes with you in words of flattery? God will judge. For it is written: *Not only they who do evil, but also they who approve of them, shall be condemned.*

15. I know not what more I can say, or express, concerning the departed ones of the children of God whom the sword has stricken with

such dire cruelty. For it is written: *Weep with those who weep*; and again: *If one member suffers, let all the members suffer with it.* The Church therefore wails and weeps for those of her sons and daughters not yet slain by the sword, but deported and exported to distant lands; where grave sin openly and shamelessly abounds, there freeborn men and women have been put up for sale, Christians have been reduced to slavery – and worst of all, slavery to vile, depraved, apostate Picts.

16. Therefore in sadness and grief I shall cry out: O my fairest and fondest brothers and sons, whom beyond numbering I have begotten in Christ, what shall I do for you? I am not fit to come to the aid of God or of men. The wickedness of the wicked has prevailed over us. We are turned as it were into foreigners. Maybe they do not believe that we have received one and the same baptism, or that we have one and the same God as Father? For them it is a matter of disdain that we be Irish. As Scripture says: *Have you not one God? Why have you abandoned each one of you his neighbour?*

17. Therefore I grieve for you, I grieve, my dearest ones. But then again, I rejoice within myself. I have not laboured for nothing, nor has my exile been in vain. This crime so horrendous, so unspeakable, has indeed been perpetrated, but thanks be to God, my baptized believers, you have gone from this world to paradise. I can see you: you have begun your migration to where there shall not be night any more, nor mourning, nor death; but you shall skip for joy like calves loosed from their bonds, and you shall tread down the wicked, and they shall be ashes under your feet.

18. You, therefore, shall reign with the apostles and the prophets and the martyrs. You shall take possession of everlasting kingdoms, as Christ himself testifies when he says: *They shall come from the east and from the west and sit at table with Abraham and Isaac and Jacob in the kingdom of heaven. Outside shall be the dogs and the sorcerers and the murderers;* and: *As for liars and perjurers, their lot shall be in the lake of everlasting fire.* Not without cause does the apostle say: *Seeing that the righteous man shall only with trouble be saved, the sinner then and the impious transgressor of the law – where will he find himself?*

19. Coroticus then and his miscreants, rebels against Christ, where shall they discover their place to be, sharers out of young Christian women as booty for the sake of a wretched temporal kingdom which will pass away in a moment of time? As a cloud or smoke that is scattered by the wind, so shall deceitful sinners perish at the presence of the Lord; but the just, strong and unchanging, shall banquet with Christ; they shall judge nations, and rule over wicked kings forever and ever. Amen.

20. I testify before God and His angels that all shall be as He has made it known to my own unlearned self. It is not my words that I have set forth in Latin, but the words of God, and of His apostles and prophets, who have never lied. *He who believes shall be saved, but he who does not believe shall be condemned* – it is God who has spoken.

21. I request with the greatest gravity – whatever servant of God agrees to be the bearer of this letter – that it be on no account withdrawn or hidden from anybody, but rather be read before all the communities, even in the presence of Coroticus himself. But if God inspires them to return, at some time or another, to a right mind towards God, so that even at a late hour they repent of such an impious deed – murder of the brethren of the Lord – and so release the baptized women captives they previously seized: if God thus inspires them, so that they deserve to live unto God and be made whole here and in eternity, peace be to them with the Father and the Son and the Holy Spirit. Amen.

# Translation into Irish of the two letters

# An Fhaoistin/Dearbhú Grásta

1. Mise Pádraig, peacach róthútach, an té is lú de na fíréin go léir, agus an té is mó ar a bhfuil dímheas ag a lán; mac mé do Chalprann, deochan, mac Potitus, sagart; bhí cónaí ar m'athair i mbaile Bannavem Taburniae mar bhí gabháltas aige taobh leis; ansiúd a gabhadh mé. Bhíos tuairim is sé bliana déag an uair sin. Níorbh aithnid dom an fíorDhia agus dá bharrsan tugadh i mo chime mé go hÉirinn fara na mílte sin duine. Sin é a bhí tuillte againn mar "thugamar cúl le Dia" agus "níor coimeádamar a aitheanta" agus ní rabhamar umhal dár sagairt agus iad ag tabhairt comhairle ár slánaithe dúinn. "D'imir an Tiarna cuthach a fheirge orainn agus scaip sinn i measc an nginte iomadúla fiú go himeall an domhain," mar a bhfuilim go dearóil anois i measc na gcoimhthíoch.

2. Is ansin a "d'oscail an Tiarna m'aigne ainchreidmheach" le go gcuimhneoinn, má ba mhall féin é, ar mo pheacaí agus "go n-iompóinn ó mo chroí go hiomlán chun mo Thiarna Dia. Dhearc sé ar m'uiríisleacht" agus rinne trócaire ar m'óige agus ar m'aineolas, agus chumhdaigh mé sular bh'aithnid dom é, agus sula raibh tuiscint agam nó fios maitheasa agus oilc, agus chosain mé agus thug sólás dom mar a dhéanfadh athair dá mhac.

3. Ní féidir liom mar sin fanacht i mo thost, "ná níor chóir dom", faoin oiread sin tabhartas agus an méid sin grásta a dheonaigh an Tiarna a bhronnadh orm "i dtír mo dhaoirse". Nuair a dhéanann Dia sinn a cheartú agus é féin a chur in aithne dúinn, is é an cúiteamh is dual uainn ná "a éachtaí a mhóradh agus a mholadh" os comhair "an uile chine faoi íor na spéire go léir".

4. Mar níl aon Dia eile ann, ná ní raibh riamh, ná ní bheidh go deo, ach Dia an tAthair gan ghiniúint gan tús, ar uaidh gach tús, arb ann gach ní, de réir an teagaisc a fuaramar; agus a Mhac-san, Íosa Críost, a dhearbhaímid a bhí fara an Athair i gcónaí, a gineadh ón Athair roimh thúsú an domhain go spioradálta dolabhartha, roimh an uile thosach; is tríd a rinneadh an uile ní sofheicthe agus dofheicthe; rinneadh duine de; chloígh sé an bás agus glacadh leis sna flaithis fara an Athair; "thug seisean dó gach cumhacht os cionn gach ainm dá bhfuil ar neamh ar talamh agus faoin talamh; agus admhaíodh gach teanga dó gurbh é Íosa Chríost an Tiarna agus Dia". Creidimid agus táimid ag súil lena theacht gan mhoill "ina bhreitheamh ar bheo agus ar mhairbh le cúiteamh a dhéanamh le cách de réir a ngníomhartha. Agus dháil sé an Spiorad

Naomh, tabhartas agus geall na beatha síoraí, go fras orainn". Eisean a sholáthraíonn creidmhigh agus géillsinigh le go mbeidís "ina gclann ag Dia agus ina gcomh-oidhrí le Críost". Eisean a dhearbhaímid agus a adhraimid, aon Dia amháin i dTríonóid an ainm naofa.

5. Óir is é an Tiarna féin a dúirt trí bhéal an fháidh: "Glaoigh orm lá do bhuartha, agus saorfaidh mé thú agus mórfaidh tú mé." Agus deir sé arís eile: "Is uasal é éachtaí Dé a fhoilsiú agus a dhearbhú."

6. Cé gur lochtach mé ar a lán bealach, mar sin féin is mian liom go mbeadh a fhios ag mo bhráithre agus ag mo ghaolta cén sórt duine mé le go mbeadh ar a gcumas dúil m'anama a léirthuiscint.

7. Nílim aineolach faoi fhianaise mo Thiarna a fhógraíonn sa salm: "Millfidh tú an lucht inste bréag." Deir sé arís: "An béal bréagach, maraíonn sé an t-anam." Agus deir an Tiarna céanna sa soiscéal: "Gach focal gan bhun dá labhróidh daoine, tabharfaidh siad cuntas ann lá an bhreithiúnais."

8. Ba láncheart dom mar sin faitíos a bheith orm le barr sceimhle agus critheagla roimh an mbreithiúnas sin an lá úd nuair nach mbeidh sé ar chumas aon duine é féin a cheilt nó a chur i bhfolach ach go dtabharfaimid go léir cuntas fiú sna peacaí is suaraí os comhair chúirt ár dTiarna, Críost.

9. Dá bhrí sin is fada ó chuimhníos ar scríobh, ach ba leasc liom é go dtí seo, mar gurbh eagal liom titim faoi theanga lucht na cúlchainte. Mar níl foghlaim orm mar atá ar dhaoine eile a fuair sárdheoch as tobar an dlí agus na scríbhinní naofa le chéile ar chomhthomhas, agus nár mhalartaigh a dteanga riamh óna n-óige ach iad de shíor ag cur barr feabhais uirthi. Mise, áfach, níorbh fholáir dom mo chaint agus m'urlabhra a mhalartú ar theanga iasachta ionas gur furasta a chruthú as blas mo scríbhinne a laghad oiliúna agus teagaisc sa léann a fuaireas, óir tá sé ráite: "tríd an teanga a aithnítear an t-eagnaí, agus a thuiscint agus a eolas agus a theagasc san fhírinne".

10. Ach cén tairbhe dom an leithscéal fiú más de réir na fírinne é, go mór mór má ghabhann dánaíocht leis? Seo mise anois i mo sheanaois ar thóir rud nár sholáthraíos dom féin i m'óige. Choisc mo pheacaí orm an rud a bhí léite agam a dhaingniú i m'aigne. Ach cé atá ag géilleadh dom fiú má deirim arís a bhfuil ráite cheana agam? I m'óganach dom, sea agus mé geall leis i mo bhuachaill amhulcach, gabhadh mé sularbh eol dom cad ba chóir dom a lorg nó a sheachaint. Inniu féin dá bhrí sin tá scáth agus

critheagla orm m'aineolas a nochtadh mar nach féidir liom mé féin a chur
in iúl i bhfocla don mhuintir atá oilte sa ghontacht, – sé sin le rá, de réir
mar is tnúth le mo spiorad agus le m'anam, agus sa chiall a nochtann mo
mheanma dom.

11. Ach dá mbronnfaí ormsa mar a bronnadh ar dhaoine eile,
is cinnte, ar mhaithe le cúiteamh, nach i mo thost a bheinn. Agus más
dóigh le daoine áirithe, b'fhéidir, go bhfuilim, sa ghnó seo, do mo bhrú
féin chun tosaigh, mise i m'aineolas is i mo thutbhéalaíocht, tá sé scríofa
freisin: "Is tapa a fhoghlaimeoidh teangacha briotacha conas síocháin a
labhairt". Nach móide go mór is cóir dúinne fonn cainte a bheith orainn
ós rud é, mar atá ráite, gur "litir ó Chríost" sinne "ag breith an tslánaithe
go himeall an domhain", agus más míshlachtmhar féin í mar litir, tá sí
scríofa go daingean tréan "in bhur gcroí, agus ní le dúch é ach le Spiorad
Dé bheo". Tugann an Spiorad fianaise arís fós: "fiú an tútachas féin, is
é an té is airde a chruthaigh é."

12. Mise dá réir sin, a bhí ar dtús i mo dheoraí tútach gan
léann, "nach fios dó conas soláthar don lá amárach", tá a fhios seo go lán-
daingean agam, go mba chosúil mé, sular íslíodh mé, le cloch ina luí go
doimhin sa láib; agus tháinig "an té atá cumhachtach" agus le barr
trócaire thóg sé suas mé, agus, fairis sin, d'ardaigh sé in airde mé agus
chóirigh ar barr an bhalla mé. Uime sin tá sé ina dhiandualgas orm glaoch
go hard le cúiteamh éigin a dhéanamh don Tiarna ar son an méid sin
tabhartas dom ar an saol seo agus ar feadh na síoraíochta, nach féidir le
haigne an duine iad a mheas.

13. Dá bhrí sin déanaigí ionadh sibhse, idir mhór agus bheag,
ar a bhfuil eagla Dé, agus sibhse, a ollúna tiarnúla, éistigí agus scrúdaígí
é seo. Cé ghríosaigh an t-amadán seo, mise, as measc an dreama a
dhealraíonn a bheith eagnaí agus oilte sa dlí, agus éifeachtach i gcaint agus
i ngach uile ní agus cé spreag mise thar dhaoine eile, mise a bhfuil
drochmheas ag an saol mór orm, le go mbeinn ar an duine – dá mba
amhlaidh a bheadh! – a dhéanfadh, "le hurraim agus le hómós gan
urchóid", leas an chine ar sheol grá Chríost chucu mé, agus a bhronn
orthu mé le mo shaol, más fiú mé é, sé sin go bhfónfainn daoibh go
humhal agus go hionraic?

14. De réir an chreidimh a fuaireas ón Tríonóid, dá bhrí sin,
tá sé de dhualgas orm, comhairle a dhéanamh, tabhartas Dé agus an sólás
síoraí a chur in iúl gan aird ar chontúirt, ainm Dé a leathadh i ngach áit
le misneach gan scáth ná eagla, ionas go bhfágfainn, tar éis mo bháis,
oidhreacht ag mo bhráithre agus ag mo chlann mhac a bhaisteas sa Tiarna
– an oiread sin míle duine!

15. Níorbh fhiú mé é, ná níorbh é an saghas sin mé go ndeon-
fadh an Tiarna é seo dá shearbhónta bocht; tar éis an méid sin cruatan
agus callshaoth, i ndiaidh mo bhraighdeanais, go mbronnfadh sé ormsa an
oiread sin grásta ar mhaithe leis an bpobal sin tar éis mórán blian – sin
rud nach raibh coinne ar bith agam leis riamh i m'óige ná níor thaibhsigh
sé dom.

16. Ach tar éis teacht go hÉirinn dom, bhínn gach lá ag
aoireacht tréad, agus ba mhinic sa lá mé ag guí; bhí grá agus eagla Dé ag
dul i neart ionam níos mó agus níos mó, bhí mo chreideamh ag borradh
agus mo spiorad á shuaitheadh i dtreo go ndeirinn suas le céad urnaí sa
lá agus an oiread céanna geall leis san oíche fiú agus mé sna coillte agus
faoin sliabh. Mhúsclaítí mé chun urnaí roimh bhreacadh an lae sa
sneachta, sa sioc, sa bháisteach, ach ní bhraithinn aon deasca dá bharrsan
ná ní bhíodh aon leisce orm, murab ionann agus mar a fheicim anois; mar
bhí an Spiorad ar fiuchadh ionam an uair úd.

17. Agus oíche amháin ansiúd i mo chodladh dom chuala guth
á rá liom: "Maith mar a dhéanann tú troscadh, is gearr go rachaidh tú go
dtí do thír dhúchais." Agus arís i gcionn tamaill bhig chuala guth á rá
liom: "Féach, tá do long ullamh." Ní i ngar dom a bhí sí, ach, b'fhéidir,
dhá chéad míle uaim; agus ní raibh mé riamh ansiúd, ná níorbh aithnid
dom aon duine ann. Theitheas liom go gearr ina dhiaidh sin, d'fhágas an
fear ar chaitheas sé bliana fairis, agus ar aghaidh liom trí chumhacht Dé
a bhí do mo stiúrú ar bhealach mo leasa; níorbh eagal liom dada nó gur
shroicheas an long úd.

18. An lá a tháinig mé, chuir an long chun farraige, agus dúrt
go raibh agam costas an turais leo. Ach ní raibh an captaen sásta agus
thug freagra feargach giorraisc: "Is fánach agat é a bheith ag iarraidh
teacht linn." Nuair a chuala mé an méid sin, d'imíos uathu le filleadh ar
an mbothán mar a raibh mé ag cur fúm, agus ar an tslí dom chrom mé
ar urnaí agus sula raibh m'urnaí críochnaithe agam chuala mé duine acu
agus é ag glaoch in ard a chinn orm: "Brostaigh agus tar, mar tá an dream
seo ag glaoch ort." Agus d'fhilleas orthu ar an toirt, agus thosaigh siad
ar a rá liom: "Tar, mar glacaimid leat le muinín; déan muintearas linn mar
is áil leat"; an lá sin dá réir sin dhiúltaigh mé a gcíocha a dhiúl (ag achainí
dom) de bharr eagla Dé, ach ina áit sin, bhíos ag tnúth leis go dtiocfadh
cuid díobh chun creidimh in Íosa Críost, mar ginte ab ea iad. Is mar sin
a d'éirigh liom faru agus sheolamar láithreach bonn.

19. Tar éis trí lá thángamar i dtír agus thaistealaíomar trí
fhásach ar feadh ocht lá fichead, agus theip ar an mbia agus sháraigh an

gorta iad; agus lá eile chrom an captaen ar labhairt liom mar seo: "Féach,
a Chríostaí, deir tú gur mór agus gur uilechumhachtach é do Dhia. Cén
fáth mar sin nach féidir leat guí ar ár son? mar táimid i mbaol báis de
ghorta. Is ar éigean a fheicfimid duine beo go deo arís." Dúirt mé leo le
misneach: "Iompaígí le creideamh ó chroí go hiomlán chun an Tiarna, mo
Dhia, mar níl aon n. dodhéanta aige, ionas go gcuirfidh sé bia in bhur
dtreo nó go mbeidh sibh sách; óir is aige atá an fhlúirse i ngach áit." Agus
le cúnamh Dé, is mar sin a bhí. B'shiúd tréad muc ar an tslí os comhair
ár súl, agus mharaigh siad a lán acu, agus d'fhan siad ansin dhá oíche;
beathaíodh go maith iad, agus cothaíodh a gcolainn, mar bhí teipthe ar
a lán acu agus iad fágtha leathmharbh le hais na slí. Agus ina dhiaidh seo
thug siad barr buíochais do Dhia, agus fuair mé onóir ina láthair agus ón
lá sin ar aghaidh bhí bia go raidhsiúil acu. Fuair siad mil fhiáin freisin
agus thairg siad roinnt dom, agus dúirt duine acu: "Mar íobairt atá sí á
tairiscint." A bhuí le Dia, níor bhlaiseas pioc di.

20. An oíche chéanna agus mé i mo chodladh chuir Sátan
cathú dian orm, rud a mbeidh cuimhne agam air "fad bheidh mé sa
cholainn seo". Thit sé anuas orm mar a dhéanfadh carraig mhór agus níor
fhan brí i mball de mo bhallaí beatha. Ach cén chaoi ar rith sé liomsa agus
mé chomh haineolach sa spiorad glaoch ar Eilias? Agus lena linn sin
chonaic mé an ghrian ag éirí sa spéir agus le linn dom a bheith ag glaoch
"A Eilias, a Eilias", in ard mo chinn, féach! thaitin dealradh na gréine orm
agus sciob sí léi an t-ualach go léir díom. Creidim gurb é Críost mo
Thiarna a d'fhóir orm agus go raibh a Spiorad an uair sin ag glaoch ar
mo shon agus tá súil agam gur mar sin a bheidh i lá mo dhuainéise, de réir
mar a deir sé sa soiscéal: "An lá úd," dearbhaíonn an Tiarna, "ní sibhse
a labhraíonn ach Spiorad an Athar a labhraíonn ionaibh".

21 Agus gabhadh mé uair eile fós tar éis mórán blian. Bhíos
ina dteannta dá réir sin an chéad oíche. Chuala teachtaireacht dhiaga á rá
liom: "Beidh tú ina dteannta go ceann dhá mhí." Is mar sin a bhí; trí fichid
oíche ina dhiaidh sin "d'fhuascail an Tiarna mé óna gcrúba".

22. Fiú agus sinn ar an aistear chuir sé cóir bia agus tine agus
leapa gan taise orainn gach lá nó gur bhaineamar daoine amach ar an
deichiú lá. Mar a dúirt mé romhainn thaistealaíomar tríd an bhfásach ar
feadh ocht lá fichead, agus an oíche úd ar bhaineamar daoine amach, ní
raibh greim bia fágtha againn.

23. Agus arís faoi cheann beagán blian bhí mé sa Bhreatain le
mo thuismitheoirí; ghlac siadsan liom mar mhac, agus d'impigh siad ó
chroí orm, ar a laghad anois tar éis dom an oiread sin cruatan a fhulaingt,

gan imeacht uathu choíche. Agus ansin chonaic mé i bhfís oíche fear, agus é mar a bheadh ag teacht ó Éirinn, agus Victoricus mar ainm air; bhí dlús gan áireamh litreacha aige agus thug sé ceann acu dom agus léas tosach na litreach a ghabh: "Glór na nGael". Agus fad a bhí tús na litreach á léamh os ard agam, shíleas gur chuala ar an nóiméad sin glór na ndaoine úd a raibh cónaí orthu taobh le Coill Fhochlaid (Vocluti) atá le hais na mara thiar; agus mar seo a ghlaoigh siad amhail is dá mba d'aon ghuth: "Impímid ort a ógánaigh (naofa), teacht agus siúl arís inár measc." Bhíos croíbhrúite go mór agus níor fhéadas a thuilleadh a léamh agus ansin dhúisíos. A bhuí le Dia gur dheonaigh an Tiarna dóibh tar éis a lán blian de réir mar a ghlaoigh siad.

24. Agus oíche eile – cé acu ionam istigh, nó taobh liom, "níl a fhios agam, ag Dia atá a fhios" – rinne siad amhlaidh go ríshoiléir i mbriathra a chuala mé ach nár fhéad mé a thuiscint ach ag deireadh na hurnaí gur fhógair sé: "An té a thug a anam ar do shon, eisean atá ag labhairt ionat." Agus, leis sin, dhúisíos faoi lúcháir.

25. Uair eile fós chonaic mé é ag guí ionam istigh, agus bhíos faoi mar a bheinn i mo chorp istigh, agus chuala mé é os mo chionn, sé sin os cionn an duine inmheánaigh, agus bhí sé ansiúd ag guí go tréan agus ag osnaíl; idir an dá linn bhí mearbhall agus ionadh orm agus bhíos ag iarraidh a dhéanamh amach cérbh é a bhí ag guí ionam istigh; ach ag deireadh na guí d'fhógair sé gurbh é an Spiorad é, agus dhúisíos leis sin agus chuimhníos ar a ndúirt an t-aspal: "Tagann an Spiorad i gcabhair ar laige ár nguí, mar ní eol dúinn conas an ghuí féin a dhéanamh mar is cóir; ach déanann an Spiorad féin idirghuí ar ár son le hosnaí nach féidir a chur i bhfocail"; agus arís "Déanann an Tiarna, ár n-abhcóide, idirghuí ar ár son."

26. Agus nuair a thug cuid de mo sheanóirí fúm, iad ag teacht agus ag athchasadh mo pheacaí liom in aghaidh m'easpagóideachta duaisiúla, is cinnte gur buaileadh go trom mé an lá úd, i dtreo gur dhóbair dom titim abhus agus thall go deo; ach rinne an Tiarna anacal ar an gcoimhthíoch agus ar an deoraí le barr cineáltais ar son a ainm; agus ba thréan é a chúnamh dom agus an bhróg ag luí orm, i dtreo nár thit mé go hainnis faoi tháir agus faoi tharcaisne. Táim ag guí Dé "nach gcuirfear ina leith é mar pheaca".

27. Tar éis tríocha bliain fuair siad faill ar chúis a chur i mo leith, gníomh a d'admhaíos sula rabhas i mo dheochan. De bharr suaitheadh agus crá croí ligeas mo rún leis an gcara ba dhlúithe agam rud a rinne mé in aon lá amháin, ní hea ach in aon uair an chloig amháin,

i m'óige, mar nach raibh smacht agam fós orm féin. "Níl a fhios agam, ag Dia atá a fhios", an raibh cúig bliana déag slán agam an tráth sin, agus gan creideamh i nDia beo agam, agus ní mó a bhí sin agam ó bhíos i mo naíonán, ach mé ag caitheamh mo shaoil sa bhás agus sa díchreideamh nó gur smachtaíodh go mór mé "agus gur íslíodh i gceart mé le gorta agus nochtacht" agus sin gach lá.

28. Ar an láimh eile, ní as mo stuaim féin a bhíos ag cur chun bealaigh go hÉirinn agus mé faoin am sin anonn geall leis i mblianta an cheiliúrtha, ach ba é mo leas é sin, mar cheartaigh an Tiarna mé idir an dá linn, agus chóirigh sé mé i dtreo go mbeadh bail orm inniu a b'fhada uaim tráth: go mbeinn ag déanamh cúraim agus ag saothrú ar mhaithe le slánú daoine eile, mise nár smaoinigh fiú orm féin an uair úd.

29. Dá bhrí sin, an lá a dhiúltaigh an mhuintir atá luaite romhainn mé, an oíche sin chonaic mé i bhfís oíche scríofa os mo chomhair amach: "gan an onóir". Idir an dá linn chuala mé guth diaga á rá liom: "D'fhéachamar le míghean ar ghnúis a leithéid seo" (luadh é as a ainm). Agus ní hé a dúirt: "D'fhéach tú le míghean," ach "d'fhéachamar le míghean," amhail is dá mbeadh sé á nascadh féin liom, mar a dúirt sé: "An té a bhaineann libhse, baineann sé le mac imreasan mo shúile."

30. Dá bhrí sin beirim buíochas don té a neartaigh mé i ngach ní mar nár thoirmeasc sé orm an t-aistear a bhí curtha agam romham ná an obair a bhí foghlamtha agam ó Chríost an Tiarna, ach a mhalairt, gur bhraitheas ionam féin neart nár bheag uaidhsean agus gur promhadh mo dhílse os comhair Dé agus daoine.

31. Mar sin deirim go dána nach bhfuil mo choinsias do mo chiontú anois agus nach mbeidh thall; tá Dia mar fhinné agam "nár inis mé bréag" sa chuntas a thug mé daoibh.

32. Ach is amhlaidh is mó atá brón orm faoin gcara is ansa liom a rá is gur thuilleas a leithéid de scéal a chlos. An té ar chuir mé fiú m'anam ar a iontaoibh! Fuaireas amach ó chuid de na bráithre roimh an gcruinniú inar cuireadh m'ainm chun cinn – ní rabhas i láthair, ná ní rabhas fiú sa Bhreatain, ná ní mé a b'údar leis – go mbeadh sé ag brú mo chúise ar aghaidh agus mé as láthair. Dúirt sé féin fiú liom ó bhéal: "Féach ní mór tú a ardú go céim na heaspagóideachta," rud nárbh fhiú mé é. Ach cad a tharla dó ina dhiaidh sin gur thug sé náire phoiblí dom os comhair cháich, idir olc agus mhaith, a rá is go raibh siúd maite cheana aige dom dá dheoin le fonn, agus maite chomh maith ag an Tiarna "ar mó é ná cách"?

33. Is leor a bhfuil ráite agam. Ach mar sin féin níor chóir dom an tabhartas a bhronn Dia orm i dtír mo dhaoirse a cheilt, mar san am sin is ea a chuaigh mé sa tóir air le dúthracht agus ansiúd a fuaireas é, agus chosain sé mé ar an uile urchóid, de réir mar a chreidim, "ar son a Spioraid atá ag lonnú ionam" agus atá ag oibriú ionam go dtí an lá inniu féin. Dánaíocht arís! Ach tá a fhios ag Dia dá mba duine a déarfadh é seo liom, b'fhéidir go bhfanfainn i mo thost as ucht grá Chríost.

34. Uime sin gabhaim buíochas gan staonadh do Dhia a choinnigh dílis mé i lá mo chathaithe i dtreo go n-ofrálfainn inniu dó mar bheoíobairt mo bheatha do Chríost mo Thiarna, "an té d'fhuascail mé ó mo chruatain go léir", ionas go ndéarfainn: "Cé hé mé, a Thiarna, nó cad é mo ghlaoch?" gur oibrigh do dhiacht chomh tréan i gcomhar liom i dtreo "go molfainn is go mórfainn d'ainm" go misniúil i measc na gciníocha i gcónaí inniu cibé áit ina mbím; agus go ndéanfainn sin ní amháin in am an tséin ach in am na cúngrachta. Fágann sin nach foláir dom glacadh le cibé olc maith a tharlaíonn dom, gan buaireamh aigne agus buíochas a bhreith i gcónaí le Dia, an té sin a thaispeáin dom gur chóir géilleadh dó le hiontaoibh dobhogtha. Eisean a d'éist le mo ghuí ionas go raibh sé de mhisneach agam, dá aineolaí mé, sna laethanta deireanacha seo tabhairt faoin saothar seo atá chomh naofa agus chomh hiontach i dtreo go ndéanfainn aithris, a bheag nó a mhór, ar na daoine sin ar thairngir an Tiarna fúthu fadó go ndéanfaidís a shoiscéal "a chraobhscaoileadh mar fhianaise do na ginte uile roimh dheireadh an tsaoil". Is mar sin, más ea, a chonaiceamar, agus is mar sin a cuireadh i gcrích. Féach, is finnéithe sinn gur craoladh an soiscéal chomh fada ó bhaile nach bhfuil duine i gcéin thairis.

35. Ba liosta le háireamh iomlán mo shaothar ina gceann is ina gceann, nó ina gcoda. Inseoidh mé i mbeagán focal conas mar a shaor Dia le barr cineáltais go minic mé ó dhaoirse, agus ón dá ghábha déag ina raibh m'anam i mbaol, seachas na chomchealga iomadúla "a théann díom a chur i bhfocail". Ná ní chuirfidh mé masmas ar mo léitheoirí. Ach Dia, a bhfuil fios gach ní aige fiú sula dtarlaíonn siad, tá sé mar fhianaise agam air gur minic a thug ráiteas diaga foláireamh domsa, fág gur bochtán agus dílleachta mé.

36. "Cén fáth ar tugadh an eagna seo domsa," agus gan í ionam féin, mise "nárbh eol dom líon mo laethanta" agus nach bhfuair blas ar Dhia? Cén fáth ar tugadh ina dhiaidh sin tabhartas chomh mór, chomh folláin dom le Dia a aithint nó a ghráú, seachas le go gcaillfinn mo thír dhúchais agus mo mhuintir?

37. Agus is iomaí bronntanas a bhí á dtairiscint dom le deora agus olagón, agus ghoilleas orthusan agus ar chuid de mo sheanóirí i

gcoinne mo thola. Ach, faoi threoir Dé, níor aontaíos ar aon tslí ná níor ghéilleas dóibh. Ní liomsa a bhuíochas sin ach le Dia a rug an bua ionam agus a sheas ina n-aghaidh go léir, i dtreo gur tháinig mé chuig na ginte in Éirinn chun an soiscéal a chraobhscaoileadh agus chun maslaí a iompar ó dhaoine gan chreideamh; "chun go gcloisfinn tarcaisne mo dheorantais á chasadh liom"; chun géarleanúint go tiubh fiú go géibheann a fhulaingt; agus chun mo shaoirse a reic ar mhaithe le daoine eile. Agus más fiú mé é, táim réidh le fiú m'anam a thabhairt, gan cheist agus le lántoil, ar son a ainm, agus is san áit sin is mian liom mo shaol a chaitheamh go bás má cheadaíonn an Tiarna sin dom.

38. Óir is mór mé i bhfiacha ag Dia a bhronn orm an oiread sin grásta gur athghineadh na sluaite do Dhia tríomsa, agus gur cóineartaíodh iad ina dhiaidhsin; agus gur oirníodh cléirigh i ngach aon bhall dóibh – do phobal is é sin a bhí ag teacht go nua chun creidimh agus a ghlac an Tiarna chuige ó imill an domhain, mar a gheall sé fadó trína fháithe: "Tiocfaidh na ginte ó imill an domhain agus déarfaidh siad: "Nach déithe bréige a sholáthraigh ár n-aithreacha dóibh féin, agus gan aon tairbhe iontu?" Agus arís: "Tá tú ceaptha agam le bheith i do sholas do na náisiúin, ionas go mbeidh tú i d'údar slánaithe go himeall an domhain."

39. Agus is ansin is mian liom fanacht le gealltanas an té úd nach bhfeallann riamh go deimhin mar a gheallann sé sa soiscéal: "Tiocfaidh siad anoir agus aniar agus beidh siad ina suí chun boird le hAbrahám, agus le hÍosác agus le Iacób", de réir mar a chreidimid go bhfuil na creidmhigh le teacht ón domhan mór.

40. Dá bhrí sin is cóir dúinn ar ndóigh, iascach go maith agus go dícheallach mar a chomhairlíonn agus a mhúineann an Tiarna á rá: "Tagaigí i mo dhiaidh, agus déanfaidh mé iascairí ar dhaoine díbh." Agus deir sé arís trí na fáithe: "Féach, táim ag seoladh a lán iascairí agus fiagaithe uaim a deir Dia", agus mar a leanas. Uime sin tá sé de dhualgas trom orainn ár líonta a leathadh i dtreo go ngabhfaí lear mór agus mathshlua daoine do Dhia agus go mbeadh cléir i ngach áit leis an bpobal atá ina chall, agus ag tnúth leis, a bhaisteadh agus a spreagadh mar a deir an Tiarna sa soiscéal agus é ag comhairliú agus ag teagasc á rá: "Imígí dá bhrí sin, déanaigí deisceabail de na náisiúin uile, á mbaisteadh in ainm an Athar agus an Mhic agus an Spioraid Naoimh, ag múineadh dóibh gach ní atá ordaithe agam a choinneáil. Agus féach, táim in éineacht libh go dtí deireadh an tsaoil." Agus deir sé arís: "Imígí faoin domhan uile agus fógraígí an soiscéal don chruthaíocht uile. An té a chreidfidh agus a bhaistfear slánófar é; ach an té nach gcreidfidh, daorfar é." Agus arís eile:

"Fógrófar an dea-scéal seo na ríochta ar fud na cruinne go léir mar fhianaise do na náisiúin uile, agus ansin a thiocfaidh an deireadh." Agus arís fógraíonn an Tiarna roimh ré tríd an bhfáidh á rá: "Sna laethanta deireanacha, arsa an Tiarna, doirtfidh mé amach mo Spiorad ar an uile dhuine, agus déanfaidh bhur gclann mhac agus bhur n-iníonacha tairngreacht. Feicfidh bhur bhfir óga aislingí agus déanfar taibhrimh do bhur seanóirí. Doirtfidh mé mo Spiorad sna laethanta sin fiú amháin ar m'óglaigh agus ar mo bhanóglaigh, agus déanfaidh siad tairngreacht." Agus deir sé in Óseá: "Glaofaidh mé 'mo phobal' ar phobal nach liom, agus 'an mhuintir a fuair trócaire' ar an mhuintir nach bhfuair trócaire. Agus san áit a ndúrthas 'ní muintir liom sibhse', glaofar 'clann Dé bheo orthu', ansiúd."

41. Cé mar a tharla in Éirinn, más ea, na daoine nach raibh riamh aon aithne ar Dhia acu agus gan á adhradh acu i gcónaí go dtí seo ach íola agus nithe míghlana – cé mar a rinneadh pobal Dé díobh le déanaí agus a ghlaoitear clann Dé orthu, agus atá clann mhac na nGael agus iníonacha na ríthe le feiceáil ina manaigh agus ina maighdeana ag Críost?

42. Bhí fiú aon chailín uasal beannaithe amháin ann de chine Gael, a raibh barr scéimhe uirthi agus í in aois mná; bhaisteas féin í. Tar éis cúpla lá tháinig sí chugainn le haon aidhm amháin, lena insint dúinn go bhfuair sí scéala ó theachtaire Dé a thug mar chomhairle di a bheith ina hóigh le Críost agus druidim i gcóngar Dé. A bhuí le Dia, sé lá ina dhiaidh sin ghlac sí leis le barr díograise fónta. Agus déanann ógha uile Dé mar an gcéanna, agus ní de dheoin a n-aithreacha é, ach iad ag fulaingt géarleanúna agus maslaí gan bhonn óna dtuismitheoirí. Dá ainneoin sin is ea is mó a mhéadaíonn ar a líon, agus ní heol dúinn cé méid dár gcine féin a rugadh ansiúd a ndearnadh ógha díobh, agus de bhreis air sin tá baintreacha agus lánúna a chleachtann an aontumha. Díobh siúd is iad na cumhala is mó atá faoi chruatan; bíonn fiú sceimhle agus bagairtí á bhfulaingt gan stad acu. Ach thug an Tiarna grásta dá lán dá ionailtí mar, bíodh is go gcrostar orthu é, leanann siad a lorg go tréan.

43. Dá bhrí sin, dá dteastódh uaim iad a fhágáil ansin agus imeacht chun na Breataine – nach orm a bhí an fonn, dála duine a bheadh ag triall ar a thír dhúchais agus ar a thuismitheoirí, agus ní hé sin amháin é ach an Ghaill a bhaint amach ag fiosrú na mbráithre agus le gnúis naoimh mo Thiarna a fheiceáil; tá a fhios ag Dia gur mhór mar ba mhian liom é, ach "táim i mo chime ag an Spiorad" atá á dhearbhú má dhéanaim é seo go bhfógróidh sé ciontach mé agus is eagal liom an saothar ar chuireas tús leis a chailleadh, fág nach mise a chuir tús leis ach Críost an

Tiarna, an té a d'ordaigh dom teacht agus a bheith faru an chuid eile de mo shaol, más é toil an Tiarna é agus má chosnaíonn sé mé ón uile drochbhealach ionas nach ndéanfainn peaca ina láthair.

44. Sin é mo dhualgas, dar liom, ach nach bhfuil aon iontaoibh agam asam féin "fad a bheidh mé sa chorp básmhar seo"; mar is tréan é an té atá gach lá ag iarraidh mé a chlaonadh ón dílse agus ón ngeanmnaíocht a chuireas romham go deireadh mo shaoil le barr deabhóide, gan cur i gcéill, do Chríost an Tiarna. Ach tá an cholainn naimhdeach de shíor ag tarraingt chun an bháis, is é sin chun na n-ainmhianta a shásamh go haindleathach. Tá mo chuid eolais easnamhach agus dá réir sin níor chaitheas beatha gan locht dála creidmheach eile. Ach admhaím do mo Dhia agus ní lasaim le náire os a chomhair, mar ní bréag dom é, ón uair a chuireas aithne air i m'óige, bhí grá agus eagla Dé ag borradh ionam agus, trí ghrásta Dé, "choinnigh mé an creideamh go dtí seo".

45. An té arb áil leis é, déanadh sé gáire agus tugadh sé masla, ach ní fhanfaidh mé i mo thost ná ní cheilfidh mé na comharthaí agus na hiontais a thaispeáin an Tiarna dom na blianta fada roimh theacht i gcrích dóibh, ós dó is eol gach ní fiú roimh thús na n-aimsirí saolta.

46. Ba chóir dom dá bhrí sin buíochas a ghabháil gan staonadh le Dia a mhaith go minic mo dhíth céille agus m'fhaillí dom, agus nár ghabh fearg mhór liom é níos mó ná aon uair amháin; mar ceapadh mé mar chúntóir dó, ach nár aontaíos gan mhoill de réir mar a foilsíodh dom agus mar a bhí an Spiorad á chur i mo cheann. Agus rinne an Tiarna trócaire orm na mílte míle uair mar d'aithin sé orm go rabhas ullamh ach nach raibh a fhios agam cad ba cheart dom a dhéanamh maidir leis na nithe úd sa chás ina rabhas, mar bhí a lán daoine ag toirmeasc na toscaireachta seo agus iad ag caint eatarthu féin mar seo ar mo chúl agus ag rá: "Cén fáth go bhfuil sé siúd á shá féin i mbaol i measc naimhde nach eol dóibh Dia?" Ní le mailís a bhí sin á rá acu, ach nach raibh bun ná barr leis dar leo, rud a dhearbhaím féin, de bharr mo thútachais mar a thuigeas. Níor aithníos féin go luath an grásta a bhí ionam an uair úd; tuigim anois mar ba chóir dom a dhéanamh níos luaithe.

47. Anois mar sin tá cuntas ionraic tugtha agam do mo bhráithre agus do mo chomhsheirbhísigh a chreid ionam de bharr "a bhfuil fógartha agus a bhfuil á fhógairt agam" ag daingniú agus ag neartú bhur gcreidimh. Uch nach mbeadh spriocanna níos airde agaibh agus bearta níos tréine á gcur i gcrích agaibh! Sin í an ghlóir atá romham, mar "glóir athar é an mac eagnaí".

48. Tá a fhios agaibhse agus tá a fhios ag Dia cé mar a mhair mé in bhur measc ó m'óige i dílse na fírinne agus i ndúthracht chroí. Fiú maidir leis na ginte a mairim ina measc, chuir mé le m'fhocal dóibh, agus cuirfidh mé. Tá a fhios ag Dia nach ndearna mé calaois ar aon duine acu, ná ní chuimhneoinn air, ar son Dé agus a eaglaise, le heagla go músclóinn géarleanúint dóibhsean agus dúinn go léir, agus go dtabharfaí masla d'ainm an Tiarna tríomsa, óir atá scríofa: "Is mairg don té a maslaítear ainm an Tiarna tríd."

49. Óir "más aineolach féin ar gach ní mé", mar sin féin, thugas iarracht mé féin a chosaint fiú ar na bráithre Críostaí, ar ógha Chríost, agus ar na mná cráifeacha a bhíodh ag iarraidh bronntanaisí a thabhairt dom dá ndeoin féin, agus a chaitheadh cuid dá n-ornáidí ar an altóir. Thugainn ar ais arís dóibh iad agus bhídís míshásta liom mar go ndéanainn amhlaidh. Ach ba le dóchas na síoraíochta a rinne mé é le go gcoinneoinn mé féin slán go cáiréiseach i ngach ní ar a shon, ionas nach bhfaighidís mé féin ná ministreacht mo sheirbhíse mídhílis ar aon slí agus nach dtabharfainn faill do dhíchreidmhigh, fiú sa ghnó is suaraí, tromaíocht nó cúlchaint a dhéanamh.

50. Ach, b'fhéidir, nuair a bhaisteas an oiread sin míle duine, go raibh mé ag súil le hoiread is leathscreaball ó dhuine acu? "Insigí dom é agus tabharfaidh mé ar ais daoibh é". Nó nuair a d'oirnigh an Tiarna cléirigh i ngach áit tríd an suarachán seo agus gur bhronnas an mhinistreacht orthu ina aisce, má d'éiligh mé oiread agus praghas mo bhróige ó aon duine, "tugaigí fianaise i m'aghaidh agus tabharfaidh mé ar ais daoibh é."

51. Ina áit sin is amhlaidh a dhíolas ar bhur son le go nglacfaidís liom; agus rinne mé taisteal in bhur measc féin agus go forleathan trína lán contúirtí ar bhur son, fiú go dtí na réigiúin i gcéin thar mar nár mhair aon duine agus nár shroich aon duine riamh níos sia, le baisteadh a bhronnadh nó cléirigh a oirniú nó pobal a chóineartú. Rinne mé é sin go léir, trí fhéile an Tiarna, le cúram agus le barr lúcháire, ar mhaithe le bhur slánú.

52. Idir an dá linn thugaim bronntanais do na ríthe seachas tuarastal a íoc lena gclann mhac a bhíonn ag taisteal liom; ach mar sin féin ghabh siad mé féin mar aon le mo chompánaigh agus bhí fonn róchraosach orthu an lá sin mé a mharú, ach ní raibh an t-am tagtha fós; sciob siad leo gach a bhfuair siad againn, chuir siad mé féin i ngeimhle iarainn; ach ar an gceathrú lá déag shaor an Tiarna mé óna lámha, agus tugadh ar ais dúinn gach ar bhain linn ar son Dé agus na gcairde dlútha a bhí soláthraithe againn roimh ré.

53. Tá a fhios agaibh féin cé méid atá íoctha agam leis an lucht ceannais sna dúichí go léir ar a mbíodh mo thriall mós minic. Is dóigh liom nach lú ná luach cúigear déag ar scaip mé orthu, ionas go mbainfeadh sibhse taitneamh asam agus go mbainfinnse taitneamh asaibhse i gcónaí i nDia. Ní aithreach liom é ná ní leor liom é. "Táim ag caitheamh go fóill agus caithfidh mé níos mó." Tá ar chumas an Tiarna a dheonú dom níos déanaí "go gcaithfinn mé féin ar son bhur n-anama".

54. Féach! "dearbhaím daoibh ar m'anam i bhfianaise Dé nach bhfuilim ag insint éithigh" agus nach d'fhonn go mbeadh sé ina ócáid plámáis nó brabúis atá scríofa agam chugaibh. Ní mó ná sin atáim ag súil le honóir ó aon duine agaibh. Is leor liomsa an onóir nach bhfeictear fós ach a gcreidtear inti ó chroí; "is dílis an té a gheall; ní thugann sé a éitheach choíche".

55. Ach feicim mé féin ardaithe thar coimse ag an Tiarna cheana féin ar an saol seo; agus níorbh fhiú mé é, ná níorbh mé an sórt sin go dtabharfadh sé é seo dom; mar tá a fhios go dianmhaith agam gur fearr a oireann bochtaine agus tubaiste dom ná saibhreas agus só. Ach bhí "Críost an Tiarna freisin bocht ar ár son"; agus mise, an t-ainniseoir dearóil, fiú má shantaím saibhreas, níl a leithéid agam; agus "ní ag tabhairt breith orm féin atáim", mar gach lá bím ag brath ar bhás nó caimiléireacht a imirt orm, nó mé a ghabháil i mo chime, nó mí-ádh éigin a theacht sa mhullach orm. "Ach ní heagal liom aon cheann díobhsan" de bharr gealltanais na bhflaitheas, mar táim caite agam féin isteach i lámha Dé uilechumhachtaigh atá i réim i ngach áit, mar a deir an fáidh: "cuir do chúram faoi choimirce Dé agus cothóidh seisean thú."

56. Féach, "tiomnaim m'anam anois do mo Dhia sárdhílis a bhfuilim i mo thoscaire dó" dá shuaraí mé. Ach ós rud é "nach bhféachann sé ar phearsa seachas a chéile", mise a thogh sé mé don oifig seo, as measc na muintire ba lú aige, le súil go mbeinn i mo mhinistir aige.

57. Ach "cé mar a dhéanfaidh mé cúiteamh leis an Tiarna ar son gach ar bhronn sé orm"? Cad a déarfaidh mé nó cad a gheallfaidh mé don Tiarna? – mar níl ar mo chumas ach ar thug sé féin dom. Ach "scrúdaíodh sé an croí agus an aigne", mar go santaím go hiomlán agus thar fóir, agus go bhfuilim réidh, le go dtabharfadh sé dom a chailís le hól faoi mar a dheonaigh dóibh siúd eile a ghráigh é.

58. Dá bhrí sin nár lige mo Dhia dom go gcaillfinn go deo a phobal a bhailigh sé chuige féin in imigéin an domhain. Guím chun Dé go mbronnfadh sé an bhuanseasmhacht orm, agus a dheonú go ndéanfainn finné dílis dó go dul anonn dom, ar son mo Dhé.

59. Má éirigh liom riamh aon mhaith a léiriú i mo shaol ar son mo Dhé a ghráim, impím air a dheonú dom m'fhuil a dhoirteadh leo siúd atá ina ndeoraithe agus ina mbraighde ar son a ainm, fiú dá rachainn gan adhlacadh féin, nó go sracfaí mo chorp ball ar bhall ó chéile go lánainnis ag madraí nó ainmhithe allta, nó go n-alpfadh éanlaith an aeir é. Táim lándeimhin de, dá dtarlódh sin dom, go mbeadh m'anam gnóthaithe agam chomh maith le mo chorp, mar, gan aon amhras, aiséireoimid an lá úd i ngile na gréine, sé sin, i nglóir Chríost Íosa, ár Slánaitheoir, mar chlann Dé bheo agus "mar chomh-oidhrí Chríost, a bhfuil macasamhla a dheilbhe-sean le teacht orthu"; óir "is uaidh-sean agus tríd-sean agus is ann-san" atáimid le bheith i réim.

60. An ghrian seo a fheicimid éiríonn sí gach lá ar mhaithe linn faoi réir Dé, ach ní thiocfaidh sí i réim choíche ná ní mhairfidh a gile; ach lucht a hadhartha freisin, beidh droch-chríoch orthu faoi phéin go hainnis. Sinne, áfach, an dream a chreideann agus a adhrann an fhíorghrian, Críost, nach bhfaighidh bás choíche, agus "nach bhfaighidh an té a dhéan-faidh a thoil bás ach oiread", ach "mairfidh sé go deo mar a mhaireann Críost go deo", Críost a rialaíonn le Dia an tAthair uilechumhachtach, agus leis an Spiorad Naomh, roimh na haoiseanna agus anois agus le saol na saol. Amen.

61. Féach táim chun éirim m'fhaoistine a chur in iúl go hachomair arís eile. Is é m'fhianaise "os comhair Dé agus a aingeal naofa le fírinne agus le hardú croí", nach raibh riamh aon chúis agam, seachas an soiscéal agus a ghealltanais, le filleadh ar an gcine úd arb ar éigean a d'éirigh liom éalú uathu roimhe sin.

62. Ach impím orthu siúd a chreideann i nDia agus arb eagal leo é, cibé duine ar dheoin leis an scríbhinn seo a chum Pádraig, an peacach gan oiliúint is é sin, in Éirinn, a iniúchadh nó glacadh léi, nach ndéarfadh aon duine choíche gurb é mise, le m'aineolas go léir, a b'údar le cibé beagán a rinneas nó a d'fhoilsíos de réir thoil Dé; ach bígí den tuairim agus bíodh sé á chreidiúint mar lomchlár na fírinne, go mba thabhartas ó Dhia é. Agus sin í m'fhaoistin roimh bás dom.

# An Litir ag Coinnealbhá Corotícus

1. Mise Pádraig, peacach gan oiliúint ag cur fúm in Éirinn, fógraim gur easpag mé. Táim lándeimhin de gur ó Dhia a fuaireas a mbaineann liom. Dá bhrí sin is ar son grá Dé atá cónaí orm i measc na nginte barbaracha, i mo choimhthíoch agus i mo dheoraí. Is finné é Dia gur mar sin atá. Ní hé gur mhian liom aon ní a scaoileadh thar mo bheola ar shlí chomh dian ná chomh géar sin, ach tá dúthracht do Dhia do mo thiomáint agus spreag fírinne Chríost mé de bharr grá comharsan agus clainne, ar thréig mé mo thír dhúchais agus mo thuismitheoirí agus mo shaol go bás ar a son. Más fiú mé é, mairim do mo Dhia, d'fhonn na ginte a theagasc cé gur beag é meas roinnt daoine orm.

2. Is le mo láimh féin a scríobhas agus a chumas na briathra seo lena seachadadh agus lena gcur agus lena seoladh go saighdiúirí Chorotícus. Ní deirim chun mo chomhshaoránach, ná chun comh-shaoránaigh na Rómhánach naofa, ach chun comhshaoránaigh na ndeamhan de bharr a ndrochbheart. Maireann siad sa bhás dála naimhde, i gcomhar le Gaeil agus le Cruithne agus le díchreidmhigh. Lucht fola iad agus fuil ar sileadh leo, fuil Chríostaithe neamhurchóideacha a ghin mé ina sluaite do Dhia agus a chóineartaigh mé i gCríost.

3. Amárach an lae a ungadh na nuabhaistigh le criosma agus éadach geal an bhaiste orthu – bhí an chumhracht fós ar a n-éadan agus ár agus eirleach á imirt go míthrócaireach orthu faoi bhéal claímh an dreama a luamar – chuir mé litir le sagart naofa, fear a d'oileas ó bhí sé ina naíonán, agus cléirigh ina choimhdeacht, á iarraidh orthu roinnt den chreach nó cuid de na cimí baiste a ligean linn; ní dearna siad ach fonóid fúthu.

4. Dá bhrí sin ní eol dom cé acu is mó is ábhar caointe – an mhuintir a maraíodh, nó an mhuintir a ghabh siad, nó an mhuintir atá gafa go daingean ina líon ag an diabhal. Beidh siad faoi dhaoirse ag ifreann mar aon leis i bpionós síoraí mar, "an té a dhéanann peaca, is daor é, ar ndóigh, agus tugtar mac an diabhail air".

5. Dá bharrsan bíodh a fhios ag cách arb eagal leis Dia nach bhfuil aon pháirt liomsa ná le Críost mo Dhia, "a bhfuilim i mo thoscaire ar a shon", ag lucht fionaíle athar nó máthar, "faolchúnna craosacha a alpann pobal Dé mar a bheadh arán ann", mar a deir an scrioptúr: "Scrios lucht an oilc do dhlí, a Thiarna", dlí a bhí curtha go sármhaith agus go cáiréiseach aige in Éirinn sna blianta deireanacha, agus a bhí ag borradh faoi ghnaoi Dé.

6. Nílim ag léim thar líne. Táim i bpáirt leo siúd "a ghlaoigh sé agus a réamhchinntigh" chun an soiscéal a fhógairt, i lár géarleanúintí nár bheag, go himill an domhain, bíodh go bhfuil an namhaid in éad linn trí ansmacht Chorotícus; ní heagal leis-sean Dia ná a shagairt, iad siúd a thogh sé agus ar ar bhronn sé an chumhacht dhiaga is airde agus is oirirce, "go mbeadh ceangal ar neamh orthu siúd ar a gcuirfidís ceangal ar talamh".

7. Dá bhrí sin sibhse atá "naofa agus umhal ó chroí", táim ag impí oraibh go dúthrachtach, ní ceadmhach lútáil ar a leithéid, ná bia ná deoch a chaitheamh faru, ná ní ceart glacadh le déirc uathu nó go ndéana siad leorghníomh le Dia le haithrí dhian ag sileadh na ndeor, agus go saora siad seabhóntaithe Dé agus cumhala baiste Chríost, a bhfuair sé bás agus ar céasadh ar chrois é ar a son.

8. "Diúltaíonn an té is airde do thabhartais na n-olc. An té a ofrálann íobairt as maoin na mbocht is cuma é nó an té a bheadh ag íobairt an mhic i láthair an athar." "An mhaoin a bhailigh sé go héagórach," a deir an Scrioptúr, "déanfar í a aiseag as a ghoile; tá aingeal an bháis á tharraingt leis, déanfaidh confadh na ndragan é a stolladh, maróidh teanga an nathair nimhe é, alpfaidh an tine dhomhúchta é." Uime sin: "Is mairg dóibh siúd a líonann iad féin le nithe nach leo". Nó: "Cá fearrde duine go ngnóthódh sé an domhan go léir dá ligfeadh sé a anam féin ar ceal?"

9. Ba fhadálach mar ghnó é gach téacs a spíonadh nó a lua ceann ar cheann, agus faisnéis a lorg i dtaobh an sórt sin sainte ar fud an dlí go léir. Coir mharfach í an tsaint. "Ná santaigh cuid do chomharsan. Ná déan marú." Ní féidir aon dúnmharfóir a bheith fara Críost. "Gach duine ar fuath leis a bhráthair féin, is mar dhúnmharfóir a áirítear é." Nó: "An té nach dtugann grá dá bhráthair fanann sa bhás." Nach mó go mór is ciontach an té a thruailligh a lámha le fuil chlann Dé, an mhuintir a ghnóthaigh sé dó féin le déanaí ar imeall an domhain le cabhair mo spreagadh-sa dá shuaraí mé.

10. An é gur tháinig mé go hÉirinn gan Dia nó ar ghnóthaí saolta? Cé a chuir iallach orm? "Cuireadh ceangal orm sa Spiorad" gan aon duine de mo chineál féin a fhiosrú. An uaim féin a shníonn an trócaire bhúidh seo atá á cleachtadh agam i leith an chine úd a ghabh mar chime mé tráth agus a rinne creach ar sheirbhísigh theaghlach m'athar idir fhir agus mhná? Ba shaoránach mé de réir na colainne; ba dhecurion m'athair. Dhíolas m'uaisleacht ar mhaithe le daoine eile, rud nach náir liom agus nach aithreach liom. I mbeagán focal, is daor mé i gCríost do chine

deoranta ar son glóire do-inste "na beatha síoraí atá i gCríost Íosa ár dTiarna".

11. Agus mura n-aithníonn mo mhuintir féin mé, "ní bhfaigheann fáidh onóir ina thír dhúchais". B'fhéidir nach "den aon chró sinn agus nach é t-aon Dia céanna atá mar athair againn?". Mar a deir an Scrioptúr: "An té nach bhfuil liom, tá sé i m'aghaidh, agus an té nach gcnuasaíonn liom, scaipeann." Ní oireann sé: "Leagann duine ar lár, tógann duine eile. Ní hé mo thairbhe féin a lorgaim." Ní domsa a bhuíochas ach do Dhia "a chuir an díogras seo i mo chroí" go mbeinn "ar dhuine de na fiagaithe nó de na hiascairí" a thairgir Dia fadó a bhí le teacht sna laethanta deireanacha.

12. Tá olc ar dhaoine chugam. Cad tá le déanamh agam, a Thiarna; Níl meas madra orm. Sin iad do chaoirigh i mo thimpeall á stolladh agus á gcreachadh ag na foghlaithe a luamar faoi ordú Chorotícus na drochaigne. Is fada ó ghrá Dé an té a bhraithfeadh Críostaithe isteach i lámha na nGael is na gCruithne. D'alp "faolchúnna craosacha" tréad an Tiarna agus é ag borradh thar barr in Éirinn de thoradh ár ndíograis saothair. Ní féidir liom a bhfuil de chlann mhac na nGael agus d'iníonacha rí ina manaigh agus ina n-ógha le Críost a áireamh. Ar an ábhar sin "ná bí sásta go ndéanfaí éagóir ar na fíréin", ná ní bheifear sásta leis ach oiread le hifreann.

13. Cé acu de na naoimh nár ghráin leis bheith ag spraoi nó ag caitheamh fleá lena leithéidí? Tá a dtithe lán acu de chreach na gCríostaithe marbh; ar a mbradaíl is ea a mhaireann siad. Ní thuigeann siad, na hainniseoirí, gur nimh mharfach an bia atá á thairiscint acu dá gcairde agus dá gclann mar nár thuig Éava gurb é an bás dáiríre a bhí á thabhairt aici dá fear. Mar sin atá ag lucht déanta an oilc go léir; tá an bás síoraí á shaothrú acu mar phionós.

14. Is nós é seo ag Críostaithe Rómhánacha na Gaille: seolann siad fir chráifeacha, oiriúnach don ghnó, chun na bhFrancach agus chun na náisiún eile le dlús áirithe míle solidí le cimí baiste a fhuascailt. Déanann tusa a mhalairt, iad a mharú agus a dhíol le cine deoranta nach eol dóibh Dia; tá tú mar a bheifeá ag tabhairt baill Chríost suas do dhrúthlann. Cén dóchas i nDia atá agat nó ag aon duine atá ag réiteach leat nó ag déanamh béil bháin leat? Dia a thabharfaidh breith. Óir tá sé scríofa: "Ní hiad sin a dhéanann an t-olc amháin a dhaorfar, ach iad siúd a aontaíonn leo chomh maith."

15. Ní fheadar cad tá le rá agam nó le cur le mo chaint agam faoi chlann Dé atá marbh, iad sin a chuaigh faoi bhéal an chlaímh chomh

cruálach sin. Tá sé scríofa: "Bígí dobrónach le lucht an dobróin," agus arís: "Má bhíonn tinneas ar bhall amháin, bíodh na baill go léir ar chomhphian leis." Dá bhrí sin tá an Eaglais "ag caoineadh agus ag éagaoineadh a clann mhac agus iníon" nár mharaigh an claíomh fós ach atá fuadaithe agus díbeartha san imigéin mar a bhfuil an peaca ag borradh go follas, go tréan agus go mínáireach; ansiúd a díoladh saoránaigh, a cuireadh Críostaithe i ndaoirse, go háirithe ag na Cruithne, a shéan an creideamh, an dream meirleach is táire agus is coirpe ar fad.

16. Dá bhrí sin glaoim in ard mo chinn go brónach doilíosach: A bhráithre agus a chlann is sciamhaí agus is ansa liom, agus "a ghin mé i gCríost" in bhur líon gan áireamh, cad tá le déanamh agam daoibh? Ní fiú mé teacht i gcabhair ar Dhia ná ar dhaoine. "Tá an lámh in uachtar ag urchóid na n-urchóideach orainn." Tá ionann agus coimhthígh déanta dínn. B'fhéidir nach gcreideann siad gurb é an t-aon bhaisteadh amháin atá faighte againn, ná gurb é an t-aon Dia amháin atá mar athair againn. Is náireach leo gur Éireannaigh sinn. Mar a deir an Scrioptúr: "Nach aon Dia amháin atá agaibh? Cén fáth ar thréig gach duine a chomharsa?"

17. Dá bhrí sin, táim ag caoineadh ar bhur son, a mhuintir mo chléibh, agus ag sileadh na ndeor; ach arís tá áthas croí orm; ní raibh mo shaothar in aisce, nó m'oilithreacht gan toradh. Fág gur tharla coir chomh huafásach chomh do-inste sin, buíochas le Dia, a chreidmheacha baiste, tá sibh gafa anonn ón saol seo go Parthas. Is léir dom sibh; tá cromtha agaibh ar an aistear chun na háite "nach mbeidh oíche ná brón ná bás ann a thuilleadh; ach beidh sibh ag súgradh mar a bheadh gamhna a scaoileadh as a laincisí, agus gabhfaidh sibh de chosa ar na hurchóidigh agus beidh siad mar dheannach faoi bhur gcosa".

18. Beidh sibhse i réim, más ea, leis na haspail agus leis na fáithe agus leis na mairtírigh. Bainfidh sibh na flaithis shíoraí amach de réir mar a thugann sé féin fianaise á rá: "Tiocfaidh siad anoir agus aniar agus beidh siad ina suí chun boird le hAbrahám agus le hÍosác agus le Iacób i ríocht na bhflaitheas. Lasmuigh a bheidh madraí agus lucht asarlaíochta agus dúnmharfóirí"; agus "lucht na mbréag agus na leabhar éithigh, a bheith sa linn tine shíoraí is dán dóibh". Ní gan fáth a deir an t-aspal: "Más ar éigean a shábhálfar an fíréan, cá bhfágfar an peacach agus coirpeach bhriste an dlí?"

19. Ar an ábhar sin, Corotícus agus a chuid coirpeach, dream nach ngéilleann do Chríost, cá bhfeicfidh siad iad féin má tá mná baiste á roinnt acu mar dhuaiseanna ar mhaithe le ríocht shuarach shaolta a sceinneann thart i bpreabadh na súl? "Dála an scamaill nó an deataigh a

scaiptear le gaoth, sin mar a shíothlóidh peacaigh fhealltacha ó láthair ghnúis an Tiarna; beidh fleá ag lucht na córa go daingean teann" fara Críost; "tabharfaidh siad breith ar na náisiúin" agus rialóidh siad ar dhrochríthe trí shaol na saol. Amen.

20. "Tugaim m'fhianaise os comhair Dé agus a aingeal" gur de réir mar a chuir sé in iúl domsa d'ainneoin m'aineolais, a bheidh. Ní hiad mo bhriathra féin ach briathra Dé agus na n-aspal agus na bhfáithe a chuireas i láthair i Laidin, agus, ar ndóigh, b'fhada uathu riamh an bhréag. "An té a chreidfidh, slánófar é, ach an té nach gcreidfidh daorfar é. Dia a dúirt."

21. Impím go dúthrachtach, cibé searbhónta Dé ar fonn leis an litir seo a iompar, nach mbainfear uaithi nó nach gceilfear í ar aon duine, ach a mhalairt, go ndéanfar í a léamh i láthair na dtreibheanna go léir, agus i láthair Chorotícus féin. Má spreagann Dia iad le teacht ar mhalairt tuisceana faoi Dhia i dtreo, dá mba mhall féin é, go ndéanfaidís aithrí uair éigin sa bheart ainspianta a rinneadar – bráithre an Tiarna a eirleach – agus na mná baiste atá gafa cheana a scaoileadh saor, i dtreo go mb'fhiú iad maireachtáil do Dhia agus an slánú a bhaint amach anseo agus go deo, síocháin dóibh leis an Athair, an Mac, agus an Spiorad Naomh. Amen.

# *Part III*

# Commentary Section on the Theological Dimension of St Patrick's Letters

# *Chapter One*

# St Patrick's theology in detail

1. Introduction

2. St Augustine in controversy with the Pelagians and Semi-Pelagians

3. St Patrick's *Confession of Grace*
(a) His theology of personal conversion
(b) His theology of merit in the economy of grace
(c) His theology of mission
(d) St Patrick's theology and his faith-life

4. St Patrick's *Letter excommunicating Coroticus*

# Chapter One

# St Patrick's theology in detail

## 1. Introduction

St Patrick's character, attitudes and labours manifest an implicit many-faceted theology. Although his *Confession of Grace* and *Letter excommunicating Coroticus* are brief, through them we know the kind of person he was and, although they were written with specific purposes, they are so clearly and fully reasoned that they provide a cross-section of his whole theological understanding. They are astonishingly valuable indeed as a scripture of both his faith-life (i.e. his *life* with Christ, unseen but present, and, in and through Christ, with God the Father and the Spirit) and his belief-faith (i.e. what he *assented* to as revealed truth).

He shows a real sense of the presencing of Christ and of God's providence in his life. He has absolute trust in God's loving care for him, is full of love for God, of joy and pride in his missionary vocation and of gratitude to God for the gift of it. So great is his prayerfulness and feeling for prayer that talking to God and of God are as natural to him as breathing in the air, as enjoying, contemplatively, the warmth and light of the sun. Everything in his life is understood as being a gift from God, both in its small beginnings and in its growth, and perseverance too, is to be prayed for. In his later years, the years of the *Confession* and *Letter,* looking back on a life crowded with bodily and spiritual trials, crowded equally with great joys, he had come to see the pattern: the golden thread of God's loving Providence woven into it all.

Theologically, as a writer, he expresses his life in St Augustine's theology of grace, in a theology of human unworthiness and divine vocation which is Pauline in inspiration, and in a theology of mission that is solidly grounded in Scripture but not at all prominent in his day. In addition, the document of excommunication gives us a good glimpse of the Churchman engaged in due process of ecclesiastical law.

Although he does not discuss the contemporary Pelagian controversy, his theology expresses the mind of the Church on it. It is important then to note, in essence, this controversy.

## 2. St Augustine in controversy with the Pelagians and Semi-Pelagians

The controversy centred on the mysterious integration of divine grace and human freedom. Once we appreciate that here we are in the realm of mystery, not of explanation, we can avoid binary polarizing questions such as: are we a puppet in God's hands or are we really free and capable of merit? Even then we are still confronted with a question: to what extent are we to allow our experience and ideas of human freedom to mediate any conclusions about the providential workings of divine grace? These exercised an axiomatic influence within the reasoning of Pelagians and Semi-Pelagians. For them human autonomy (under, of course, the Lordship of God) was a fundamental principle for theological reasoning about divine grace. Such a principle invalidated any theological statement in which the term, grace, was made to refer to some direct divine influence on man's exercise of free choice. And it thereby abolished an essential ineffable mysteriousness in the integration of grace and freedom: there were really limits to the integration and therefore corresponding limits to the mystery.

The essential point and strength of Augustinian theology was to emancipate the concept, divine grace, from axiomatic control by human principles. To use this concept properly we must move more towards the mystery of our creaturehood, our living and moving and having our being in God, than towards our own experience of self-direction. The latter simply cannot mediate positive knowledge of divine action in our lives. In our affirmations then we must allow ourselves to be guided by Sacred Scripture and by a sense of our own mysterious creaturehood. The Augustinian tradition is indeed associated with definite *formal* affirmations of the strongest nature, in contrary opposition to the affirmations of Pelagianism. But its essential strength and comparative acceptability does not lie in the affirmations but in its achievement of directional truth when it says: human bounds cannot be set to divine grace. Any other direction diminishes divine action and is self-biasing towards falsehood and heresy, as was the case with Pelagianism.

In this attitude St Patrick is theologically and whole-heartedly Augustinian. As a Churchman we find him unhesitating in identifying himself with strong affirmations which had been made by St Augustine when violent opposition to this teaching was aroused in Gaul during the second decade of the fifth century.

## 3. St Patrick's *Confession of Grace*

Here he presents his whole life as the manifest working of divine grace in him. Further, in one passage which has puzzled scholars, it is possible that he was calling the attention of Pelagians to his life as a case history which completely rebutted their heresy.

The theology of the *Confession of Grace* is presented in the following pages in its many facets, as a theology of personal conversion, a theology of merit in the economy of grace and as a theology of mission. Also, this theology is seen in relationship with faith-life. Finally, the *Letter* is appraised as a document imposing excommunication on Coroticus and his followers.

Always the intellectual quality is Patristic in inspiration. Further, the Latin and idiomatic flavour of the writing is Patristic rather than classical. This is a significant fact in the translation and interpretation of texts and in any intellectual appraisal of St Patrick himself.

### (a) *His theology of personal conversion*

Conversion, the living orientation of the person towards God, takes place by divine grace, and in his own case this was manifestly so to himself. God had converted him. Assessing his spiritual condition in boyhood he says that he was dead in sin and unbelief (1, 12, 13, 27, 28) and only God could deliver him. We must interpret him here as meaning exactly what he says and not diminish his presentation, for an entire argument is built on it. On the eve of being ordained deacon we find him troubled in conscience, about going forward to receive Holy Orders because of a sin in boyhood. His own picture is clear: the face of God had transformed him from a sinner heading for eternal damnation.

First God "humbles" him by the severe chastisement of captivity, daily hunger and nakedness (27, 1, 3). They having humbled Patrick, God bestows on him the gift of faith, of repentance, of conversion to himself, pardoning his sins (2, 32). Further, God guards the newly converted, protecting him and consoling him (2). Patrick now, by the grace of God, grows in the divine gifts to him: in the love and fear of God, in prayer and in faith (16, 44).

In chapter 2, St Patrick describes the action of God which delivered him as from death: "The Lord opened my unbelieving mind so that even at that late hour I should remember my sins and turn with all my heart to the Lord my God". This sentence corresponds to St Augustine's use of a text in Sacred Scripture, Acts 16:14, concerning Lydia, a seller of purple goods, in the city of Philippi. The text, in the

Revised Standard Version, is "The Lord opened her heart to give heed to what was said by Paul". The Latin Vulgate also has the word *heart* (*cor*). But the version used by Augustine had the word *sensum* (*mind*) and St Augustine draws on the text to support his thesis that God *effects* faith in us: He opens our unbelieving minds. Thus He called Lydia *effectively* to faith. St Augustine uses the text for the first time (428-429 A.D.) when defending his views against opponents in Gaul. His great admirer, Prosper of Aquitaine, with a friend Hilary, both laymen, had written urgently for help and he replied with *De praedestinatione sanctorum* and *De dono perseverantiae.*

Afterwards Prosper frequently employed the Scripture text in St Augustine's version and use of it. It seems clearly the background to St Patrick's opening statement in ch. 2: "And there the Lord opened my unbelieving mind" ("et ibi Deus *aperuit sensum* incredulitatis meae"). And of course it is a detail in the weighty case that his theological education and preparation for ordination was in Gaul.

Early (4) in the *Confession of Grace* a credal statement, a formulation of belief-faith, appears. A sentence towards the end is clearly Augustinian in inspiration and directly anti-Pelagian:

> And He poured out the Holy Spirit upon us abundantly, as gift, and pledge of immortality, who *makes* believers and listeners *in order that* they shall be sons of God and fellow heirs with Christ.

The words emphasised are an exact translation of the Latin: they say exactly what the Latin says: but they have appeared strange to translators, unaware that as they stand they have a definite theological source and an exact significance. The received translation has been: ". . . who makes those who believe and obey become sons of God and joint heirs with Christ", i.e. the transformation is not *into* people who believe but *of* people who already believe.

It is in the two works already cited that St Augustine first employs the bold expression: "God makes believers". It appears twice: in *De praedestinatione sanctorum*, n.34 and in *De dono perseverantiae*, n.67. In the former Augustine asks: how are we to interpret St Paul in Ephesians 1:4? The text is:

> Blessed be the God and Father of our Lord Jesus Christ, who has blessed us in Christ with every spiritual blessing in the heavenly places, *even as he chose us in him before the foundation of the world . . . (sicut elegit nos in ipso ante mundi constitutionem).*

Does God choose us in and through foreseeing that we will believe (*"praescivit Deus credituros"*), or in and through his being about to make us believers (*"facturas fuerat ipse credentes"*). Augustine's answer is the latter: otherwise Christ could not have said: "you have not chosen me, but I have chosen you". In *De dono perseverantiae* n.67 we are told that:

> just as God made the man Christ Jesus, without any preceding merits of his, in such wise that he neither contracted original sin, nor committed by his own will any sin, so too God, without any preceding merits of theirs, *makes believers* (*facit credentes*) in Christ, in order that he may remit all their sins.

Incontrovertibly, we have here, in these two tracts of Augustine, written for circulation in Gaul, the doctrinal and literary inspiration for the phrase we get in Patrick's Credal Statement: "who *makes* believers and listeners *in order that* they shall be sons of God and fellow heirs with Christ". Indeed one of the reasons for the Credal Statement being in the *Confession of Grace* must be that it contained an article aimed at semi-Pelagianism, this article being added in Gaul to the statement not earlier than Augustine's tracts in the late 420s.

St Patrick's presentation of his life as a manifestation of grace seems to become pointedly and vigorously anti-Pelagian in ch. 13. He wishes his brothers in the ministry, and the many thousands of his spiritual sons and daughters whom he has baptized in Ireland, to learn the lessons of his experience and reflection on God's gracious dealings with him. On this note he addresses those "great and small who fear God". But he includes also, in the address, *et vos, domini, cati rhetorici*. Who are these particular people? To us the reference is certainly obscure. To the original readers it must have been reasonably clear. Very possibly "domini" (masters) is a term which could easily be made refer to Pelagians as they argued that we are self-directive beings, masters in our own actions and omissions. Literally rendered then the obscure text would be *"crafty rhetoricians (rhetorici cati) making yourselves out to be masters (domini)"* or "self-styled masters".

The text is certainly open to this interpretation. With it, the obscure passage not only loses its obscurity but assumes a somewhat climactic irony. The readers, experiencing already the vigour and cogency of St Patrick's reasoning, would not find this theological *coup de gras* surprising, just after they had learned (12) how Patrick had been "like a stone lying in deep mire" and how "He who is mighty came and . . . lifted me up, and, more than that, truly raised me aloft and placed me on top of the wall".

### (b) His theology of merit in the economy of grace

His theological understanding of human merit is the key to his powerful defence against accusations of being unworthy and unqualified – of being the wrong person for the office and labours of a bishop. In language and doctrine the defence corresponds very closely to St Paul's letters to the Corinthians.

Let us first note the general theological context and also principles expressed by St Paul in a situation which, in many respects, was similar to that of St Patrick.

Although the economy of salvation is one of divine revelation, of divine presencing and divine grace, the tradition of this economy is entrusted to the people of God themselves. Thus human unworthiness is intrinsic to the Church which is a very concrete reality, a definite body of people (*ecclesia*) whose function it is to proclaim, conserve and facilitate the divine transformation of persons and of social life which began with the Incarnation. A co-worker with God is necessarily unqualified and unworthy; further, in ecclesiastical life as in any other context, the same probabilities apply to his or her being also inferior, rather than excellent, in human competence, temperament and character. This is a description which is applicable, even-handedly, to bishops and priests, to lay and religious.

After St Paul had evangelized Corinth and departed, dissensions and antagonistic criticism of himself developed. A particular group was discrediting him and aimed to take his place. He had to defend his mission to Corinth and re-establish his full authority there as father of the Church. His self-vindication has the quality of absolute simplicity and sincerity, marked by a balanced presentation of doctrine, of self-revelation and of autobiographical detail.

At the very opening of each letter he states his office and dignity as an apostle. Opposing him, his critics were confronting the will of God: he had not called himself; his vocation was divine: no merit or competence of his had determined God's choice. And his sufficiency was from God and from God alone: ". . . our sufficiency is from God who has qualified us to be ministers of a new covenant" (2 Co 3:5-6). In criticizing him, his opponents were unwittingly drawing attention to the divine origin and nature of everything Christian: an apostolate manifested not the power and working of human persuasion but the power and working of God: "we have this treasure in earthen vessels, to show that the transcendent power belongs to God and not to us" (2 Co 4:7).

What was proof that God was with him in his apostolate? In 2 Co 11, 12 he presents as evidence all that he endured and was enabled to endure including the pain of misrepresentation; also signs, wonders and mighty deeds, visions and revelations; there was a divine seal on his apostolate – the flourishing churches that resulted:

> You yourselves are our letter of recommendation, written on our hearts, to be known and read by all men; and you show that you are a letter from Christ delivered by us, written not with ink but with the Spirit of the living God, not on tablets of stone but on tablets of human hearts (2 Co 3:2-3).

The evidence that he was not driven by self-interest was his disinterestedness in the service of God:

> For we are not like so many, peddlers of God's word . . . the love of Christ controls us, because we are convinced that one has died for all; therefore all have died. And he died for all, that those who live might live no longer for themselves but for him who for their sake died and was raised (2 Co 2:17; 5:14-15).

Finally, St Paul knew and affirmed that ultimate *corroboration* must be sought from his own conscience speaking in the sight of God (2 Co 1:12; 2:17), and from God himself as his witness (2 Co 11:31). Ultimate *judgement* would come from the Tribunal of Christ:

> For we must all appear before the judgement seat of Christ, so that each one may receive good or evil, according to what he has done in the body (2 Co 5:10).

Turning to St Patrick's *Confession of Grace*, we find a self-vindication that is structured very theologically. In a series of articles published in the *Irish Ecclesiastical Record*, 1948-1949, Fr D. S. Nerney, S.J., argued that it was carefully grounded in Scripture and the Magisterium. In language and doctrine St Paul's Second Letter to the Corinthians was the main Scriptural influence and provided the model used by St Patrick. Also relevant, in arguing with opponents, who prided themselves on possessing a superior *human* ability to evangelize successfully, were interventions from the Magisterium of the Church in the Pelagian controversy. Fr Nerney notes that St Patrick was able to fortify his apology with practically the whole body of doctrine defended by the Church. He also points out a significant correspondence between chapters 10 and 2 of the *Confession* and canon 5 of the XVI Council of Carthage (418) which condemned Pelagianism.

St Patrick's opening argument is in close correspondence with St Paul and is quite remarkable for its theological force. Fr Nerney summarizes:

His accusers contended, at least by inference, that God has respect to persons in calling to the apostolate: he takes the wise and good, not sinners, or rude, uneducated men. Realising that this was an inversion of the right order of divine vocation and an infringement of the Catholic doctrine of grace, St Patrick answered with St Paul that God chose the foolish and weak things of the world to confound the wise and mighty; and with St Augustine that men are not called by God because they are good, but to be good: *non enim electi sunt quia boni fuerunt, qui boni non essent nisi electi essent* [they are not chosen indeed because of their goodness, seeing that they would not be good unless they had been chosen] (*In Joann*, Tract 86, 2).[1]

Of course St Paul could claim a personal vocation and mission, received immediately from Christ himself, a claim that was accepted by St Peter and other apostles of Christ. St Patrick received the commission to his apostolate mediately from the Church. But the force of the argument is not thereby diminished. Perhaps the fullest and most concise formulation of the underlying theology is 2 Co 13:4:

Even though it was in weakness that Christ was put to death on the cross, it is by God's power that he lives. In union with him we also are weak; but we shall live with him by God's power.

St Patrick's vocation had its own unique features indeed. His first invitation came in a vision of the night:

And once more, after a few years I was in Britain with my family, who received me as a son, and sincerely begged of me that at least now, after all the many troubles I had endured, I should not leave them to go anywhere. And there, truly, I saw in a vision of the night, a man coming as it were from Ireland, whose name was Victoricus, with countless letters, and he gave me one of them, and I read the beginning of the letters, which ran: 'The Voice of the Irish'; and as I was reading the beginning of the letter aloud I thought I heard at that very moment the voice of those who lived beside the wood of Voclut, which is near the Western sea, and thus they cried out as with one voice: 'We beg you, holy youth, to come and walk once more among us'. And I was greatly troubled in heart and could read no further, and so I awoke. Thanks be to God that after many years the Lord granted them according to their cry (23).

---

1. *Irish Ecclesiastical Record* 72 (1949), p. 110.

This was confirmed in a vision censuring the verdict which rejected him as bishop:

And so, on that day when I was rejected by the above-mentioned persons – that night I saw a vision in the night, I looked, [and] before my face was a writing that stripped me of my honour. And as I looked at it I heard a divine voice say to me: 'We have seen with disapproval the face of so-and-so' (designated by name). Nor did He say: '*You* have seen with disapproval', but '*We* have seen with disapproval' as if He had associated Himself with me. As He said in Scripture: *He who touches you is as one who touches the apple of my eye* (29).

And it was confirmed again by a communication from Christ himself concerning his future work:

That is why I give thanks to Him who in all things gave me strength, so that He did not hinder me from the journey I had decided on, nor from that work of mine which I had learned from Christ my Lord, but rather did I feel in myself no little power from Him, and my fidelity was approved before God and men (30).

He was converted from unbelief and disobedience to the service of God (1, 2, 27, 36). The conversion began with his captivity which was a punishment from God; and his vocation to evangelize was imperative, like St Paul's. "For necessity is laid upon me. Woe to me if I do not preach the Gospel" says St Paul (1 Co 9:16). And St Patrick says:

As a result, then, even if I should wish to leave them and make a journey to Britain – I would most dearly love to make that journey so as to see my homeland and family; not only that, but also [to proceed] as far as Gaul to visit the brethren and see the face of the saints of my Lord: God knows I greatly desired it – still I am bound by the Spirit, who testifies to me that if I do this He will pronounce me guilty; and I am afraid of losing the labour I began, and not I but Christ the Lord, who ordered me to come and be with those people for the rest of my life – if God wills it, and keeps me from every evil way, so that I sin not in His sight (43).

From this starting point of divine vocation, St Patrick develops in detail the evidence of God's preparation and protection of him. His life is of course a rich source of such evidence which is duly divided and presented in Pauline divisions of (a) "signs, wonders and mighty deeds" (15, 17, 19, 21, 22, 23, 30, 34, 35, 52); the greatest wonder indeed is that God had used him: (13); (b) all the sufferings, labours and dangers that he was enabled to endure (16, 17, 26, 27, 32, 34, 35, 37, 52, 55); (c) visions and revelations (17, 20 21, 23, 24, 29, 30); (d) the flourishing Christian communities which he had founded, his seal of divine approval (11, 14, 38, 41, 42, 50, 51); (e) his disinterestedness in the service of God, manifesting him as a person motivated, not by any desire for gain but from the charity of Christ (13, 37, 48, 49, 50, 51, 53, 59).

He acknowledges, and appeals to, the ultimate sources of corroboration for his evidence: his own conscience (48), God as his witness (24, 31, 33, 43, 44, 48) and the day of judgment at the Tribunal of Christ (8).

We have seen the strong bone structure of St Patrick's self-defence. But for the Patristic spirit which clothes the bones with flesh and breathes passionate life into them, the *Confession of Grace* itself must be read. The following sample quotations are a thin cross section of St Patrick's argumentation and language – vigorous, self-revealing, sincere and always well proportioned, logically, for what needed to be either refuted or proved:

> I am Patrick, a sinner, unlettered, the least of all the faithful, and held in contempt by a great many people (1) . . . assuredly before I was humbled I was like a stone lying in deep mire; and He who is mighty came and in His mercy lifted me up, and, more than that, truly raised me aloft and placed me on top of the wall (12) . . . And before daylight I used to be stirred to prayer, in snow, in frost, in rain (16) . . . I saw in a vision of the night a man coming as it were from Ireland, whose name was Victoricus, with countless letters, and he gave me one of them (23) . . . He [God] came powerfully to my aid when I was being walked upon (26) . . . for many were trying to forbid this mission of mine; they were even talking among themselves behind my back, and asking: "Why is that fellow thrusting himself into danger among a hostile people who do not know God" (46) . . . daily I expect to be slaughtered, or defrauded, or reduced to slavery or to any condition that time and surprise may bring. (55) . . . one more time, let me briefly set down the theme of my confession. I testify in the Truth, and in exultation of heart before God and His holy angels, that I never had any reason other than the Gospel and its promises for ever returning to that race from whom in an earlier time, I had barely made good my escape from captivity (61).

### (c) His theology of mission

Early in his *Confession of Grace* (6) St Patrick says that he wants his brethren and kindred to perceive the sacred purpose of his soul. His mission to Ireland was God's idea, not his own. God had promised in the Old Testament and in the New that he would gather a people to himself from the ends of the earth. He would send apostles to gather them. Ireland was at the limit of the earth and God was now through Patrick fulfilling his promise by gathering to himself a people from among the Irish:

> We were gravely bound, then, to spread our nets, so that a great multitude and throng should be caught for God, and that everywhere there should be clergy to baptize and exhort a needy and thirsting people, as the Lord in the Gospel admonishes and teaches, saying: *Go therefore now, make disciples of all nations, baptizing them in the name of the Father and of the Son and of the Holy Spirit, teaching them to observe all that I have commanded you: and lo, I am with you always, to the close of the age.* And again He says: *Go, therefore into all the world and preach the Gospel to the whole creation. He who believes and is baptized will be saved: but he who does not believe will be condemned.* And again: *This Gospel of the kingdom will be preached throughout the whole world, as a testimony to all nations; and then the end will come.* And again the Lord announces beforehand through the prophet: *And in the last days it shall be, God declares, that I will pour out my Spirit upon all flesh, and your sons and your daughters shall prophesy, and your young men shall see visions, and your old men shall dream dreams; yea, and on my menservants and my maidservants in those days I will pour out my Spirit; and they shall prophesy.* And *in Hosea He says: Those who were not my people I will call 'my people' and her who had not received mercy I will call 'her who has received mercy'. And in the very place where it was said: 'You are not my people', they will be called 'sons of the living God'* (40).

For St Patrick the missionary apostolate is, in all aspects, a gratuitous grace of God both to the apostle and to the evangelized. And he gives unwearying thanks to God for his own apostolate and earnestly prays for perseverance in it (3, 34, 38, 51, 58). He sees and affirms himself as the apostle of Ireland, mysteriously chosen by divine providence to be commissioned by the Church. His life is enveloped in the consciousness of being under orders from Christ, to bring the Gospel to the Irish. This is the key which gives us access to and understanding of his unflinching steadfastness and confidence as he faces criticism of his mission.

Theologically, he was original, for his times, in the emphasis he placed on the unlimited aspect of the call which Christ issued, to bring the Gospel to all the *unevangelized.* Missions to barbarians outside the Roman frontiers were not a feature of the early Church. From his *Letter excommunicating Coroticus* we know that many Britons looked askance at the mission to the Irish, indeed some were hostile to the very idea of it. We can understand, if we cannot respect the grounds for this. Britain had been Romanised (which in that age meant, for the western world, civilised) for some centuries. Ireland, never Romanised, was a barbarian island. Its people, barbarians, were regarded as, thereby, inferior. Of Coroticus and his soldiers St Patrick himself, says: "For them it is a matter of disdain that we be Irish" (*Letter,* 16). Between Irish and Britons there were also the recurring hostile forays to and from across the Irish Sea.

St Patrick attempts to win his Christian brethren and kinsmen in Britain from their attitude by arguing – again on principles drawn from Augustine's theology of grace – that his mission to the Irish is a divinely ordained enterprise which, by implication, it would be flying in the face of God to oppose. He understood his own vocation as coming from the universal salvific will of God:

> I am exceedingly in debt to God, who granted me so great a grace that through me a multitudinous people should be reborn in God, and afterwards confirmed; and that clerics should everywhere be ordained for them – for a people newly coming to belief whom the Lord took from the uttermost parts of the earth, as long ago He had promised through His prophets: *To you the nations will come from the uttermost parts of the earth and say, Our fathers got for themselves worthless idols, and there is no profit in them.* And again: *I have set you to be a light for the Gentiles, that you may bring salvation to the uttermost parts of the earth* (38).

This theological understanding imbued his own obedience to divine grace with the added human joy of whole-hearted accord. His going outside the Romanised world, in order to evangelize and baptize at the ends of the earth, was not only an obedience to his divine vocation: he could not conceive himself as ever wanting a different specific vocation.

As well as the Scriptural proof, there was concrete evidence of there being a divine call to evangelize the uttermost, barbarian, parts of the earth, evidence that it was "the love of Christ [which] brought" (13) himself, in particular, to Ireland. This evidence was the new Christian community which arose and flourished:

I journeyed among you, and everywhere, in your interest, in many dangers, even to the remotest parts beyond which nobody lived, and whither no-one had ever come to baptize, or ordain clerics, or confirm the people; by gift of the Lord I did it all diligently and most gladly, for the sake of your salvation (51) . . . Consequently, then, in Ireland, they who never had knowledge of God, but up till now always worshipped only idols and abominations – how they have lately been made a people of the Lord and are called children of God; sons of the Scotti and daughters of chieftains are monks and virgins of Christ! (41) . . . my brethren and sons whom I have baptized in the Lord – so many thousands of people (14). (Cf. also *Confession*, 38, 42, 50; *Letter*, 2, 3, 5, 16.)

Thus St Patrick's theology of mission emphasizes two fundamental truths:

(i) there is a divine command to bring the Gospel to the uttermost places and peoples on earth:
(ii) the manifest working of grace testifies to divine co-operation and so is a seal of divine approval on any particular mission.

St Peter, himself, invoked this truth in his reply to those who criticised him when he began to baptize Gentiles: "As I began to speak, the Holy Spirit fell on them just as on us at the beginning. And I remembered the word of the Lord, how he said, 'John baptized with water, but you shall be baptized with the Holy Spirit'. If then God gave the same gift to them as he gave to us when we believed in the Lord Jesus Christ, who was I that I could withstand God? When they heard this they were silenced. And they glorified God saying, 'Then to the Gentiles also God has granted repentance unto life'" (Ac 11:15-18).

### (d) St Patrick's theology and his faith-life

One of his purposes in writing the *Confession of Grace* was to proclaim the faith and to strengthen and confirm it in the thousands of Irish he had baptized:

In proportion, then, to the faith which I have received from the Trinity, it is my duty . . . to make known the gift of God . . . fearlessly and confidently to spread God's name everywhere; so that even after my death I may leave a legacy to my brethren and sons whom I have baptized in the Lord – so many thousands of people (14) . . . I have given an honest account to my brethren and fellow servants, who have believed me because of what I have proclaimed and am proclaiming in order to strengthen and confirm your faith. My desire is that you strive after greater things, and do more excellent deeds. This will be my glory, because a wise son is the glory of his father (47).

In appraising how instructional, on faith-life itself, the *Confession of Grace* is, it is important to see both St Patrick's method of instruction and the important truths and lessons which he either directly communicated or implied.

As we have already adverted to, briefly above, faith-life is a form of human living with Christ, in the medium of our minds and hearts. Christ being the Incarnate God, his presencing to us is both divine and human; and it is a presencing with his Father and with the Holy Spirit, his Spirit, for God is triune and indivisible. St Patrick's method of strengthening the faith in everyone whom he wanted his *Confession of Grace* to reach, was to present his own faith-life. Propositional statements about an interior presence of Christ, of God, of the Spirit, are not entirely absent (4, 33, 57, 62). But characteristically, the *Confession of Grace* is pure acknowledgment of the grace, in himself, from God, of faith-life. And indeed just as there is more moral truth contained, informally, in the being and life of an excellent moral person than could ever be conveyed by him or her in formal doctrine (however valuable and necessary in its own right), so too faith-life is illuminated in a unique and incomparable way by St Patrick's personal "confession of grace".

For faith-life came to him as a slave, destitute, abject and alone. In his case the transition to faith-life was a *felt* transition, i.e. he experienced it in its reality as a transition, a foretaste indeed of the transition, in death, to eternal life. It came to him as a felt liberation from bonds of slavery, a crossing out of darkness into light, a spiritual transformation, when God presenced himself in his mind and heart and he became orientated towards God, in love and prayer, daily and nightly, in all weathers and hardships.

St Patrick is not silent about any aspect of his faith-life as it developed – his prayer, his feelings, his readiness and responsiveness to Christ; also his visions and the revelations made to him:

And there [in Ireland] the Lord opened my unbelieving mind, so that even at that late hour I should remember my sins and turn with all my heart to the Lord my God (2) . . . And he poured out the Holy Spirit upon us abundantly as gift and pledge of immortality, who makes believers and listeners in order that they shall be sons of God and fellow heirs with Christ (4) . . . more and more the love of God and the fear of Him came to me, and my faith increased, and my spirit was moved so that in one day I would pray as many as one hundred times, and in the night nearly as often, even while I was staying in the woods and on the mountain; and before daylight I used to be stirred to prayer, in snow, in frost, in rain (16) . . . and I heard a divine voice telling me: 'For two months you will be with them' (21, cf. 20) . . . And on another night – I do not know, God knows, whether it was in me or beside me – very distinctly, in words which I heard and could not understand, except at the end of the prayer He thus declared Himself: 'He who gave His life for you, He it is who is speaking in you'; and at that I awoke rejoicing. (24, cf. 25, 29 35) . . . He did not hinder me from the journey I had decided on, nor from work of mine which I had learned that from Christ my Lord (30) . . . I grieve for my best friend, that he should have given cause for our hearing such a statement from the Lord (32) . . . He preserved me from all iniquities (so I believe) through the grace of His indwelling Spirit, who has worked to this day within me (33) . . . It was not I but God, who overcame in me and resisted all these things (37, cf. 43, 62) . . . I shall not be silent, nor do I hide the signs and wonders which were shown to me by the Lord many years before they came to pass, by Him who knows all things even before the beginning of time (45) . . . [God] who on more than one occasion held back from vehement anger with me (46) . . . Let Him search my heart and mind, for with desire I desire, and ready I would be, to drink of His chalice, as He granted it to many others who loved Him (57).

For St Patrick, phenomena which excite our wonder can be expected at the level of faith-life. But it is faith-life itself that is primarily extraordinary; it is the grace of graces. And so, side by side with his own visions and revelations, he is careful to narrate the story of a newly baptized convert, the message to her from God, and the fruitfulness of her faith:

And there was even one Scottic girl of noble birth, blessed, very beautiful, full grown, whom I baptized; she came to us a few days afterwards for one reason only: to tell us she had received a message from a messenger of God who instructed her to become a virgin of Christ and to draw close to God. Thanks be to God, six days later she most laudably and eagerly laid hold of that life (42).

Implicit in St Patrick's whole approach to grace is the certainty that no human bounds can be set to its possibilities, its working or its effects. Accordingly, faith-life is open to all the possibilities of what we would now call mystical experience and mystical prayer. But it is not dependent on them for its value. In its essence it is our life with God and it can remain so, with or without being graced with peaks and depths and intensities of mystical experience. The deprivation of deprivations is not to have really crossed the threshold at all, into the life of grace.

Once again he is being very Augustinian in his outlook. For St Augustine, it is not any individual phenomenon which is primarily wonderful. Creation itself is the miracle of miracles, and the economy itself of grace is the grace of graces. There is really only one miracle: the creation and salvation of the world; everything is an integral part of this work of God and so the particular phenomenon we marvel at is not really extraordinary:

> God himself has created all that is wonderful in this world, the great miracles as well as the minor marvels I have mentioned, and he has included them all in that unique wonder, that miracles of miracles, the world itself.[2]

In his First Letter to the Corinthians, St Paul, the other major literary influence on St Patrick, writes: "The world as we know it is passing away" (7:31). It is interesting that one of the Scriptural texts (Mt 24:14) which St Patrick uses (40) to support his missionary work at the "uttermost parts" of the earth, links the preaching of the faith *everywhere* with the end of the world. He, himself, does not speak of the world ending physically, but he does present it as passing away in another sense which, patristically, is a deeper, allegorical sense of Scripture:

> Consequently, then, in Ireland, they who never had knowledge of God, but up till now always worshipped only idols and abominations – how they have lately been made a people of the Lord and are called children of God; sons of the Scotti and daughters of chieftains are monks and virgins of Christ! (41).

What is passing away is not reality but its shroud of darkness, the form under which we live in it. What is appearing now in Gospel light is reality under the Lordship of Christ. Our world is seen with Christ, our Divine Saviour, as centre; and pagan countries like Ireland, respond with dedications and consecrations to him. The dynamism of faith-life brings them into union with Christ and, in Christ, with the indivisible Triune God. As the Second Vatican Council puts it: ". . . as sons united in the Son we can cry out in the Spirit 'Abba, Father'" (*Constitution on the Church in the Modern World*, 22).

2. *The City Of God*, Book 21, Ch IX, translation by H. Bettenson (London, 1972).

On a last analysis, faith-life is seen to join together the order of nature and the order of grace. In it nature and grace enjoy their common orientation to God. Human persons (described so aptly by Plato as "in-between" beings) see in God the Truth and Goodness they so naturally desire. And, freely, they abandon themselves, obedientially, to this attraction.

Towards the end of his *Confession of Grace* (60), St Patrick proclaims the transformation of Ireland with the passing away of sun worship and its replacement by faith-life with the true Sun, Christ:

> For that sun which we see [with our bodily eyes] rises daily at God's command for our sake; but it will never reign, nor will its splendour abide; but all who adore it will come, as unhappy men, unhappily to punishment. We, on the other hand, [are a people] who believe in the true Sun and adore Him, Christ, who will never perish. And neither will he who does His will; but he will abide for ever, as Christ abides for ever, He who with God the Almighty Father and with the Holy Spirit reigns before all ages, as now, and for ever and ever. Amen.

The severe wording here, in the repudiation of sun-worship, reminds us of the dark mystical experience which St Patrick had towards the end of his escape from captivity in Ireland. It was, for him, an immediate concrete experience of the power of Satan and it reminds us further of St Paul's continual harassment from an angel of Satan (2 Co 12:7-10). St Patrick was saved by Christ, present in the experience as the rising sun:

> The very same night I was sleeping when Satan mightily put me to the test − I shall remember it as long as I am in this body. He fell upon me like a huge rock, and I could not move a limb. But whence did it occur to me, ignorant in spirit, to call upon Helias? And while this was happening I saw the sun rise in the heavens, and as I was crying out: 'Helias, Helias', with all my strength, lo, the splendour of that sun fell on me and promptly shook all heaviness from me; and I believe that I was aided by Christ my Lord, and that His Spirit was even then crying out on my behalf . . . (20). [The Latin word he would use for Elijah is *Helias* (vocative *Helia*) and the Greek word for the sun is *helios*.]

Beiler points out that a certain fusion of *Helias* and *helios* was quite common in Christian art and literature in St Patrick's time. He goes on:

The sun that dispelled Patrick's nightmare was, of course, understood by him as the *sol verus* (the Messianic *Sol Justitiae* – Mal 4:2).
Here again we have the very interesting parallelism of a Christian
tradition conceiving of Christ, the Creator of the sun, as the sun of
our salvation (*Sol Salutis*) opposed to the pagan and Imperial sun-
god (*Sol Invictus*).[3]

In his Christmas Sermons, Augustine contrasted Christ with
the pagan *Sol Invictus*.
Thus taking into consideration what is explicit and what is
implicit in St Patrick's presentation of faith-life, one must appraise it as
being highly and effectively instructional, typically Patristic and, in particular, Augustinian in spirit.

### 4. St Patrick's *Letter excommunicating Coroticus*

In his articles "A Study of St Patrick's Sources"[4] Fr D. S.
Nerney, S.J., compared this letter with a letter of excommunication written by Pope Innocent I. The latter's pontificate lasted from Dec. 20th, 401
A.D. until his death, March 12th, 417 A.D. He was one of the greatest
popes of the early centuries and contributed very much to the development
of the concept of Roman primacy. The collection of some forty-four
extant letters of his is of great importance. In his letter, *Inter Ceteras* (ep
30), to the Fathers of the Council of Milevis he condemns Pelagius and
Caelestius and declares that these "Founders of novelties . . . are to be
deprived of ecclesiastical communion until they recover their senses".
Although a precise doctrine was not developed in the early
centuries, a real power to excommunicate was acknowledged and it was
used, e.g. by St Paul in the church at Corinth (1 Co 5:1-10; and 2 Co
13:1-3). St Patrick and Pope Innocent are dealing with matters as far apart
as murder and heresy. But their letters share a common structure. Fr
Nerney puts it:

> The general procedure is the same: a description of the misde-
> meanour; the excommunication of the principals, of their accessories,
> with a specific reference to their exclusion from the common life of
> the community; and finally a promise of rehabilitation on due repen-
> tance.[5]

---

3. *The Works of St Patrick* (Newman Press and Longmans, Green and Co., London, 1953), p. 84.
4. *Irish Ecclesiastical Record* 72 (1949), p. 24 ff.
5. Ibid., p. 24.

Both writers use the same Pauline text (Rm 1:23) in applying their excommunication to accessories, and both use the image of fierce wolves coming in and not sparing the flock, an image that occurs in St Paul's speech to the elders of Ephesus (Ac 20:29).

The indications are that St Patrick's letter of excommunication was drawn up carefully and competently, in a manner that agreed, in idiom, style and structure with the See of Rome. Although it is very moving, both in its denunciation and in its expression of grief, it bears scrutiny also as an official document issued by an experienced Churchman.

## Chapter Two

# St Patrick's Letters: The Literary Genre, Use of Scripture and Patristic Ethos

1. The literary genre of St Patrick's pastoral letters
(a) The confessional-autobiographical genre
(b) Patrick's *Confessio* and Augustine's *Confessiones*

2. The significance of St Patrick's wide use of Scripture
(a) Introduction: the world of Scripture
(b) Scripture as boundless in its symbolization of the experience of God-with-us
(c) The Bible in the life of the Early Church
(d) St. Patrick's use of Scripture

3. The particular period of the Fathers evidenced in St Patrick's letters
(a) Introduction
(b) The Latin Fathers of the Fourth and Fifth centuries
(c) The main Western Fathers appearing in the Patristic Apparatus to St Patrick's pastorals, considered according to regions:
   (i) Italy
   (ii) Gaul
   (iii) Spain
   (iv) North Africa
(d) Summary conclusion

4. A note on excommunication in the Early Church

# Chapter Two

# St Patrick's Letters: The Literary Genre, Use of Scripture and Patristic Ethos

## 1. The literary genre[1] of St Patrick's pastoral letters

### (a) The confessional-autobiographical genre

It is a fundamental critical principle that a literary document cannot be adequately understood and evaluated without understanding the literary genre to which it belongs. That principle is now as well established for religious and biblical books as it is for secular literature. And so it holds also for the understanding and evaluating of St Patrick's *Confessio*, and hence of its author, his genius and stature. And that, not just of Patrick and his *Confessio* in isolation at an ancient moment in time. For in writing his *Confessio* Patrick is in organic continuity with a millenarian tradition, a tradition that had a long history before him and was to have a long history after him, right down into modern times. And (to make the point at once) his *Confessio* is not just any casual link in the tradition. After the outstanding contribution of the great Augustine to the genre Patrick's is the most explicit, developed, and vibrant in early Christianity – due regard, of course, being had to the difference of scale between foothills and mountains.

I have labelled the genre more fully as 'Confessional-*Autobiographical*'. It is obvious enough that Patrick's *Confessio* is autobiographical – as Augustine's is – although, equally obviously, and again like Augustine's – not in the exhaustively factual genre of modern autobiography. The reason in both cases is that the facts, in the sense of the external events of a life, are not the principal point of the exercise in a *confessio*. They are necessary of course, but only as the 'plot', the 'structure of events', is necessary as the armature to carry the deeper inner meaning of a drama or a novel – or of a human life-story. As such the external facts of the life will not be exhaustive but selected, selected in function of their charge of significance, as all art and all scientific enquiry

---

1. For a brief survey see A. Solignac in *Oeuvres de Saint Augustin*, vol. 13, *Les Confessions*, Livres I-VII (Desclée De Brouwer, 1962) pp. 36-45; – confessedly indebted to Pierre Courcelle, *Antécédents autobiographiques des Confessions de Saint Augustin*, in *Revue de Philologie*, 31 (1957), pp. 23-51; cf. also Courcelle's *Les Confessions de Saint Augustin dans la tradition littéraire: antécédents et postérité* (Études Augustiniennes, Paris, 1963).

must select if it is to see beyond the multiplicity of phenomena into a unity of pattern and meaning.

Now the deepest and most comprehensive significance of the 'confessional' genre is the narrated quest, finding, meditation and profession of this meaning, in the pattern retrospectively perceived in the process of a life lived. A genre designated by the radically religious name of 'confession' because the narrative is in the first place before God and to Him, the ultimate source of both existence and the providence and light that gives existence pattern and meaning. Patrick was the stone lying in the mud . . . until God lifted him up and set him on top of the wall (cf. *Conf.* 12). 'Let me make return to the Lord then for all His bounty to me'' (*Conf.* 57). "Late have I loved Thee, O Beauty so ancient and so new; late have I loved Thee! . . . Thou wert with me but I was not with Thee. I was kept from Thee by those things [which Thou has made], yet had they not existed in Thee they would not have existed at all . . . [but] Thou didst send forth Thy beams and shine upon me and chase away my blindness . . ." (Augustine, *Conf.* X 27, 38).

Is Patrick's account of his life and mission in fact a *confessio* in the sense we have explained? It might seem a strange question to ask, but it has been argued that Patrick's *Confessio* is not a *confessio* in the Augustinian sense (e.g. C. Mohrmann, *The Latin of Saint Patrick*, pp. 4-6).[2]

A genre with an autobiographical axis may incorporate many strands. And certainly one strand in Patrick's *Confessio* is an *apologia pro vita sua*, against clearly indicated if ill-defined opponents of his mission in Ireland. The need to answer those critics might even have been the immediate occasion of his writing, as Kingsley's accusations were the immediate occasion of Newman's *Apologia*. But in the genius of an Augustine or a Newman the narrower immediate occasion will not prevent the work becoming something greater in the writing. On the contrary, in fact, it is likely to provide the release and the occasion for expansion into a larger theme. With all due regard to differences of scale the same would apply to the welling genius of the Patrick we know from the *Confessio*.

But in this question we are not dependent on the imprecisions of mere conjecture. Already in chapter 3 Patrick gives us a *confessional* reason for his writing, namely that he cannot stay silent, nor is it fitting that he should, about the great favours and graces he has had from the Lord in the land to which he came first as a captive. This is the context for his explicit statement in chapter 9 that he "*long ago* thought of writing", but had "hesitated until now", for fear of what critical tongues would say about his literary limitations.

2. Where see the reference to John J. O'Meara, "The *Confessio* of Saint Patrick and the *Confessions* of Saint Augustine," *Irish Ecclesiastical Record* 85 (1956), pp. 190-197.

Further, it is in this same confessional context that he uses the very word *confiteri* four times in chapters 3-5, three of them in quotations from Scripture (the scriptural roots of *Confessio* we shall see later − as also the relevance of words such as *exaltare* and *magnificare* used in these chapters). Mohrmann does address these words, but, in the light of the context we have described, her interpretation of them is very strained. All the more so in light of Patrick's use of the term *confessio* to describe his work in the two concluding chapters in which he explicitly sums up its contents. True, she says that "there is nothing in this summing up of the contents of his work that points to the *threefold* [my emphasis] *confessio*" − she is referring to the three subjects of *confessio*, confession of sin, of praise, and of faith, as we shall understand them later and as exemplified in St. Augustine's *Confessions*. Her statement may be true if we read the concluding summary without any context. When we read the *Confessio* as a whole it is hard to see how it could be interpreted as having no confession of sin (*Ego Patricius peccator . . .* I am Patrick, a sinner − opening words of the work). And no confession of praise? The word may not be there, but what is the theme of the whole work if not the praise of God, for the wonderful works He has done for, in, and through the lowly Patrick? And is not this the meaning of the phrase used to state the theme of the work in chapter 3: "to *exalt* and *confess* His wonderful deeds . . ." (*exaltare et confiteri mirabilia eius. . .*). There is a parallel summary thematic statement in the explicitly confessional and consciously eloquent chapter 34: "Who am I, Lord, or what is my calling . . . that today among the nations I steadfastly exalt and glorify Your Name (*exaltarem et magnificarem nomen tuum*) wherever I am . . .?"

And as for the confession of faith, it is easy to see it in the great credal proem of chapter 4, analogous in its power and placing to Augustine's great opening descant on God in the first five chapters of his *Confessions*: "Great art Thou, O Lord, and greatly to be praised . . ."

Through what we have been saying so far the nature of the confessional genre has emerged in its main lines. Because it is the fruit of life and lived experience it is an 'existential' genre − hence its tang of reality and the perennial interest of its greatest examples. Furthermore that perennial interest is one purpose of the writer. For while the confession is principally a religious exercise, before God and addressed to Him, it is also before men and addressed to them as an existential example for their benefit. "In proportion, then, to the faith which I have received from the Trinity, it is my duty to make it known . . . fearlessly and confidently to spread God's name everywhere; so that even after my death I may leave a legacy to my brethren and sons whom I have baptized in the Lord . . ." (*Conf.* 14; cf.6). "I confess not only before You . . . but also in the ears of the believing sons of men, companions of my joy and sharers of my mortality, my fellow citizens, fellow pilgrims . . ." (Augustine, *Conf.* X 4, 6).

That perennial interest and value is all the greater in so far as the existential experience is of ultimate questions of meaning and their resolution, resolution not merely by abstract thinking but also at the deeper level of profound personal experience with the whole of the author's being. Hence the greatest confessions are those of great converts, converts in the full original sense of that word, a complete 'turning round' of an existence, as we see it in an Augustine, a Patrick, a Newman . . . "I lost my normal consciousness for a moment and my delirium was lulled to sleep; and I awoke to see your infinity in a totally different way . . ." (Augustine, *Conf.* VII 14, 20). "And there the Lord opened my unbelieving mind so that even at that late hour I should remember my sins and turn with all my heart (*converterem toto corde*) to the Lord my God . . ." (Patrick, *Conf.* 2; cf. 33). And in the case of such converts as Augustine and Patrick the 'turning round' is made all the more intense, profound and complete by the higher light of mystical experiences (Augustine, *Conf.* VII 10, 16 and 17, 23; Patrick, *Conf.* 17, 20, 23-25). Even in the more placid Newman we can point to his youthful sense of the unreality of the material world. "My imagination ran on unknown influences . . . I thought life might be a dream, or I an Angel, and all this world a deception, my fellow angels by a playful deception concealing themselves from me, and deceiving me with the semblance of a material world".[3]

That excerpt from Newman illustrates the nature of those 'ultimate questions of meaning' from which I said arise the questions, experiences and resolutions that provide the material of the confessional narrative. They are firstly metaphysical, and ultimately religious, questions about the origin and nature of man, the purpose of his existence, his relation to an ultimate explanatory Ground of reality. It is natural therefore that the great confessions should ultimately centre on the two great poles of reality, on what Newman calls "the thought of two and two only supreme, and luminously self-evident beings, myself and my Creator" (*Apologia*, p. 98). "What then do you desire to know?", wrote Augustine in his first confessional work. "I desire to know God and my soul" (*Soliloquia* I 2, 7). "I became a great enigma to myself", he later wrote about his youthful "discovery" of death and the black pall of mystery and apparent futility it spread over existence (*Conf.* IV 4, 9). Even the "rustic" Patrick sees the pattern of his life enveloped in mystery, and is moved to ask (in words borrowed from Scripture): "Who am I, Lord, or what is my calling, that you made known such divine power to me?" (*Conf.* 34, in a variant reading).

3.  J. H. Newman, *Apologia pro Vita Sua.* (Collins: Fontana Books, London and Glasgow, 1959), p. 96.

It is within and from this larger theme, this deeper experimental, existential knowledge of the self and of God, that there arise those more specific motifs of confession that we mentioned earlier, confession of sin, of praise (including thanksgiving), and of faith. In the domain of the discovery of God thanksgiving, praise and faith hardly need explanation. Confession of sin might not seem to need explanation either—since the normal pattern of the confessional narrative is that of a conversion out of error and sinfulness into the light of truth and the life of grace. It is the Augustinian pattern, and the Patrician pattern too.

But in fact the rationale of the confession of sin goes deeper. It is rooted in the confessional awakening to the reality of sin at a deeper level and in a more experiential way. It represents the primordial and universal correlative of the experience of the transcendent numinous, the *mysterium tremendum*, the Holy. It generates the confessional cry of Isaiah before Yahweh and the seraphs: "What a wretched state I am in! I am lost, for I am a man of unclean lips . . ." (Is 6:5). It generates the cry of Peter falling at the knees of Jesus: "Depart from me, O Lord, for I am a sinful man" (Lk 5:8). It generates Augustine's awed recognition of the gulf between the self and the totally Other of God in his first mystical experience. "When first I knew Thee, Thou didst lift me up so that I might see that there was something to see, but that I was not yet the man to see it. And thou didst beat back the weakness of my gaze, blazing upon me too strongly, and I was shaken with love and with dread. And I realised that I was far from Thee in the region of unlikeness . . ." (*Conf.* VII 10, 16).

Essentially the same two correlatives make up the numinous experience that Patrick describes in *Conf.* 20. "That very same night I was sleeping when Satan mightily put me to the test—I shall remember it as long as I am in this body. He fell upon me like a huge rock . . . And while this was happening I saw the sun rise in the heavens, and as I was crying out: 'Helias, Helias', with all my strength, lo, the splendour of that sun fell on me . . . and I believe that I was aided by Christ my Lord . . ." (cf. 59-60).

It is not surprising then that the greatest confessions are written by authors who temperamentally are 'pilgrims of the absolute', who suffer the metaphysical[4] *inquietudo* of the Augustinian restless heart. "Thou hast made us oriented towards Thyself, and our hearts are unquiet until they rest in Thee" (Augustine, *Conf.* I 1, 1). And it is that 'totalising' range of the passionate questioning and resolution of existence that makes St. Augustine's *Confessions* the supreme example of the genre, 'a possession for ever'. That range determines the very framework of the book. For

4. Cf. R. Guardini, *The Conversion of Augustine* (Sands & Co., London, Glasgow, 1960), chap. X: "Amazement over Existence".

its autobiographical questioning of the meaning of existence begins not just with infancy and birth but in 'the dark backward and abysm of time' – before birth. "Therefore, O God, tell me I beg You, . . . whether my infancy followed on some other age of my life that had passed away before it. Was the time I spent in my mother's womb such another age? . . . And before that again, O God of my joy? Was I anywhere? Was I anyone? There is none to tell me . . ." (*Conf.* I 6, 9). And the book ends with an exploration of the opposite pole of temporal existence. From the mystery of origins before time it is projected forward into the mystery of destiny beyond time in eternity. "What man will give another man the understanding of this . . .? Of You we must ask, in You we must seek, at You we must knock. Thus only shall we receive, thus shall we find, thus will it be opened to us" (*Conf.* XIII 38, 53).

Patrick's *Confessio* has the same framework, from birth to "before I die". He does not go into the mystery of origins, but he is not unworthy of comparison with Augustine in the cadenza leading up to "before I die". ". . . Without any doubt we shall rise on that day in the glory of the Sun: that is to say, in the glory of Christ Jesus our Redeemer . . . For that sun which we see [with our bodily eyes] rises daily at God's command for our sake: but it will never reign, nor will its splendour abide . . . We on the other hand, [are a people] who believe in the true Sun and adore Him, Christ, who will never perish. And neither will he who does His will; but he will abide for ever, as Christ abides for ever . . ." (*Conf.* 59-60).

The transcendent range of the confessional genre is often thought to be due uniquely to the genius of Augustine. And of course without that genius we would not have the genius of the *Confessions*. But the work of genius is often the final fruiting of a long historical development. That is the case with Augustine's and Patrick's *Confessions*, and with the Christian confessional genre in general. Its taproot goes down deep and far back into Christianity's own taproot, Judaism and the Old Testament. A concordance will reveal that 'confess' is one of the thematic words of the Bible – along with related words like 'praise', 'magnify', 'glorify', etc. That is scarcely surprising, given that the overall theme of the Bible is precisely those two supreme (and extreme) poles of reality that Augustine and Newman isolate, the self and God, I and Thou, the creature and his Creator.

Hence the invocation by the Psalmist[5] to "come and exult in the Lord . . . Let us come before His face in confession (*in confessione*) . . ."

---

5. The *unity* of Augustine's *Confessions* has been sought in the leitmotivs from the Psalms; see G. N. Knauer, *Psalmenzitate in Augustins Konfessionen* (Vandenhoeck und Ruprecht, Göttingen, 1955); cf. the function of Ps 90 in St Thomas More's *Dialogue of Comfort against Tribulation*.

For in His hands are the depths of the earth,
and the heights of the mountains are His,
For His is the sea, and He made it,
and the dry land was moulded by His hands,
Come, let us bow down and adore,
and bend the knee before the God who made us
(Ps 94, Vulg.).

Confess to the Lord (*confitemini Domino*), for He is good,
and His love is everlasting . . .
(Ps 117, Vulg.).

Praise of the power and the glory of God as revealed in the order and splendour of the cosmos is the theme of some of the great poetico-religious excursuses in the Bible, e.g., Sirach 42:15ff and Job 36:22ff. But the confession of the infinite Creator as revealed in the cosmic splendour entails confession of the opposite polar deep of the infinite littleness of the lonely individual human soul, because

He has fathomed the deep and the heart,
and seen into their devious ways
(Si 42:18).

It entails confession of the fact that while He fathoms all deeps He remains Himself unfathomable. That is the final word of Job, at the end of his own totalising face-to-face between his soul and God about the burden of the mystery of existence. It is in effect a confession, and a confession, once again, that implicitly conjoins confession of praise, faith (despite the mystery), and sin (his own sin in questioning the mystery).

I have been holding forth on matters beyond my understanding,
on marvels beyond me and my knowledge . . .
I knew You then only by hearsay;
but now having seen You with my own eyes,
I retract all I have said,
and in dust and ashes I repent
(Jb 42:3-6).

In fact the main lines of the life-story of the great Old Testament prophets provide a close analogy to the main lines of the great confessions. They too turn on those two supreme poles of reality, the individual soul and the transcendent God. The prophets undergo the awesome experience of being personally touched by God, and called to a great mission. But the touch reaches down into what Augustine calls the abyss of human consciousness, of human interiority, and becomes a fire in the heart and a torment in the soul. And the great call and the great mission become a great suffering. And yet the *misère* of the call and the mission and the suffering becomes a *grandeur* and a glory to be 'confessed'. It is the seraphic cautery of Isaiah's live coal (Is 6:6ff ), Jeremiah's "fire burning in my heart, imprisoned in my bones" (Jr 20:9),

> The effort to restrain it wearied me,
> I could not bear it (ibid).

And yet

> Sing to the Lord,
> praise the Lord
> for he has delivered the soul of the needy . . .
> (Jr 20:14).

We have been saying that the taproot of the Christian confessional genre goes back down deep into Judaism and the Old Testament. Yet that is not its only root. A complete explanation of its genesis demands that we draw attention, if only cursorily, to what it owes to certain elements in the evolution of Greco-Roman civilization.

For the sake of simplicity in a brief account we can take as a starting point the statement, already conventional in the classical world, that philosophy had two beginnings; one with the Ionian Greeks of Asia Minor, the so-called Ionian 'physicists'; the other with the Pythagoreans of Southern Italy. The point of mentioning this distinction is that, once more, it is analogous to those two extreme poles of reality, the individual soul and the transcendent God. For the concern of the Ionian philosophers was outward-directed, occupied with the metaphysics of the external phenomenal world, the cosmos and its ultimate Ground. The Pythagoreans, on the other hand, turned inward, into existential concern with man's own soul. We might sum up their rationale in the Gospel question: "What will it profit a man to gain the whole world if he suffer the loss of his own soul?" (Mk 8:36).

It was Plato who finally systematized this existential concern with man's spiritual dimension, with what he called the therapy of the soul, and thereby put into Western civilization a permanent awareness of the spiritual dimension of man and a permanent concern with its exploration. It was Plato's inspirational mentor, Socrates, who "was the first to call philosophy down from the heavens and set her into the cities of men, and bring her also into their homes and compel her to ask questions about life and morality and things good and evil" (Cicero, *Tusculan Disputations* V 4, 11 – based on Plato's *Phaedo* 96ff). Socrates had repeated in his own life the original Pythagorean conversion away from outer reality to existential spiritual concern with inner reality, with man and his soul.

It was from this spiritual orientation that philosophy ever afterwards in the Greco-Roman world took on a dimension of meaning to which the only adequate analogy is the *religious* life in Christian terms. Philosophical truth was not to be attained at the end of a cerebral syllogism, but only in the illumination that comes at the end of a quest that was a way of life, an 'ascetic' way of life, the 'philosophic life', the *bios philosophikos* of contemplation.[6] So highly was it esteemed as an ideal that there came into existence a genre of philosophical writing called the *protreptic*, which consisted of an exhortation to turn to that way of life. And so close was the parallel to the religious life that there was even the phenomenon of 'conversion' to the philosophic life,[7] that Clement of Alexandria could appropriate the title of *Protreptic* for one of his Christian writings, and that Christianity itself could be conventionally referred to as the 'true philosophy'.

That is the background without which we cannot fully understand a whole stretch of Augustine's life and *Confessions*, beginning in the experience of his nineteenth year as described in *Conf.* III 4,7, passing through the project of joining a philosophic 'community' as described in *Conf.* VI 14, 24, coming to a resolution in the great Christian conversion scene in the garden at Milan (*Conf.* VIII 11, 25ff), and culminating in the beginning of the journey back to Africa, there to live the 'philosophic life' in its Christian metamorphosis (*Conf.* IX 8, 17). For the *Hortensius* of Cicero that changed Augustine's life in his nineteenth year was a 'protreptic', an 'exhortation' to the 'philosophic life' (to which Cicero himself had turned at a critical moment of 'awakening' in his own life). And the extraordinary effect it had on Augustine was a true 'conversion'. "I had begun that journey upwards by which I was to return to You" (*Conf.* III 4,7).

That Greco-Roman 'philosophic life' already produced its own 'confessional' soul-histories independently of Christianity, but we cannot go into them here,[8] beyond pointing to the well-known instance of the *Meditations* of Marcus Aurelius. Our concern here is to point to the double strand of development, the biblical and the classical, that leads up to the final masterpice of Augustine's *Confessions*. He is also a sufficient illustration of the actuality of the two strands in the making of his soul-

6.  Cf. classic statements in Plato's *Seventh Letter*, 341 bc and 344 c.
7.  Cf. A. D. Nock, *Conversion* (Oxford Paperbacks, 1961).
8.  Cf. G. Misch, *A History of Autobiography in Antiquity* (Routledge & Keegan Paul, London, 1950).

history and in the making of the *Confessions*. And before him there are others, such as the 'philosophic' quest of Justin Martyr, described in his *Dialogue with Trypho*, or the soul-history with which Hilary of Poitiers prefaces his *De Trinitate*.

The supreme example of Augustine provides the definitive model for those who come after him. One that is profoundly influenced by Augustine's model is the *Eucharisticos* of Paulinus of Pella, grandson of Ausonius of Bordeaux in Roman Gaul, written in old age in 459 – about the time when Patrick would be writing his *Confessio*. We would like to know definitively whether Patrick also was influenced by Augustine's model. Suffice it here to say that there are very close parallels, and secondly, that it would be surprising if Patrick could use the word *confessio* so frequently and explicitly without any awareness of the great tradition of the genre within which he is writing, a tradition to which he was close, in time and space, as shown by Paulinus' *Eucharisticos* in the Gaul with which Patrick was certainly acquainted.[9]

The rest is history, the unbroken later history of a genre which, more than any other, explores the answer to the Psalmist's question: "What is man, that You should be concerned with him?" (Ps 8). The Psalmist's own answer already anticipated Augustine's *grande profundum* and *abyssus humanae conscientiae* (*Conf.* IV 14, 22 and X 2, 2). "Man is a *profunditas*, and his heart an abyss" (Ps 63:7, Vulg.).

Among the great explorations that come to mind are Boethius' *Consolation of Philosophy*, Abelard's *Historia Calamitatum*, Dante's *Vita Nuova*, St. Thomas More's *Dialogue of Comfort against Tribulation*,[10] St. Teresa of Avila's *Life*,[11] Newman's *Apologia*, George Moore's *Confessions of a Young Man*,[12] Joyce's *Portrait of the Artist as a Young Man*, and, right in the middle of our twentieth century, the nearest ever to an Augustine *redivivus*, Thomas Merton in his *Seven Storey Mountain*.

That is the great tradition in which Patrick's *Confessio* is a great link.[13]

9. On Patrick's *Confessio*, in the context of those of early Christianity, see Pierre Courcelle, *Les Confessions de Saint Augustin dans la tradition littéraire*, pp. 211-213; also Misch, op. cit., pp. 678-681.
10. Considered in one of its multiple meanings, i.e. as an ultimate spiritual testament – like Patrick's *Confessio*, and in the tradition of Boethius' *Consolation*.
11. A turning-point in her spiritual life was the discovery of Augustine's *Confessions* – see her *Life*, Chapter 9.
12. To vary the menu a little!
13. It is also the first link between Ireland's literary tradition and that of Romano-Christian Europe; see Thomas Finan, "Hiberno-Latin Christian Literature", in James P. Mackey (ed.), *An Introduction to Celtic Christianity* (T. & T. Clark, Edinburgh, 1989); see also E. Malaspina, *Patrizio e l'acculturazione latina dell'Irlanda* (Japadre, L'Aquila, 1984).

## (b) Patrick's Confessio and Augustine's Confessiones

In our account of the confessional genre, and its long tradition, to which St. Patrick's *Confessio* belongs, we referred to St Augustine's *Confessiones* as the supreme exemplar and the definitive model for later Christian writers in the genre. "We would like to know definitively," we said, "whether Patrick also was influenced by Augustine's model . . ." We referred to "close parallels," and expressed the opinion that "it would be surprising if Patrick could use the word *confessio* so frequently and explicitly without any awareness of the great tradition of the genre within which he is writing . . ."[14] The question of Augustinian influence on Patrick is one we have to address more explicitly, however tentatively, especially in a work like the present one, which points up reasons for believing that, *inter alia*, Patrick was a man of wider reading and learning than has usually been thought.

It is a question that has been argued by scholars on and off, *pro* and *contra*, ever since Misch in 1950 asserted that "there are plenty of echoes of Augustine to be found in Patrick's *Confessio*."[15] Ludwig Bieler[16] agreed, if not quite so confidently. So did Pierre Courcelle,[17] after more methodical juxtaposition of parallel texts from Augustine and Patrick. In strong disagreement were Christine Mohrmann,[18] and especially J. J. O'Meara.[19] The latter takes up systematically the parallel texts cited by both Bieler and Courcelle, and in every case finds a Patrician reminiscence either unproven or explicable by a common source (usually the Scriptures, which the language of both writers constantly echoes), or by the fact that there is only a limited number of ways of describing essentially the same situations and of expressing essentially the same feelings – of which, given the nature of the genre, there are necessarily many that are common to Patrick and Augustine. O'Meara's conclusion therefore is that "even if Patrick had heard of, or even read, Augustine's *Confessions*, his own

14. Page 131ff.
15. Georg Misch, *A History of Autobiography in Antiquity* (Routledge & Kegan Paul, London, 1950), pp. 189-93.
16. "The Place of St. Patrick in Latin Language and Literature", in *Vigiliae Christianae* VI (1952), pp. 65-98, especially p. 69 ff.
17. *Les Confessions de saint Augustin dans la tradition littéraire* (Études Augustiniennes, Paris, 1963), pp. 211-13.
18. Christine Mohrmann, *The Latin of Saint Patrick* (Institute for Advanced Studies, Dublin 1961), p. 4ff.
19. In two contributions: "The Confession of St. Patrick and the Confessions of St. Augustine", in *Irish Ecclesiastical Record* 85 (1956), pp. 190-197 (taking up Bieler): and "Patrick's *Confessio* and Augustine's Confessions" (taking up Courcelle), in *Latin Script and Letters, A.D. 400-900: Festschrift Presented to Ludwig Bieler*, edited by John J. O'Meara and Bernd Naumann (Leiden, 1978), pp. 44-53.

document reveals no sure echo of it . . ."[20] This in reply to Bieler, and similarly in reply to Courcelle – "Patrick's *Confessio* shows no reliable indication of literary dependence on Augustine's *Confessions* . . ."[21] And finally Hanson and Blanc, in their *Sources chrétiennes* edition of Patrick's writings, give up the ghost on the question – all those efforts to find an Augustinian influence in Patrick *sont restés stériles.*[22]

I do not think the case is at all as bad as that. It is probably true that there is no 'echo' of Augustine in Patrick extended and sustained enough to be definitively probative of literary dependence. On the other hand if along with Misch we can find – as arguably we can – 'plenty' of what looks like less extended 'echoes' of Augustine in Patrick, we have a stronger argument from convergent probabilities. Even then of course such convergence will never give proof without residue – converging indeed, like some beautiful mathematical curves, but never quite reaching 'the line'.

To that extent then the comparison of parallel texts may well be a *voie sans issue* – especially when the Patrician texts are so little extended and sustained. The way out might be through a different methodology. And that is precisely what was opened up by Peter Dronke, in an article that is one of the most liberating contributions to the question.[23]

Starting from considerations of method he rejects as inadequate the one adopted by previous scholars. "I do not think the aptest way to test if there is a direct relation between the *Confessio* and Augustine's *Confessions* is by printing a series of sentences in parallel columns with similar phrases in each column italicized."[24] Such a method works only when there is question of direct dependence on "an immediate model or source", as, for instance, when Shakespeare used Plutarch as a quarry (transforming his material of course) in writing some of his Roman plays. But Patrick's relation to Augustine need not be of that kind, and probably was not. It is unlikely that Patrick had Augustine's *Confessiones* to hand while he composed his *Confessio.* But he could have read the work in earlier years in the course of his studies, especially on the Continent. What Patrick in his old age would retain from that reading would not *necessarily* be identifiable phrases and sentences (though that too would be *possible*)

20. "The Confession of St. Patrick and the Confessions of St. Augustine", p. 197.
21. "Patrick's *Confessio* and Augustine's Confessions", p. 52.
22. R. P. C. Hanson and C. Blanc (eds.), *Saint Patrick: Confession et Lettre à Coroticus* (Paris, 1978), p. 50.
23. "St. Patrick's Reading", in *Cambridge Medieval Celtic Studies* I (Summer 1981), pp. 21-38.
24. A method indeed overworked by Courcelle – and as it happens, notoriously in a study of the famous garden conversion scene in Augustine's *Confessions*, VIII 8, 19ff. See his *retractatio* in *Les Confessions de saint Augustin . . .*, pp. 191-197.

but rather a vivid indelible memory, a memory of an impression all the more vivid in a reader who was himself too a *grand converti*, "a memory of love and of longing as for something of which he had once caught the fragrance" (to use Augustine's own remembering, *Conf.* VII 17, 23).

When Patrick came to *confess* his own life all those years later the influence of Augustine's *Confessions* would be in the way they helped him to *shape* that confessing, "the way in which a man, while telling about himself, telling . . . of the circumstances of his life, and confessing his own sinfulness, sees God as the indwelling presence in his life, the guiding force of his destiny, and is moved to proclaim this to the world and again and again to give thanks for it."[25] In Augustine Patrick could recognize himself, and even perhaps "[find] the stimulus" for his own *Confessio*.

The method that will assess the possible presence of pervasive informing influence of that kind is necessarily more complex than that of juxtaposing parallel sentences to isolate precise verbal reminiscences.

"We should have to consider the 'inner form' of a certain kind of work [in this case the confessional genre] – its characteristic conceptions; how the elements in the work are organized (its *conjointure*); the interpretation of life that is mirrored in the work; distinctive kinds of trains of thought . . .; distinctive modes of expression . . . To indicate such things is a more delicate task than ranging verbal parallels – but it can be done . . ."[26]

Applying this method to Patrick's *Confessio* Dronke focuses on a few illustrative passages in which, on this hypothesis, Patrick may have been under Augustinian influence in the *form* – the "range of syntactic patterns" – as well as in the matter – "certain deeply-focused moments from the *Confessions*, ones in which Augustine evoked key episodes in his life," ones that may have helped Patrick to "organize certain movements of his own thought". One pair of such passages is Patrick's regretful but providentially interpreted escape from the master with whom he had spent six years in slavery (ch. 17), and Augustine's similarly coloured escape from his mother to sail for Rome (*Conf.* V 8, 15). Another set of parallel moments are the visionary experiences of Patrick (ch. 20 and 23-5) and Augustine (*Conf.* VII 10, 16 and VIII 12, 28-29). In common they have violent spiritual experience, transcendent light, introspective questioning, a voice heard and a call to "take and read" a decisive message, compunction of heart, 'conversion', and the consequent shattered inability to "read any further".[27]

25. Dronke, art. cit., p. 26.
26. Ibid., p. 24ff.
27. *Amplius non potui legere* (Patrick, *Conf.* 23); *nec ultra volui legere* . . . (Augustine, *Conf.* VIII 12, 29).

Such passages describe decisive moments in the life-histories of those *grands convertis*, but they remain 'moments' – along with others selected more randomly by Dronke. The method used by Dronke in their study calls for application on a larger scale – in a comparison of the two *Confessions* in terms of larger structures, master ideas, thematic strands, etc. Some of these have already been noted by implication in the analysis and illustration of the confessional *genre*. But the present topic demands more detailed treatment of such terms of comparison.

In that section on the confessional genre it was shown how its drive is towards a metaphysico-theological *totalisation*, towards a comprehensive understanding of a human existence, under God and *sub specie aeternitatis*, in the *depths* of its inner life and in its *extension* from the mystery of origins and birth on to death, and beyond death into the mystery of eternal destiny.[28] It is easy to show that this is the cadre of Augustine's *Confessions*, from the opening Book, especially I 6, 7ff, and the final Book XIII, especially its conclusion.[29] Patrick's *Confessio* is framed between the same two great poles of reality, from origins and birth to that 'sense of an ending' in his "confession before I die", and in the faith that extends beyond death into the Christ "who will never perish", the guarantor that neither will he perish who does Christ's will, but rather "will abide for ever, as Christ abides for ever" (*Conf.* 60).

Between those two extreme poles life for Patrick is what it was for Abraham (Gen 12; cf. Patrick, ch. 23, 28, 37, 43) and so often is for Augustine, a call . . . to leave country and family and father's house . . . to go out on a journey and a pilgrimage, into an exile that is more spiritual than physical, into a bondage that is more to a mission than to a master. "The Lord graciously spared the alien and stranger (*proselito et peregrino*)[30] for His Name's sake . . ." (ch. 26); "He did not hinder me from the journey (*profectione*) I had decided nor from that work of mine which I had learned from Christ my Lord . . ." (ch.30). He would love to revisit his country and parents, but he is "bound by the Spirit" (*alligatus Spiritu*) in opposition to that human desire (ch. 43). He does not want to lose the people he has gained for God in his exile (ch. 58). And as he looks back he is able to rejoice that his journeying abroad (*peregrinatio mea*) "has not been in vain" (*Letter*, 17).

---

28. Page 136.
29. The project is explicitly stated in *Conf.* XI, 2, 3: "Let me confess to you whatsoever I shall find in your books . . . from the first beginning (*ab usque 'principio'*), when you made the heavens and the earth, right up to our everlasting reign with you in your Holy City."
30. The equivalent terms are used also in the *Letter*, ch. 1.

This theme of life as exile and pilgrimage is a commonplace in Augustine. It is a major unifying thematic strand in the *Confessions*.[31] "I had begun to arise in order to find my way back to you," he says of his awakening, after discovering the *Hortensius* of Cicero, and, doubtless, thinking of the Prodigal Son as he writes (*Conf.* III 4, 7). Human life is a complex of "sorrowful roads" through which we must pass with "multiplication of sorrow and grief for the sons of Adam" (*Conf.* I 9, 14). It is a "region of deprivation" (*Conf.* II 10, 18). It is "a vast and terrible sea traversed with difficulty even by those who embark on the ship of the Cross" (*Conf.* I 16, 25). We come to "supreme peace" only when we have crossed over the "insubstantial waters" of the world (*Conf.* XIII 7, 8). It is in that context that his sailing from Carthage to Rome after deceiving his mother became such a vibrant symbol of human life and the Providence that governs it. "I lied to my mother, and to such a mother, and so got away. But this also you have mercifully forgiven me, saving me from the waters of the sea . . . to bring me to the water of your grace" (V 8, 15) "I had come into the depths of the sea and had lost confidence and all hope of discovering truth" (VI 1, 1).

In all this the over-arching figure is the same as Patrick's, the journey in and into exile, the pilgrim way, the *peregrinatio*, the way to "the eternal Jerusalem, for which your people sigh in their *peregrinatio* all the way from departure to home-coming" (IX 13, 37). "O lovely and luminous house . . . let me keep sighing for you in my *peregrinatio* . . ." (XII 15,21). The way is still in the dark of faith, but "in this our *peregrinatio* we have received a pledge that we are already light . . . and children of the light . . ." (XIII 14, 15).

In Patrick the exile is a consequence of turning and *going away from* God, so that the *peregrinatio* is a turning back and returning. "We had forsaken God (*a Deo recessimus* – Is 59:13) and did not keep His commandments . . . God brought to bear upon us the wrath of His anger and scattered us among many peoples, even unto the uttermost part of the earth, where now, in my lowliness, I dwell among strangers" (*Conf.* 1). It is logical that the beginning of the *peregrinatio* back should be a *remembering*, a *turning round* and a *conversion* to God. "And there the Lord opened my unbelieving mind, so that even at that late hour I should remember my sins (*vel sero rememorarem . . .*) and turn with all my heart (*converterem*) . . . to the Lord my God . . ." (*Conf.* 2).

That sentence reminds us at once of a sentence in Augustine that is all compact of the longing remembering of the exile in Ps 41. "Because our soul was troubled within us we remembered you, Lord (*commemorati sumus . . .*), and light was made" (*Conf.* XIII 12, 13).[32] But in

31. See G. N. Knauer, "Peregrinatio animae", in *Hermès* 85 (1957), pp. 216-248.
32. Cf. XII 10, 10.

Augustine as in Patrick this remembering and returning is the correlative of an original forgetting and turning away. In Augustine it is a fusion of elements from Platonist as well as scriptural sources which in the *Confessions* construct an all-pervading dialectic – often reinforced by Augustine's stylistic wordplay. Let one example suffice out of the many possible.

Recalling his youthful genius in his studies he asks what use it all was when he was straying (*errarem*) so far from God, or what harm was the slower intelligence of some of his companions when they, unlike himself, "were not withdrawing (*recederent*) far away from you . . ."

> "It is with you that our good ever lives, and because we have been averted (*aversi*) from there we have become perverted (*perversi*). Let us now revert (*revertamur*) to thee, Lord, that we be not overturned (*evertamur*), because it is with you there abides our good without defect, the Good that is Yourself. And we have no fear of there being no place for us to return to (*redeamus*) because we ourselves fell down from there (*ruimus*); for our own absence does not make our home fall down too (*ruit*), the home that is your own Eternity" (IV 16, 31).

As we know especially from Augustine and Patrick the confessional genre is addressed to God. More than that, it is a religious exercise, a confession of praise, thanks and unworthiness. More than that again, it is not only an account of the experiential knowledge of God acquired from his perceived working in the pattern of a life. It is also a sustained project of coming to know Him better, because the confessional project, the complete understanding of self and of the life on which it reflects, is *sub specie aeternitatis* and from a God's-eye view – in His light we shall see light. The project is expressed in Augustine's first confessional sketch – to know self and to know God, for only by knowing God can we know the goal and *bonum* of the self, and the present condition of the self in relation to that goal and *bonum*.[33] "I am still in many things imperfect", says Patrick (*Conf.* 6). "Do not abandon the work you have begun", prays Augustine, "but perfect what is still imperfect in me" (*Conf.* X 4, 5). And in any case the quest for God can be the only goal of what we have seen both authors describe as a 'return' to what they 'turned away' from, a *peregrinatio* back to the Beginning where is the true home and the true *bonum*.

There is then a quest and a finding of God. But first, how and where does it begin? In both, in the starting point and in the process, we find parallels between Patrick and Augustine.

"You made us orientated towards yourself", says Augustine, "and our heart is restless until it rests in you. Grant me, Lord, to know

---

33. *Soliloquia*, I 1, 1 and I 2, 7; cf. *Conf.* X 1, 1.

and understand which is the first movement towards you, to invoke your aid (*invocare te*) or to proclaim your praises (*laudare te*), and whether knowing you must come before invoking your aid. But who can invoke your aid without knowing you? Or is it that you must be first invoked (*invocaris*) in order to be known? But how shall they invoke you who have not believed in you?" And so on in a typical piece of Augustinian dialectical flyting (*Conf.* I 1, 1).

Patrick comes faster to that point. "For the Lord himself said through the prophet: 'Call upon me (*invoca me*) in the day of your trouble, and I will deliver you, and you shall glorify me.'" That last phrase functions as an immediate transition from *invocation* to *confession*. A transition confirmed in the next sentence: "And again He says: 'It is honourable to reveal the works of the Lord and to confess them'" (*confiteri*: *Conf.* 5; Ps 49:15 and Tb 12:7).

Patrick's first 'discovery' of God was in the isolation – should we say the 'desert'? – of his six years in the land of his captivity, as described in *Conf.* 16 "The love of God and the fear of Him came to me and my faith increased and my spirit was moved (*fides augebatur at spiritus agebatur*)" – a play of words and sounds that he could learn from many a passage in Augustine's *Confessiones*.

Looking back on this experience in chapter 33 Patrick describes it more explicitly as a *seeking* and a *finding* of God. "Then I earnestly sought Him, and there I found Him (*tunc fortiter inquisivi eum, et ibi inveni eum*)".

Even if it has scriptural echoes it is still a striking parallel to find that this formula in the same two words, *quaerere* and *invenire*, seeking and finding, is recurrent in Augustine's *Confessiones*. Already in answer to the opening dialectic on the question of *how* God is to be found and known: "by seeking Him (*quaerentes*) they find Him (*inveniunt*), and finding Him they shall praise Him . . ." (*Conf.* I 1,1). The formula is used *passim* in the long analysis of the 'way' of the 'ascent' to 'where' God is to be 'found'. 'We are not your God,' say the voices of nature, 'search above us' (*Conf.* X 6, 9). "I shall transcend the faculty of memory also – to find you where . . . to find you where?" (*Conf.* X 20, 29). "See how much space I have covered in my memory seeking you, Lord, and – I have not found you outside it . . ." (*Conf.* X 24, 35). "Where then *did* I find you, to come to know you?" (*Conf.* X 26, 37). "Late have I loved you . . . For behold, you were *within* me, but I was *without* – and it was there I [mistakenly] searched for you . . ." (*Conf.* X 27, 38).

The parallel between Patrick and Augustine does not end with the terminology of seeking and finding. We know that Augustine's first 'finding' was a mystical experience, described in *Conf.* VII 10, 16. The experience was a determining moment in his life, and one to which he

again and again refers back – as he is doing in the sentence quoted from
*Conf.* X 27, 38.

From *Conf.* 17 and 23-5 we know that Patrick too had 'higher'
spiritual experiences. And it is possible that a phrase in his description of
one of them echoes a sentence in Augustine's description of his own
experience. In *Conf.* 25 Patrick describes his experience of the Spirit praying within him. "I saw Him praying in me, and I was as it were within my
body, and I heard [One] above me, that is to say, above my inner man . . .
(*et audivi super me, hoc est super interiorem hominem . . .*)."

In *Conf.* VII 10, 16, following a Platonist inspiration adapted
to Christianity, Augustine takes the classical 'journey inward' to contemplative experience – "I entered into my own inner depths". "I entered,
and with the eye of my soul – such as it was – above (*supra*) that eye of
my soul, above (*supra*) my rational mind, I saw an unchangeable Light . . ."

Two elements in those experiences are common to both
accounts. One is the deep *interiority* of the experience – explicit in
Augustine, implicit in Patrick's 'inner man', and possibly even in the detail
that he was within his body (the reminiscence of 2 Co 12:2 notwithstanding). The other common element is the precision in the insistence on the
*transcendence* of the Reality perceived – 'above', *super, supra*. Augustine
returns to it to insure that its transcendence is made totally clear. "It was
not above my rational mind in the way that oil floats above water, nor in
the way that the sky is above the earth . . ." It was above because it was
the Source and Ground of Augustine's being – "it was above because that
was the Reality that made me, and I was 'below' because by It I was
made" (*Conf.* VII 10, 16). And a final parallel is in the awe-ful reaction
to the experience of something like the primordial and perennial
*mysterium tremendum*. "I was shaken (*contremui*) with love and with dread
(*amore et horrore*)," says Augustine. "I was stricken with awe and with
wonder", says Patrick. *Stupebam et ammirabam et cogitabam quis esset . . .*
where we may also note the heightened stylistics of the assonance –
employed also in Augustine's *amore et horrore*.

It is also a possibility that Patrick's *first* 'finding' of God
(*Conf.* 16) was, like Augustine's, at the level of mystical experience. Like
Augustine he looks back to that adolescent experience, all those years later
while he writes in old age. The backward look in *Conf.* 33 has already been
referred to. He refers back to it again in chapter 44 – and this time in terms
which at least *suggest* a particular moment of definitive experience, a
moment of sudden higher 'knowledge' and 'recognition'. "From the time
I came to know Him, from my early manhood, the love of God and the
fear of Him have grown in me" (*Conf.* 44).

We may note two things about the second part of that
sentence. It repeats almost verbatim the phrase used in chapter 16. And its

two terms, love and fear, *amor* and *timor*, are parallel – even if the 'pressure' is lower – to Augustine's 'love and dread' (*amore et horrore*), in *Conf.* VII 10, 16.

The opening clause of the sentence contains another intriguing parallel to another phrase in the same section of Augustine. 'From the moment I came to know Him . . .' reads in the Latin: *ex quo cognovi eum* . . . Augustine has a sentence describing the transitory and incomplete nature of his first mystical experience. "When first I came to know you you raised me up so that I should see there was Something to see, but that I was not yet the man to see it" (*Conf.* VII 10,16). In the Latin the sentence opens: *et cum te primum cognovi* . . .

The verbal parallel is even closer in a repeated phrase in *Conf.* X 24, 35f, where Augustine like Patrick is thinking back on the experience. There *didici* is substituted for *cognovi*, and the phrase becomes *ex quo didici te* . . . "From the moment I came to know you I have not forgotten you" – and the equivalent thought is in Patrick's sentence – "and up to now, through the Lord's favour, I have kept the faith." "Therefore", Augustine continues, "*from the moment I came to know you*, you have remained in my memory . . . you have deigned to abide in my memory *from the moment I came to know you.* And why should I ask in what place you abide in it, as if there were really [spatial] places there? It is a certainty that you do dwell in it, because I remember you *from the moment I came to know you*, and I find you there when I recall your memory" (*Conf.* X 25, 36).

In the context of such deep and transforming religious experience, which governs both a life and the book of that life, there is little need to explain why God and the confession of His praises should be at the centre of both. And in the light of that fact it is possible to suggest a deep structural and thematic parallel between the two *Confessions* in the great proem of incantation and invocation to God with which each *Confession* opens – Augustine over five chapters, and Patrick in the high credal profession of chapter 4. "Great art Thou O Lord, and greatly to be praised . . . And man's desire is to praise Thee . . ." (Augustine, *Conf.* I 1, 1). "For there is no other God nor was there ever before nor will there be hereafter, except God the Father, unbegotten, without beginning, from whom is all beginning . . . Him we confess and adore, one God in the Trinity of the Sacred Name" (Patrick, *Conf.* 4).

In a work like the present one that might be a suitable note on which to leave the question of Patrick's possible acquaintance with Augustine's *Confessions*. There is much more to be said, especially on the many details of Patrick's language and style which on their own may be inconclusive evidence of Augustinian influence, but seen in a larger framework become more persuasive. Consideration of a multiplicity of such details, however, may be more appropriate to an occasion other than that of the present work.

With one concluding exception, however. The confessional genre is addressed not only to God but also to men and women, with a moving concern for their condition, so that by self-revelation and example the 'confessor' may serve those whom both Patrick and Augustine repeatedly refer to, in the same terms, as brethren of their own and as fellow-servants and children of God, whom they serve by their writings, and by the self-revealing and God-revealing life which the writings 'confess'.

"Notwithstanding that I am in many things imperfect I want my brethren and kinsmen (*fratribus et cognatis meis*) to know what sort of man I am (*scire qualitatem meam*) so that they may be able to perceive the desire of my soul" (Patrick, *Conf.* 6; cf. 14). Augustine too writes to serve those who want to know "who I am" (*quis ego sim*, X 3, 3), "what kind of man I am" (*qualis sim*, X 4, 5).

> This is the fruit of my *Confessiones* – the confession not [only] of what I have been but of what I [now] am: I confess not only before you with inward exultation yet mingled with trembling, with inward sorrow yet mingled with hope, I confess, as I say, not only to You but also in the ears of the believing sons of men, companions of my joy and sharers of my mortality, my fellow citizens and my fellow pilgrims: those who have gone on before and those who will follow after and those who are my own fellow travellers on the road of life. These are Your servants, my brethren, whom You have chosen to be Your sons and my masters, bidding me to be their servant – *serviam* (Augustine, *Conf.* X 4, 6; cf. IX 13, 37).

Patrick too sees his vocation as being to serve (*deservirem*) his brethren and sons "humbly and sincerely" (*Conf.* 13). And that not only in life but by writing his *Confessio*, "so that even after my death I may leave a legacy to my brethren and sons whom I have baptized in the Lord – so many thousands of souls" (*Conf.* 14).

This too was part of his "confession before I die", as it was also part of Augustine's – "so that what my mother at her end asked of me may be fulfilled more richly in the prayers of so many gained for her by my *Confessiones* than by my own prayers alone" (Augustine, *Conf.*, IX 13, 37).

## 2. The significance of St Patrick's wide use of Scripture

### (a) Introduction: the world of Scripture

To many educated modern readers the Bible seems both familiar and strange. They are generally aware of its central importance in shaping the history of Western culture, yet they also know that this culture in its modern dress has deprived the Bible of the importance it had in times past. The language as well as the message it conveys symbolizes for them that past which they feel they must absorb if they are to understand themselves and the culture in which they live. For the Bible has been and continues to be a work of great literary power shaping the minds and lives of countless men and women for more than two millenia. Its epic stories, its powerful language and imagery have left their impact on human history, especially in cultures touched by Judaism and Christianity. For Christians though, the Bible has an importance far more profound than its impact on culture. They believe that through the events of biblical history, God speaks to them and so they reverence and love the Bible and seek to understand it as God's Word.

Although bound between two covers, the Bible is a collection of seventy three different works by different authors using different literary genres, styles and perspectives, and was composed over several centuries. Most of the forty six books that comprise the Old Testament were written in Hebrew; all of the twenty seven books of the New Testament were written in Greek. But a profound unity binds them all together – the continuing story of God's love for his people. Each author shared a conviction that God is present and active in human history and that he invites human beings to respond in faith, hope and love.

The modern reader is indebted to countless numbers of people who handed on the treasures that the Bible contains. For many centuries this transmission of the biblical tradition was performed orally. With the advent of the monarchy in Israel in the tenth century B.C., an educated class of scribes began to preserve the biblical tradition in writing as well.[34] This scholarly endeavour continued throughout the remainder of Israelite history and resulted in that literary achievement we call the Old Testament. In the New Testament period, much of the Gospel materials were first preserved in oral form and transmitted in a variety of settings such as the liturgy, early preaching and catechesis. Eventually these oral materials were gathered and put in written form by the Gospel writers. Paul's letters and the remaining New Testament texts circulated in written form from the beginning.

34. Cf. R. E. Brown, D. W. Johnson, K. G. O'Connell, "Texts and Versions," *The New Jerome Biblical Commentary*, R. E. Brown, J. A. Fitzmeyer, R. E. Murphy (eds.), (G. Chapman, London, 1990), pp. 1083-1112.

No original manuscript of any biblical book exists today. Copyists transcribed the biblical materials and made them available to succeeding generations. The earliest extant manuscripts of some Old Testament books date from the first century B.C., but most of the other early written materials from both the Old and New Testaments are papyrus fragments from the early second century A.D. More complete manuscripts of the Bible on parchment date from the third and fourth centuries. Surprising as it may seen, in spite of some variants, there is a remarkable correspondence between the various biblical texts from different periods, a testimony to the accuracy and care with which the ancient scribes handed on the biblical tradition.

Towards the end of the Old Testament period ancient translations (or versions) of biblical manuscripts into neighbouring languages began to make their appearance. The most important of these versions was the Greek translation of the Old Testament known as the Septuagint (LXX), which began in the early third century B.C. with the translation of the Pentateuch, and later came to designate the entire corpus of the Greek Old Testament translations and compositions. The Septuagint furnished the cultural milieu and literary vehicle for the preaching of early Christianity to the non-Jewish or Gentile world, and was the form in which the Old Testament was most widely circulated in apostolic times.

Throughout the early centuries of the Christian era, Greek was the written language of Western Christianity, but Old Latin (i.e. *Vetus Latina*) versions of parts of the Bible may have existed from as early as the second century. Latin Christian literature began in North Africa in the early third century, so that by the time of Cyprian (d.258) there was already a well established Latin text for parts of the Bible. By the latter part of the fourth century a great variety of Latin translations were already in existence. The extant Old Latin manuscripts are not very numerous since the success of the later Vulgate tended to eliminate them. The Old Testament is represented principally by Psalters and frequently the Old Latin version of other parts of the Old Testament is found in manuscripts predominantly Vulgate in character. Old Latin texts of the Gospels, Acts of the Apostles and the Pauline Letters are more numerous. Patristic citations of the Old Latin Bible were often made with a freedom that seems capricious to the modern mind, but in some cases at least, quotations are taken with great acccuracy from a written Bible.

From about 389 A.D. Jerome broke with the Septuagint-Old Latin tradition to provide Western Christendom with a Latin translation that came to be known as the Vulgate, based directly on the Hebrew Old Testament text preserved among the Jews. From Jerome also stemmed a translation of the Gospels which was basically a correction and adaptation of the existing Old Latin text. The extent of his influence on the remaining books of the New Testament is unclear, but by the end of the fourth century a single editor drew together the Latin texts of the New Testament that became the Vulgate form. The historical importance of the Vulgate text lies in the fact that it made use of the best available Hebrew and Greek texts and that it served to open up the Bible to the Western world to make it the most influential of books.

### (b) Scripture as boundless in its symbolization of the experience of God-with-us

The Old Testament is a record of events as experienced, narrated, transmitted, elaborated and written down to reach its present form.[35] These events were seen as important and memorable because those who had experienced them believed that in them God spoke and acted. This aspect is heightened and made luminous in the narratives. What was important was what God revealed and how humans responded. The Old Testament then, may be regarded as a narrative of the divinely willed order in the world and in society through the creative and covenanting acts of God in which he reveals himself as Creator and Saviour of humankind. Most of the narrative is concerned with the human drama of obedience and disobedience to the revealed will of God. The prophets articulate this conflict of response.

The uniqueness of Israel, then, consists in a leap in human self-consciousness and understanding. It began with the spiritual breakthrough in the life of Abraham. But the central event of the Old Testament is the revelation of the transcendent God in the Exodus-Sinai experiences. The remainder of the history of Israel is largely an attempt to work out a form of social existence in line with this revelation. This took place successively through the tribal confederacy, monarchy, critique of the prophets, post-exilic community and wisdom speculation right up to the threshold of the New Testament era. The Exodus, therefore, was something more than a haphazard escape of Israelite slaves into the desert. It was there that the tribes found their God and became his people. Israel emerged from the desert as a new type of people on the world scene and conquered the Promised Land. The memory of these events was preserved because the inbreaking of God transfigured the pragmatic events into a drama of the soul. In the solitude of the desert, the people were able to hear the voice of God who spoke to their leader Moses, and accepting God's offer, they submitted to his word and so became the people of God. A new genus of society emerged that moved in the historical arena yet with

35. Cf. E. Voegelin, *Order and History*. Vol. 1. *Israel and Revelation*. (Louisiana State University Press, Baton Rouge, 1956), pp. 134-183.

a goal beyond history. A particular people made a leap towards a more perfect attunement with transcendent divine Being and so became a new agent in history, set apart from the other surrounding nations and civilizations.

With Israel a new type of history also emerged. Israelite history as narrated in the Old Testament is primarily an account of Israel's relationship with its God, experienced by people who struggled for attunement with the transcendent God, yet with a pragmatic core as well. The course of events then became sacred history; single events became paradigms of God's ways with human beings. This means that the criteria of truth will be different for paradigmatic history than for pragmatic history. An event experienced in relation to God will be truthfully related if its essence as paradigm is carefully elaborated. Pragmatic details become less important. What is important is the will of God revealed and the agreement or disagreement of the human response with the divine will. The original account was submitted to re-working in the oral tradition to improve its paradigmatic essence by means of dramatization, until it was eventually integrated by the post-exilic editors in a body of history with its own peculiar meaning.

The Israelite experience gave rise to a new type of political society through the discovery of transcendent Being as the source of order in humans and society and so became the carrier of a new truth in history. Consequently, Israel needed a record which told of the events surrounding the discovery of the truth, and the course of Israelite history as the confirmation of that truth. The Old Testament record is an articulation of both and shows the intimate connection between the paradigmatic story and the concrete historical existence of the Israelite people. History then becomes the symbolic form of their existence and is understood as having an outer form discernible in civilizational cycles, but also as having an inner form as existence under the transcendent God. The religion of Israel is concerned with the ordering of the human soul and community living under an order discovered as true. Israelite history then becomes the form of existence in which society stands before God; it shows Israel as striving for the order of existence within the world while attuning itself with the order of being beyond the world.

The oldest motive that formed the Israelite meaning of history was the concrete, historical experience of the Exodus from bondage to freedom. The Exodus narrative then expands backwards into the patriarchal history as the pre-history of the Exodus to Abraham, the first Israelite, and beyond to include creation itself and all humankind. Nevertheless the Sinai covenant was perceived as the ultimate purpose of the Exodus and so as a centre of meaning superordinate to the meaning emanating from the Exodus experience. It was here that the Israelites were established as the people of God in obedience to his Law. The rites, cult and liturgies of Israel became the key to the process in which the meaning of the Israelite experience grew into complex form. Various traditions were welded together into a whole in the cult narrative as a literary form in which the historical events that motivated the cult were celebrated.

Beyond the traditions of the cult begins the historiographic work. The scribes of the Davidic court assembled the various traditions that made up the pre-history of the monarchy and, beyond the Patriarchs, of all humankind. Their intention was to construct a world history. After the conquest of the Promised Land, Israelite history becomes the story of obedience/disobedience to the revealed will of God. A spiritual struggle took place during the monarchy when Israel repudiated its responsibility as the people of God. The carriers of meaning then became the prophets. The great achievement of the prophets was to regain a presence under God that was on the point of being lost by the chosen people. As spokespersons for God, they interpreted the promises and demands of the covenant and kept alive a tradition that was all but forgotten. In the preaching of the prophets, the Mosaic past came alive in the present with a new vitality and meaning. Accordingly, through the prophetic activity, Israel was given a deeper understanding of the implications of the covenant and of God's ways in history.

In the post-exilic period, the Old Testament was divided into the Torah or Pentateuch which embraced the period from the creation of the world and humankind to the constitution of Israel under the covenant. The historiographic work known as the Former Prophets traced the events of the conquest, confederacy and monarchy, but subordinated them to the interpretation of the religion of the prophets. The prophetic collection or the Latter Prophets comprised the preaching and doings of the prophets themselves. The Writings embraced the post-exilic literature; Chronicles, Ezra, Nehemiah, Psalms, Wisdom and Apocalyptic literature. What finally emerged was a community that preserved the past as an eternal present for all future generations.

Conscious of being in partnership with God, the Israelites knew themselves to be called to respond to the divine presence and activity in their midst. Not only did they regard their history as a dramatic narrative of God's deeds, they also addressed God in a very personal way. The finest example of this conversation with God is found in the book of Psalms. For this reason the Psalms lie at the heart of the lived religion of the Old Testament, articulating the faith of the community at worship as its fitting and public expression. In time Israel came to realize that community under God was not tied to the land of Palestine, but it had still a long way to go to rejoin the rest of humankind from which it had separated so that the promises made to Abraham could be realized. Only with the emergence of Christianity did the sacred line fully rejoin humankind.

The appearance of Jesus Christ on the stage of history is the pinnacle of the great cycle of spiritual development that had been going on in Israel. We can speak of an extraordinary 'eruption' of the divine presence, God-among-us, in the person of Jesus of Nazareth, an eruption that passed through Jesus into society and history. To be a follower of Jesus then means being a vehicle of the ongoing divine presence in society and history.[36] For with the coming of Jesus and his effect upon his disciples, there is something new and decisive in the advance of humankind and its attunement to the divine Being. The accent has now shifted irrevocably from the perennial human search for the Divine to God's gracious descent towards us. There is a story to be told of God's drawing us to himself becoming effective in the world through Jesus Christ. It is the story of the Good News that provides answers to the questions of life and death that have never ceased to occupy human beings. This is why the evangelists felt obliged to promulgate the Good News to all humankind through the writing of their Gospels.

The Good News or Gospel is a symbolism engendered by the disciples' response to Jesus, the Son of God. Its content is the story of that event which provided the foundation for the early Christian community, i.e. the interpretation of Jesus, his identity and significance for humankind. The Gospel is then inextricably bound up with the life and death of Jesus of Nazareth, yet something about him must have impressed his followers to such an extent that his bodily presence among them appeared to be fully permeated by the divine presence. In the historical drama of revelation, the unknown God, who already spoke in fragmentary ways in the Old Testament, ultimately becomes known through the presence of Jesus. This was very much alive in the consciousness of the evangelists. Their Gospels are the articulation in language of something experienced, understood, conceived and expressed. The primary experience was the concrete historical events in the life of Jesus which were preserved, elaborated, transmitted with a deeper understanding, written down and eventually incorporated into the unique literary genre we call "Gospel" in the evangelists' own distinctive style and manner of presentation. The Gospels then are not history as detached reports of events, yet they are historical; they are not story in the sense of tales of imagination, yet they are stories. A Gospel may be described as a history-like story or a story-like history. In each of the four Gospels the essential meanings of the life and message of Jesus are explored an deepened to express a new

---

36. Cf. E. Voegelin, "The Gospel and Culture," Vol. 12. *The Collected Works of Eric Voegelin: Published Essays 1966-1985*. Edited by E. Sandoz (Louisiana State University Press, Baton Rouge, 1990), pp. 172-212.

truth about the transcendent God as "Father". This new truth of God's ways with human beings was realized in the life, death and resurrection of Jesus and called for a whole new ordering of human existence by way of response.

The Gospel narratives exercised a constitutive function in the life of the community. By accepting and responding to their story, one became a Christian, that is, one entered into a new way of life, an ontologically real order of historical existence in the present under God as a member of God's family. This new community represented a qualitatively new mode of existence as a response to Jesus' revelation in a life of faith, sacramental participation and life in the Spirit. The Church became a new agent in history, the carrier of a new truth that the inner core of history is existence under God as revealed by Jesus. This is why Luke, in addition to writing a Gospel, felt the need to write a companion volume, the Acts of the Apostles. In it he describes how the salvation of humankind promised to Israel in the Old Testament and accomplished by Jesus, has now, under the guidance of the Spirit, been extended to the Gentiles and to the ends of the earth. In telling his story Luke describes the emergence of Christianity from its origins in Judaism to a religion of world-wide status and appeal.

In his correspondence, which pre-dates the Gospels, Paul focuses more on the implications of the Jesus-event for the life of Christians. He is primarily interested in the climactic events of Jesus' life rather than in the manner of his earthly life to which, unlike the evangelists, he alludes only rarely. Instead he invited Christians to find the meaning of their existence in Jesus, the Christ. Christians are now living in the tension of the in-between; of the already of the resurrection and the not-yet of the *parousia*. In the meantime, Christ has opened up to all human beings the possibility of a new life to be lived in the Spirit who becomes the source of the Christian's faith, hope and love. Christ has effected a new union of humanity with God, a new creation. This new ontological existence, though not immediately perceptible to human consciousness, must be allowed to pervade the psychological level of existence so that one's conscious behaviour is guided by it. Living "in Christ" then is not evasion or retreat from the world to an unreal and imaginary one; it is living a new quality of life in the world that prepares the Christian for full participation in life with God through grace beyond death. For Paul, Christ is at one and the same time the true human being and the mediator of true humanity as well as God-among-us. In the light of his apostolic experience the real meaning of the universal scope of Christian salvation reached a high degree of clarity and articulation. In the epiphany of Christ, the formation of humanity in history has become transparent as a process of transfiguration through participation in God's life whose essence is love.

### (c) The Bible in the life of the Early Church

From its beginning the Church employed interpretation of the Old Testament as is already evident both from the Gospels and the New Testament Letters. When Christianity spread and crossed cultural and linguistic boundaries, Christian authors increasingly had recourse to Old Testament interpretation to respond to questions of Jews and pagans alike, and to argue against heretics. They tried to demonstrate that the Old Testament pointed towards and was superseded by the New, but that a harmony existed between them because of the underlying unity of God's plan of salvation for humankind which was brought to fulfillment in Jesus Christ (cf. Lk 24:44). Accordingly, the Bible acquires a greater density and complexity and may be compared to a huge fresco that unfolds for more than a millenium revealing its many connections and linkages.

The story of biblical interpretation in the Patristic era is a long and complex one.[37] The development in the Church of its growing collection of sacred writings, which came to be recognised as authoritative and formed the Christian Bible, sharpened the problem of the interpretation of the Old Testament and its connection with the New. Individual books now had a special relationship to each other and formed a unity. The Fathers saw that this unity rests in Christ; he is the personal key that unlocks the treasures of the Bible, giving it an "excess of meaning", i.e., one that was not confined to what an author envisioned in his local and limited circumstances and conveyed in his written work.

The most famous intellectual institution in the early Patristic period was the catechetical school (*didaskeleion*) of Alexandria. Its primary concern was the study of the Bible and gives its name to the most influential tradition in scriptural interpretation. Commentators discovered a spiritual sense underlying the written words of Scripture. In particular, they sought in the events, persons and institutions of the Old Testament signs, reflections and anticipations of subsequent epochs, the Christian era and eschatological times.

The most notable representative of the Alexandrian School was Origen (c.185-254) who set out his method of interpretation in *De Principiis*, Book IV. Origen discovered in the Scriptures three different senses corresponding to the parts of the human person then current in Neoplatonism; body, soul, spirit. The bodily or literal sense of Scripture is the straightforward historical meaning. The soul of Scripture is the moral or tropological meaning implicit in the literal sense. The spiritual sense is the figurative or allegorical meaning written for future believers. Most of Origen's work consisted of commentaries and sermons which

37. Cf. H. de Lubac, *Exégèse médiéval. Les quatre sens de l'Écriture*, 4 vols. (Aubier, Paris, 1959-64).

expounded biblical texts according to this method. Their aim was to instruct and transform the person whom Scripture addresses. The influence of Origen and the Alexandrian School was both widespread and enduring, and had a profound influence on the Fathers of the Latin tradition.

The Antiochean School and the Syrian tradition, contemporary with Origen, tended to emphasize the literal sense of Scripture. Among its later well-known representatives were Athanasius (d.373), John Chrysostom (d.407) and Theodore of Mopsuestia (d.428). Together with their Alexandrian counterparts they shared a devotion to the language and content of Scripture as significant for the lives of Christians. Their exegesis was based on grammar, close attention to the sense intended by the author, and understanding each passage in context. Their emphasis did not exclude metaphorical and allegorical meanings where it was evident that the author so intended.

The Latin tradition of scriptural interpretation began with Tertullian (c.160-215), but during the fourth century it underwent considerable influence from the East, especially through Hilary of Poitiers (c.315-367) who availed of his exile in Phrygia to familiarize himself with the works of Origen. Ambrose (340-397) adapted the works of Basil for Latin readers, but Jerome (c.347-420) was perhaps the most influential mediator of eastern traditions, having spent the last decades of his life in Bethlehem where he acquired extensive knowledge of the Hebrew language. In his later years he came to lay greater stress on the literal sense as the basis of sound interpretation. For Jerome: "Ignorance of the Scriptures is ignorance of Christ."

It was Augustine (354-430) who summed up the achievements of the Latin Patristic tradition by employing both literal and allegorical methods in his writings and sermons. Augustine was deeply influenced by Neoplatonism as was Origen and, like him, saw Scripture as a multi-layered reality. He upheld its unity and saw in the minutest details of the Old Testament a prefiguring of Christ which he epitomized in the principle: *In Vetero Testamento Novum latet, et in Novo Vetus patet* ("The New Testament lies hidden in the Old; the Old Testament is enlightened through the New"). Nevertheless Augustine emphasized the necessity of a careful and scholarly study of the text, and exegesis must be controlled by reference to the rule of faith, the orthodox teaching of the Church. The supreme test of any interpretation is conformity to the twofold Christian norm of love of God and neighbour.

The guiding theoretical principles of Patristic exegesis, therefore, distinguished four senses of Scripture: the literal or historical which flows immediately and directly from the words understood according to their current usage; the spiritual or allegorical which discovers everywhere in Scripture the mystery of Christ and so puts Him at its centre; the moral or tropological or anthropological which is instructive for the Christian life as a whole, so that the history of salvation has correspondences in the history of each person's spiritual life and guides its movements; the anagogical or eschatological which sees in Scripture the goal of the Christian journey. These were summed up in the Latin couplet:

> *Littera gesta docet; quid credas allegoria*
> *Moralis quid agas; quo tendas anagogia*

("The letter teaches what took place, allegory what you must believe, the moral sense what you must do, the anagogical sense to where you must journey.") It is possible then to interpret Scripture on several levels of meaning. Since the Bible, being the word of God, also has God for its author, the search for a fuller understanding of the biblical text was seen as legitimate and indeed necessary. And so the Fathers established various correspondences between the Old and New Testaments and between the Bible and the life of the believer. Their purpose was to attain to the fulness of God's word addressed to his people in the here and now. The various methods of interpretation were meant to facilitate that search and so the biblical commentator became the mediator of God's word through sermon, letter, commentary and treatise. The result was that the richness of Patristic biblical exegesis nourished Christian theology and mysticism for centuries to come.

Since the Bible in its deepest reality is the self-communication of God to human beings culminating in Jesus Christ, an invitation to participate in the divine life, the Fathers were convinced that this in turn called for a deep and vibrant spiritual life as a personal response. It was to facilitate this response that they expended their considerable intellectual resources so that the potentialities of God's word might be realized and made available to the Christian community.

### (d) St Patrick's use of Scripture

In the light of what we have said, it should be obvious why the Bible quickly became the language of the faith-life of the Christian community. In the Patristic literature it is used not only to provide evidence for doctrine, but also to articulate the faith-life[38] of the Fathers. With regard to St. Patrick, the number and wide range of quotations and allusions that are to be found in his correspondence serve to demonstrate that he had a deep and thorough knowledge of the biblical text; indeed a scriptural consciousness. There are very few paragraphs in his *Confession* and

38. Cf. below, ch. 3, for the distinction faith-belief and faith-life.

*Letter* in which he does not quote the Scriptures. It seems that biblical words and phrases came naturally to him, though often they are no more than snatches and half-sentences. Occasionally, though, he gives a long series of quotations. All this suggests that Patrick had fully assimilated and made his own the profound content and meaning of Scripture. He quotes from it in the conventional way and took from the Latin versions phrases which provided him with Latin words for the message he wished to convey. But Patrick used the Bible above all to articulate the faith-life that was within himself.

His quotations and allusions range widely over both the Old and the New Testaments. It should come as little surprise that his favourite source was the Psalms which articulated the living faith of God's covenanted people. Next to the Psalms Patrick quotes the epistle to the Romans most often. This is Paul's great treatise on the historical possibility of salvation, rooted in God's righteousness and love, that is now offered freely in grace to all human beings through faith in Jesus Christ. After Romans comes the Acts of the Apostles, followed by Matthew and the Corinthian correspondence. There are also numerous quotations from the other Gospels and the remaining New Testament literature, as well as from Pentateuch, Prophets and Wisdom literature. In all Patrick refers to fifty four of the books that go to make up the Bible. This in itself is quite extraordinary given that his correspondence is only two pastoral letters.

The evidence supplied by Patrick's scriptural quotations and allusions in the Biblical apparatus poses a question as to the nature and source of the biblical text he used. Generally speaking, as L. Bieler points out, he seems to quote from a text of the Bible at the point of transition from the Old Latin to the later Vulgate, i.e., partly Old Latin, partly Vulgate, and partly a transitional version. Bieler devotes two articles to this subject[39] and these represent the most thorough examination of the topic to date. We can summarize his findings as follows:

(i) Patrick's text of the Psalter is clearly Gallic (i.e., known in Gaul, but not necessarily Jerome's 'Gallican' version), later than that used by Hilary of Poitiers (mid-fourth century). It contains some certain traces of Jerome's readings.

(ii) His text of the rest of the Old Testament and of Revelation clearly predates Jerome's.

(iii) His text of Acts is pure Vulgate, with two exceptions characteristic of the *Book of Armagh*.

(iv) No certain decision can be made about his text of the other books of the New Testament. It can be said that his text here was essentially pre-Jerome, corrected by the Vulgate. A special connection with 'Celtic'

---

39. "Der Bibeltext des Heiligen Patrick," *Biblica* 28 (1947), pp. 31-58; 236-263.

texts of the Gospels (particularly with the *Book of Armagh*) cannot be established, and in the letters of St. Paul variation from the *Book of Armagh* prevails (except in Romans).

(v) A list of variants (about twelve in all) which reflect Greek readings probably indicates a new addition to our knowledge of the Latin text of the Bible.

(vi) Occasional variants (all in allusions rather than in direct quotations) indicate readings from the Fathers. There seems to be a special agreement with Cyprian.

## 3. The particular period of the Fathers evidenced in St Patrick's letters

### (a) Introduction

A rediscovery of the Fathers of the Church has initiated and inspired, almost invariably, every renewal of Christian life and culture in the West during the past millennium. It is as if these pastors and prophets of the early centuries are mighty still, and their elegant, inspiring erudition capable of permanent influence on the life of Christians and of the Church. It is enough to take but a few examples in illustration of the point. In the last century that extraordinary stirring of minds and souls in the Anglican Church that we now call the Oxford Movement was ushered in by the rediscovery of the Fathers and the application to the Church of England, on the part of a gifted coterie of Oxford professors, of the principles of Athanasius and Augustine, of Ambrose and Basil. In the thirteenth century a fresh reading of the Fathers inspired the Scholastic theologians,Thomas Aquinas, Bonaventure and Albert the Great as they attempted an original articulation of the faith in the light of the philosophy of Aristotle whose thought was then affecting both Christian and Muslim scholars. In this century the theology of the Fathers provided much of the theological inspiration for the Second Vatican Council.

Who are the Fathers of the Church? A number of criteria are called up for their identification. They belong to the earliest centuries of the Church and so are close to the events of revelation which the Scriptures describe. But they are not only close in time to Christ and his Apostles, they are also close in lifestyle and affection to Christ and his Apostles, being models for imitation and paradigms of virtue. This second criterion, however, does admit of certain exceptions. For example, neither Clement of Alexandria (+217) nor Origen (+254), who are the most creative of the early Greek-speaking writers, are listed as saints, and the idea of saintliness belongs to the notion of the Father. Thirdly, the Fathers are not only close to the era that produced the New Testament, they are also close to the faith and tradition of the Apostles of Christ and of the Early Church: they record this tradition and elaborate it in their writings with refreshing originality and, as time has told, lasting effectiveness. "The words of the holy Fathers", writes the Second Vatican Council, "witness to the living presence of this tradition, whose wealth is poured into the practice and life of the believing and praying Church".[40] Next, the Fathers are all men of the Church, the vast majority being bishops who taught and elaborated her faith. Origen and St. Jerome (+420) who were priests, and Prosper of Aquitaine (+455) a layman, are exceptions proving the rule. Finally, the Fathers are authors whose works are still extant. Indeed all of them produced works of great originality which both communicate the riches of revelation and lay the foundations of theology for which they remain beacons of light. The context of these works was often that of heresy which diluted the faith and which called forth the response of the Fathers. It is enough to think of St. Cyprian of Carthage's *On the Unity of the Catholic Church* written in 251, or of St Athanasius' *Orations against the Arians* composed to protect the teaching of the first Ecumenical Council at Nicea on the divinity of Christ. In general, the Fathers expound the apostolic tradition of the Church's life by a method that combines close personal assimilation with a daring creativity. The result is that their writings not only witness and transmit the Church's living tradition, but also contribute to its development. "The Fathers may be considered the true builders of the Church, the creators and promoters of certain indispensable structures of the Church's order, as also of a culture and of a style of life that is completely new, specifically Christian, and corresponding to the spirit of the Gospel".[41] By the standards of their time, indeed of any time, they were outstanding writers, and "all brought to the service of their thought an incomparable mastery of language".[42]

### (b) The Latin Fathers of the Fourth and Fifth centuries

The drama of the early Church largely consisted in the insertion of the Gospel into the cultures of the Roman Empire. *The Acts of the Apostles* may perhaps be seen as an inspired account of this earliest and prototypical inculturation. The Letters of St Paul, himself a rabbi and a master in Israel, as well as learned in the language and culture of Greece, are also a poignant instance of this same incarnation of the once-for-all

40. The Second Vatican Council, *Dogmatic Constitution on Divine Revelation*, 8, edited by W. M. Abbott, S.J. (Geoffrey Chapman, London-Dublin, 1966), p. 116.
41. The Congregation for Catholic Education, *Instruction on the Study of the Fathers of the Church in the Formation of Priests* (Rome, 1989), II.
42. J. Danielou and H. I. Marrou, *The Christian Centuries*, I (London, 1964), p. 304.

Gospel of Christ. In that way 'a Church from Jews to Gentiles' was formed, and the adventure of the spreading of the Gospel launched. Already by 125 A.D. the anonymous author of the *Letter to Diognetus* could describe Christians as "the soul of the Empire"[43] though they were still a numerical minority within the great commonwealth. Everywhere the Gospel went it seemed to transform the local culture. That transformation blended "the total newness of Christ" (St. Irenaeus +202) with all that was good in the local culture. Evangelization was not a destruction of the old but its recreation by its being lifted up to the level of the Gospel. This explains why St. Justin (+ 167), himself a philosopher prior to his conversion to Christianity, could describe the Gospel as the truest philosophy,[44] and this already by the middle of the second century. According to Voegelin, in the conception of Justin, "Gospel and philosophy do not face the thinker with a choice of alternatives, nor are they complementary aspects of truth which the thinker would have to weld into the complete truth in his conception; the Logos of the Gospel is rather the same Word of the same God as the *logos spermatikos* of philosophy, but at a later stage of its manifestation in history".[45] And what happened as Christianity entered the Greco-Roman world would be repeated as it entered the Ethiopian, African, Germanic and Celtic worlds.

As is well known, the Empire itself persecuted the Christians for centuries. In the middle of the third century there was a succession of persecutions by the Emperors Decius (249-51) and Valerian (257-8). The fourth century opened with the dreadful persecution of Diocletian (303-5) but closed with the legislation of Theodosius who substituted Christianity for the Roman religion. The great change was ushered in by the victory of Constantine at the Milvian Bridge in 312 and the Edict of Milan which recognised the place of the Church in the Empire. The increasing goodwill of the Emperors, however, was a mixed blessing, for "the Emperor was not always disinterested in his favours".[46] This phenomenon is perhaps most clearly visible in the fortunes of Arianism, the heresy of Arius of Alexandria who denied the divinity of the Saviour insisting "there was a time when the Son did not exist". Though condemned at the first Ecumenical Council which used the non-biblical term consubstantial (*homoousios*), the Emperors Constantine and Constantius (337-361) supported the Arian party. Athanasius of Alexandria was the champion of the Council. The heresy, perhaps the most terrible in the long history of the

43. "The Epistle to Diognetus", 6, in *Early Christian Writings* (Penguin, London, 1968).
44. St. Justin, *Dialogue*, Introduction.
45. E. Voegelin, "The Gospel and Culture" in *The Collected Works of Eric Voegelin*, Vol. 12 (Baton Rouge and London, 1990), p. 173.
46. A. Di Berardino and J. Quasten (eds.), *Patrology*, Volume IV (1986), p. 2 (henceforth *Patrology*).

Church, "penetrated into the West only by means of the favour of the Emperor. Without the intervention of Constantius there is a strong probability that the conflict would have been limited to the East".[47] Hilary of Poitiers, for example, only heard of the Creed of Nicea when driven into exile in the East by Constantius in 356. There he wrote his great work on the Blessed Trinity which gained him the title 'the Athanasius of the West'. St Patrick's work shows frequent linkage with this text.

In the episode of Hilary's banishment three factors stand out that are helpful in appreciating the Latin Fathers of the fourth and fifth centuries. These factors are the theological articulation of the faith, the influence of the Greek-speaking East on the West and the freedom of the Church within the Empire.

*(i) The Theological Articulation of the Faith*

With regard to the articulation of the faith, the great heresies of these two centuries provided the stimulus, albeit a negative one, to the Church's theological formulation of the doctrines of the Trinity, of Christ and of the Holy Spirit, as well as of grace and human freedom. It is in this context that the writings of Hilary and Ambrose, Jerome and Augustine stand out. Under the onslaught of various faith-threatening heresies these Fathers composed their many works to present the faith and to prevent the heresy. The result is a veritable forest of literature that makes the fourth and fifth centuries the Golden Age of Patristic literature. Augustine wrote his great tracts against Pelagius (+post 418 ) and Julian of Eclanum (+ca. 440) in order to defend the gratuity of grace according to which "grace is not given according to our merits".[48] It is true that "his theology of grace was the story of his life",[49] but it was the errors of Pelagius and Julian that occasioned his response for which he has since been called the Doctor of Grace. A modern scholar sums up the significance of St. Augustine's *On the Spirit and Letter* in these telling words, "The theology of Pelagius was the theology of deism: his ethics was the ethics of naturalism. There was not room in his version of Christianity for 'Christ in you, the hope of glory', nor for the real indwelling of the Holy Spirit in the believer. Augustine saw that in such a vision the Gospel has disappeared; we owe it to him that the Church has not parted company with Paul".[50] Augustine, in fact, drew his theology from the living wellsprings

47. *Patrology*, p. 3.
48. St. Augustine, *On the Grace of Christ and Original Sin*, 31; *On Correction and Grace*, 6; cf. *The Confession of Grace* (apparatus).
49. *Patrology*, p. 30.
50. J. Burnaby, *Augustine: Later Works* (The Westminster Press, Philadelphia, 1955), p. 192.

of the inspired Word of God,[51] the Church's living tradition and apostolic authority.[52]

## (ii) The Influence of the East on the West

"The East remained not only the cradle but also the womb from which proceeded the thought and spirituality that fecundated the West".[53] The Greek language became the common language of the Empire and was the medium of the faith in the West for centuries. It was not only the language of the liturgy and of letters at Rome until the fourth century, it was also the language of philosophers and the cultured circles, as well as of the merchants and the slaves coming from the East. Only at the turn of the fourth into the fifth century does Latin assert itself. Even then many of the greatest Fathers in the West continued to look to the East. Thus St Ambrose, a teacher before he was a pupil, for he was elected bishop before he was baptized, "developed an exegesis and a theology nourished by Greek sources, close to that of Origen, Athanasius and the Cappadocians".[54] He was well read in the classical Latin authors, such as Cicero. Ambrose's work, *On the Ministries*, borrows structurally from the work of the same name of the Great Roman. In this respect Ambrose resembles his famous convert and pupil, Augustine, who, in the *Confessions*, attributes his newfound love of wisdom to a chance reading of Cicero's *Hortensius*.[55] Jerome knew Greek and Hebrew, as well as Latin. He pressed his encyclopaedic knowledge of the Greek and Latin authors of antiquity into his work of translation of Scripture, exegesis and commentary, apologetics and original composition. Hilary of Poitiers based his later teaching on that of the Greeks, "which he was concerned to interpret to the West, while at the same time seeking to ensure that the East should have a better appreciation of Western points of view".[56]

Augustine is the great exception here. His knowledge of Greek was limited and he has no correspondent in the East among his letters. He was, like nearly all of the Latin Fathers, little read in the East. However, in him the West reaches its summit and his star eclipses even those of Tertullian (160-240), Hilary and all who succeed him. Augustine "has been present ever since in the life of the Church and in the mind and culture

51. *Confessions* VI, 5:7; 11:19; VII, 7:11.
52. *Confessions*, VII, 7:11.
53. *Patrology*, p. 6.
54. *Patrology*, p. 7.
55. Augustine, *Confessions*, III, 4:7.
56. H. Bettenson, *The Later Christian Fathers* (Oxford University Press, London, 1977), p. 5.

of the whole Western world".[57] His was an original synthesis between the Neoplatonism of people like Plotinus and the *Doctrina Christiana*. His great work, *The City of God*, "greatly deserves to be read today . . . as an example and stimulus to deepen the encounter of Christianity with the cultures of the peoples".[58] His thinking on grace and freedom was particularly influential in Gaul where, in 428, "he received letters from two worried admirers . . . Prosper and Hilary" of Arles. These "fearless lovers of all-or-nothing grace" elicited from Augustine in 429 two works, *On the Predestination of the Saints* and *On the Gift of Perseverance*. "Human nature could not have been raised higher".[59]

*(iii) Freedom of the Church within the Empire*

With the notable exception of Julian the Apostate (361-3), the Emperors after Constantine courted the Church. In the West, however, the Church repudiated the Erastian tendencies in this favour, but only after considerable effort. The Fathers, all of them "great and powerful personalities",[60] asserted the freedom of the Church. The altercations of Ambrose with the Emperors of his day are particularly illuminating in this respect. In 385 the Empress Justina and her son Valentinian demanded for the Arians the possession and use of the Catholic church of St Victor in Milan. Ambrose flatly refused, pointing out his reasons, "Do not, O Emperor, embarrass yourself with the thought that you have an Emperor's right over sacred things. Exalt not yourself, but, as you would enjoy a continuance of power, be God's subject. It is written, God's to God, and Caesar's to Caesar. The palace is the Emperor's, the Churches are the bishops".[61] There followed an imperial siege of bishop and people in the disputed basilica which was lifted only during Holy Week. The struggle continued the next year, with Ambrose enjoying the unqualified support of the Catholic population who saw in the bishop a successor of the apostles and in the Church a body deriving from Christ to be governed by his representatives. This body did not, indeed could not, require legitimation from the Empire. Ambrose did not hesitate to remind the Emperor that as a Christian "he was in the Church and not above the Church".[62]

57. Pope John Paul II, *Apostolic Letter on Augustine of Hippo*, 1986, Introduction, in *Origins* (October 2, 1986), p. 282.
58. Ibid., p. 285
59. P. Brown, *Augustine of Hippo* (Faber & Faber, London, 1967), pp. 400, 403; Augustine, *On the Predestination of the Saints*, 14.
60. Danielou–Marrou, op. cit., p. 304.
61. Ambrose, *Letter* 20: see J. H. Newman, *Historical Sketches*, I (Basil Montague Pickering, London, 1872), pp. 346ff, for interesting comments.
62. Ambrose, *Letter* 21.

Even when Alaric and his Visigoths sacked Rome in 410 and brought about a resurgence of sympathies for the ousted pagan deities and customs, Augustine replied with his *City of God* in which he set forth the independence of the heavenly city from the earthly one. Cardinal Newman's assessment of the Church-Empire relationship in the fourth and fifth centuries thus seems quite accurate, "As the Church resisted and defied her persecutors, so she ruled her convert people . . . As regards the Roman Emperors, immediately on their becoming Christians, their exaltation of the hierarchy was in proportion to its abject condition in the heathen period".[63]

### (c) The main Western Fathers, appearing in the Patristic Apparatus to St Patrick's pastorals, considered according to regions

It may be appropriate now to consider the Latin Fathers, appearing in the Patristic apparatus, in clusters and according to regions. As "the makers of Christendom",[64] they constitute a constellation of stars that illumines not only the now faraway sky of their days but also and more wonderful to tell very different times. They are the key to our knowledge of the daily life of the Church of these centuries, for the good reason that they inform us of its liturgical life, its faith and doctrines, its "original structure" (St Irenaeus), its struggles against heresy for the purity of the Gospel and its deepening insertion into the encircling cultures. The Fathers are therefore essential sources for a grasp of the abiding form of Christianity and the Church.

*(i)* **Italy:** *Ambrose, Jerome, Paulinus of Nola, Chromatius of Aquileia, Eusebius of Vercelli*

### Ambrose (340-397)

Ambrose is well known for the manner of his appointment as bishop of Milan in 377 as well as for his assertion of the sovereignty of the Church over against the state, and for the considerable corpus of writing he left which shows a knowledge both of Greek exegesis and theological controversies. Born into a noble family employed in the Roman administration, Ambrose received an excellent literary education. About 370 he was nominated consul of Liguria and Aemilia. Upon being acclaimed bishop, he took three years to study the Scriptures and theology

---

63. J. H. Newman, *Difficulties of Anglicans, II* (Longmans Green & Co., London, 1876), p. 201.
64. F. H. Hoare, *The Western Fathers* (Sheed & Ward, London, 1954), p. ix.

under the guidance of the priest Simplicianus. He concluded this study with a treatise on virginity, a theme that was going to recur in his writings.

Daring in his initatives, most devoted to prayer and study, concerned for the beautifying of the divine liturgy for which he composed hymns rich in melodic theological content, "Ambrose's concerns for the internal life of the church alternated with those of peace in the civil and political world".[65] With regard to the former realm, he proclaimed the truth about Christ against the Arian plague, wrote treatises on the tasks of priests (*De Officiis*), on the Sacraments (*De Sacramentis*), as well as commentaries on the books of the Bible. In his scriptural work he followed an allegorical method borrowed from Origen (+256) and Basil the Great, his contemporary. "This study, complemented by extended prayer on the Word of God, was to become the source of Ambrose's pastoral activity and preaching".[66]

The Christianity that stands out from all this work has three principal characteristics: it is dogmatic, sacramental and hierarchical. It is dogmatic in that it is based on a definite creed claiming the underpinning of divine revelation and intolerant of heresy. It is sacramental in that the worship of God lies at its core and transmits the life of the risen Christ to the faithful. It is hierarchical in that the Church is not an indiscriminate gathering but a body of apostolic origin united around the bishop.

In the sphere of the Church's relation to civil society Ambrose works for peace but champions the freedom of the Church where necessary, as we have seen. His struggles with the Emperors, who often had their own quite different perception of the place of the Church in the Empire, are justly famous. Sometimes these Emperors showed a degree of sympathy to the old religions which Ambrose disdains. The ambiguity is symbolized perhaps in the saga of the Altar of Victory which the Emperor Gratian removed from the Roman Senate in 382.

In 385 Ambrose began to attract by his preaching and reputation a young African called Augustine. It seems that the brilliant but morally wayward litterateur was first drawn by the bishop's "distinctive oratory"[67] in defence of the worth of the Old Testament against the Manichees who loved to parade the moral faults of the Patriarchs.[68] Ambrose introduced Augustine to some totally new ideas, and, in particular, to the realization that God and the soul had to be absolutely immaterial spiritual entities.[69] Of this most 'dramatic' and 'massive evolution of a metaphysician' Augustine writes, "I noticed, repeatedly, in the sermons of our bishop . . . that when God is thought of, our thoughts

65. *Patrology*, p. 149.
66. Ibid., p. 145.
67. P. Brown, op. cit., p. 83.
68. St Augustine, *Confessions*, VI 4, 6.
69. Cf. P. Brown, op. cit., p. 86.

should dwell on no material reality whatsoever, nor in the case of the soul, which is the one thing in the universe nearest to God".[70] There is a charming passage in the *Confessions* where Augustine describes the frame of mind Ambrose the preacher had produced in him as he prepared for baptism, "Ambrose is busy . . . A great hope has dawned; the Catholic faith does not teach things I thought and vainly accused it of . . . Do I hesitate to knock that other truths may be opened?" All this time Ambrose was in contact with Monica who "loved Ambrose as an angel of God, because she had learnt that it was by him that I had been brought so far".[71]

### Jerome (ca. 347-420)

Patrick's text also shows signs of contact with Jerome. Born in Stridonia in Dalmatia, Jerome is the beneficiary of an incomparable classical education, and always showed a fondness for Vergil and Cicero. Baptized only as an adult, he went on to learn Hebrew and entered the monastic way of life then flourishing. He built up friendships with Rufinus and Chromatius, both from Aquileia, and with eminent bishops in the East, like Gregory Nazianzen, patriarch of Constantinople at the time of the Second Ecumenical Council in 381. In 382 Jerome was appointed secretary to Pope Damasus, the bishop of Rome famous for his Latin epitaphs for the tombs of the martyrs in the catacombs. Later he withdrew to Bethlehem and monastic life where for thirty years he continued to translate the Scriptures. His translation, called the "Vulgate", "replaced all previous Latin versions to the extent that it imposed itself as the only authorized translation in the Latin church".[72] Of course Jerome's work was piecemeal, taking a book at a time, and spread over decades of toil. He is the true founder of scientific scriptural study. "To be ignorant of the Scriptures is to be ignorant of Christ", he wrote in his prologue to the commentary on the prophet Isaiah. In 397 a young African bishop by the name of Augustine begins a correspondence with Jerome. Augustine adopts the exegetical methods followed by Jerome. Later they were destined to join forces in the struggle with the ideas of self-redemption advocated by a brilliant British monk teaching in Rome called Pelagius.

Jerome took a keen interest in the events of the day. The fall of Rome to the Visigoths in 410 sent shockwaves through the old man who interrupted his commentary on Ezechiel to write, "My voice is faint, the sobs smother my words. She has been conquered, this city which has conquered the universe".[73] The disaster consisted in the victory of the barbarians and the apparent demise of faith and culture.

---

70. Augustine, *De Beata Vita*, i.4.
71. Augustine, *Confessions*, VI 9, 18; VI 1, 1.
72. *Patrology*, p. 264.
73. Ibid., p. 8.

## Paulinus of Nola (353-431)

Born in Bordeaux (Burdigala) and into a wealthy senatorial family, Paulinus received a splendid liberal education in the same city and under the tutelage of Ausonius, the most celebrated rhetor of the day and a refined poet. Later he travelled to Spain where he married Theresia. Her influence, as well as the tragic event of his brother's murder and his contact with Martin of Tours and Ambrose of Milan, seem to be instrumental in his decision to withdraw from the world. He was baptized in 389 and ordained priest in 394 before setting up a monastery at Nola in Campania. Ordained bishop in 409, he wrote many letters of exceptional literary quality – Jerome even compared them to those of Cicero[74] – and a collection of Poems. During the Pelagian controversy, when "the *causa gratiae* became the high-water mark of Augustine's literary career",[75] Paulinus was a special confidante of the Doctor of Grace.

## Chromatius of Aquileia (+407/8)

Chromatius belonged to the Eusebii family in Aquileia, a celebrated market town of the Empire located near Venice and which saw a remarkable flowering of Christianity in the fourth century. For some years after 370 Chromatius lived in the company of Jerome, Rufinus and Heliodorus. Jerome described the group as "a choir of the blessed" grouped around Valerian, bishop of Aquileia.[76] At the Council of Aquileia in 381 Chromatius acted as a *peritus* for his bishop whom he succeeded in 388. During his twenty years as bishop he produced many tracts and collections of homilies. His commentary on St Matthew is of rare excellence. St Patrick's text has links with it.[77] Chromatius exalts the power of the word of God. This word is sown in the soul by means of the plough of the cross; it is heavenly rain, divine salt, mercy from heaven, precious commerce and food.[78] Something of the flavour of his writing can be tasted in the opening sentence of the commentary. "The sacrament of our faith and of our salvation, although it is present in all the holy Scriptures, is expressed most especially in the Gospel preaching. In this preaching there is revealed the secret of the heavenly plan and the whole mystery of the passion and the resurrection of the Lord".[79]

---

74. Jerome, *Letter* 85, 1.
75. Brown, op. cit., p. 354.
76. Jerome, *Chronicon*, year 374, there is further information in *Letter* 7.
77. Patrick, *Confessio*, 236:2 and 239:6 (apparatus).
78. Cf. A. Quacquarelli (ed.), *Commento al Vangelo di Matteo 2*, Collana di Testi Patristici, 46 (Città Nuova Editrice, Roma, 1984), pp. 13-20.
79. Ibid., pp. 41-2.

### Eusebius of Vercelli (+370)

A Sardinian, he was the first bishop of Vercelli in southern Italy. The Arian party deposed him and sent him into exile in 355 for refusing to subscribe to the condemnation of Athanasius. His literary remains include three letters and Books I-VIII of the Pseudo Athanasian writings which go under the name of Eusebius' *De Trinitate*. Scholars divide as to the validity of the attribution of this work to Eusebius, especially in the light of its sophisticated style as seen in comparison with Athanasius and Hilary of Poitiers.

*(ii)* **Gaul:** *Irenaeus of Lyon, Hilary of Poitiers, Phoebadius of Agen, Prosper of Aquitaine and Hilary of Arles.*

### Irenaeus (ca. 140-202)

During the fourth century the Gospel spread rapidly in Gaul. While in 314 there were only twenty-two episcopal sees, by the end of the century there were seventy. As in Italy, these sees were like a network spread out evenly across the whole country.[80] In the second century, Gaul already had the glory of having the first outstanding systematic theologian of the Church. In Irenaeus of Lyons there emerges the figure of the theologian-Father of the following centuries. Irenaeus was a native of Asia Minor where he was a disciple of St. Polycarp (+155) who had been instructed by Apostles, and had had familiar intercourse with many who had seen Christ.[81] This means that Irenaeus had an exceptionally close relationship to the tradition of the Apostles. The great tide of Gnosticism threatened to sweep the faith away in its wild current in the second century. This heresy was a kind of New Age Movement, syncretistic in character and enjoying a vast diffusion throughout the Mediterranean Basin in the second and third centuries. Irenaeus, however, undertook both the exposition of the true faith and the unmasking of the new movement. The outcome of this work is his five-volume *Against the Heresies* written between 180 and 200. As "the first great champion of orthodoxy and the royal gate of patristic theology",[82] Irenaeus presents a marvellous panorama of the Apostolic Tradition. He focuses on a number of key truths: "the two Testaments come from the same God and revelation thus unfolds in a single, harmonious plan in which God progressively leads fallen men to the acceptance of salvation brought by Jesus Christ".[83] He

---

80. Danielou–Marrou, op. cit., p. 293.
81. Cf. Irenaeus, *Against the Heresies*, III, 3, 4.
82. J. Walgrave, *Unfolding Revelation* (Hutchinson, London, 1972), p. 19.
83. P. F. Beatrice, *The Fathers of the Church* (Edizioni Istituto San Gaetano, Vicenza, 1987), p. 83.

draws out a magnificent profile of Christ in this work, a Christology whose perspectives still stimulate.[84] Christ recapitulates the history of Adam's race, while in the vertical order he unites God and humankind with a view to the eventual divinization of the latter "It was incumbent upon the Mediator between God and man, by his relationship to both, to bring both to friendship and concord, and present man to God, while he revealed God to man"[85]

For Irenaeus the very life of the Church presupposes the threefold duty of fidelity to, adherence to, and transmission of the Apostolic Tradition. It is in this context that one should look for the meaning of the succession of bishops from the Apostles. Irenaeus writes with all candour, "The Apostles have given the apostolic teaching authority to bishops". Like Ignatius of Antioch, he shows special deference to the See of Rome and lists the bishops succeeding the Apostle Peter in that See. "Since it would be too long", he writes, "in this work to list the successions in all the churches, we will take the greatest and oldest church, known to all: the church founded and established at Rome by the two most glorious apostles, Peter and Paul . . . Indeed, on account of its more excellent origin, it is necessary that the entire church, that is the faithful everywhere, be in accord with this church, in whom the tradition of the apostles has been preserved for people everywhere".[86] In a further work, the *Demonstration of the Apostolic Preaching*, Irenaeus describes God's universal plan of salvation as revealed in the sending of Christ and in the mission of the Spirit-filled Church.

### Hilary of Poitiers (ca. 315-367)

Hilary, whom we have met already, emerges as an outstanding Father in the context of banishment and of the struggle for the fullness of faith. His great work, *De Trinitate*, is second only to that of St. Augustine written fifty years later. His ministry coincides with the rapid expansion of the Church in Gaul. We know that he was a friend of St Martin of Tours (316/35 – 397) who was the founder of monasteries and of a rudimentary parochial system.

Hilary wrote commentaries on St Matthew and on the Psalms. As with most of the Fathers, he read the Psalms with New Testament eyes and so in a Christological key. His words are eloquent, "There should be no doubt that the things mentioned in the Psalms ought to be understood according to their reference to the Gospel . . . In this way everything in the Psalms should be pointed both towards the knowledge of the coming and

84. Cf. H. U. von Balthasar, *The Glory of the Lord*, II (T. & T. Clark, Edinburgh, 1984), pp. 31-94.
85. *Against the Heresies*, III, 13, 7.
86. Ibid., III, 3, 1.

incarnation and suffering and kingdom of Our Lord Jesus Christ, and towards the glory and power of our resurrection".[87] It is in their ability to address things more than notions, and realities more than concepts that the Fathers stand out. Newman makes the points very well, "Here is the special use of the Fathers as expositors of Scripture; they do what no examination of the particular context can do satisfactorily, acquaint us with the things Scripture speaks of. They tell us not what words mean in their etymological, or philosophical, or classical, or scholastic sense, but what they do mean actually, what they do mean in the Christian Church and in Theology".[88]

### Phoebadius of Agen (+post 392), Hilary of Arles (401-449), Prosper of Aquitaine (ca. 390-ca. 455)

Another outstanding champion of the divinity of the Saviour in Gaul in the fourth century was the bishop of Agen, Phoebadius. It is through St Jerome that we know most about him. His *Against the Arians* is the only one of his writings still extant and consists in a refutation of the pro-Arian formula of the Council of Sirmium in 357.

The other two Fathers from Gaul appearing in the Patristic apparatus of St Patrick's texts are Hilary of Arles and Prosper of Aquitaine. The former was an organiser of the dioceses of Gaul into provinces and "exercised the role of leader of the Gallic episcopate".[89] Before becoming bishop of Arles, Hilary had been a monk of the famous monastery of Lerins, called 'the new Athens' for its learning. An outstanding preacher, he lived close to the poor and the disadvantaged. Prosper was never a priest. He was a loyal supporter of Hilary of Arles. During the Semi-Pelagian controversy in southern Gaul they elicited an intervention from St. Augustine which we have seen above. Between 432-4 Prosper was at the height of his literary prowess. A particularly interesting series of texts is one composed of responses to arguments from various quarters against St Augustine. Prosper excelled in both prose and verse.

### (iii) Spain

### Gregory of Elvira (+ca. 405)

As in Italy, France and North Africa, the Church spread rapidly in the Iberian peninsula during the fourth century. The vitality of

---

87. Hilary of Poitiers, *Tractatus super Psalmos*, Prologue 5.
88. J. H. Newman, *Lectures on Justification* (Rivingtons, London, Oxford and Cambridge, 1874), p. 121.
89. *Patrology*, p. 20.

the Church is indicated by the number of Spanish bishops who played a part in the Trinitarian disputes of the period.[90] One of these disputes was Priscillianism, which seems to have been a version of neo-gnosticism with an ascetical coloration. In this context it is possible to see the significance of Gregory of Elvira. Jerome tells us that Gregory never yielded to "the Arian depravity". He wrote an anti-Arian *De Fide* about 360 and issued a second modified edition three years later. As the title suggests, this work is doctrinal in character and has the purpose of refuting Arians and justifying the Nicene teaching on the *homoousios*. His thinking here runs close to that of his contemporary, Phoebadius of Agen with whom he shares "a conviction that if this word is eliminated, the way lies open to Arianism".[91]

*(iv)* **North Africa:** *Cyprian, Augustine*

### Cyprian (200-258)

In North Africa the remarkable third century flowering of the Gospel saw the emergence of Latin as the language of the Church. This contrasts with Rome where Latin gained the ascendancy only much later. With Minucius Felix and Tertullian (160-240), both gifted and educated Africans, the stage was set for the emergence of the Latin literature of the West. About the middle of the third century, Cyprian (200-258) became bishop of Carthage. He had received an excellent education in his youth and had become a Christian only in later life, much like Ambrose and Augustine over a century later. His episcopal ministry was going to be as eventful as it was decisive for the subsequent history of the Church. Two devastating persecutions were unleashed on the Church at this time, those of Decius (249-51) and of Valerian (257-8) in which Cyprian gave the ultimate witness.

Many Christians, however, denied their faith at this time: the *lapsi*. This created a special problem for the Church and, in particular, for Cyprian. The rigorists proposed that the *lapsi* be denied readmission to the Church once the tempest of persecution had subsided. Cyprian, however, prescribed penance as the way of re-entry to the Church "outside of which there is no redemption". And so there emerged the famous principle of Catholic theology, "He is not able to have God as Father who does not have Church as Mother". Thus Cyprian wrote the famous *On the Unity of the Catholic Church*, itself "a document of great historical value".[92] For

---

90. Danielou–Marrou, op. cit., p. 293.
91. *Patrology*, p. 88.
92. O. Davies (ed.), *Born to New Life: Cyprian of Carthage* (New City, London, Dublin, Edinburgh, 1991), p. 18.

Cyprian the unity of the Church is closely connected to the See (*cathedra*) of Rome, and the unity of the many bishops with the occupant of that *cathedra*. The theme of unity pervades the life and thought of this great bishop. Thus he writes in a commentary on the Lord's Prayer: "Our peace and fraternal harmony and a people gathered together by the unity of the Father, Son and Holy Spirit is the greatest sacrifice we can make".[93] Another text of Cyprian called the *Testimonies* "gathered together passages from the Bible used in catechesis and is one of the outstanding examples of the literary genre known as *Testimonia*".[94]

### Augustine (354-430)

In the next century the North African Church produced the great Augustine, author of a thousand works, "an incomparable man whose children and disciples we all are in a certain fashion, both in the Church and in the Western world itself".[95] Even to indicate the range of his achievements would be an enormous task. His first biographer, Possidius, when concluding his account of the bishop of Hippo amid the ruins of the city and within months of his death, was of the view that, while no one could ever read all his books, "those who gained most from him were those who had been able actually to see and hear him as he spoke in Church, and, most of all, those who had some contact with the quality of his life among men".[96] Augustine wrote on music and mathematics, on literature and philosophy, on theology and history, on spirituality, exegesis and culture. Central to this gigantic literary output in which "all the thought currents of the past meet . . . and form the source which provides the whole doctrinal tradition of succeeding ages",[97] was his search for the truth, "Truth! Truth! How the very marrow of my soul within me yearned for it!"[98] The search for the truth ended where he did not want it to end – in the Catholic Church from which the Manicheans who were radical dualists had turned him away.

What was the secret of St Augustine? Perhaps the key is to be found by following his amazing journey from moral errancy and unbelief into the fullness of Catholic faith, into what he called the "virginity" of the faith.[99] It is possible to detect three stages or levels in that conversion.

93. Cyprian, *The Lord's Prayer*, 23; see *Letter 60 to Pope Cornelius*. This text is quoted in Vatican Two, *Constitution on the Church*, 4.
94. Danielou–Marrou, op. cit., p. 196.
95. Pope John Paul II, *Apostolic Letter on Augustine of Hippo*, p. 291.
96. Possidius, *Vita*, XXXI, 9: quoted in P. Brown, *Augustine of Hippo*, p. 433.
97. Pope Paul VI, "Discourse to the Religious of the Augustinian Order", May 4th, 1970, *Acta Apostolicae Sedis* 62 (1970), p. 426.
98. *Confessions* III, 6, 10: translation by R. S. Pine-Coffin (Penguin Edition, London, 1979), p. 60.
99. *Sermons* 93, 4; 213, 7.

First, there was an intellectual conversion when, at the age of nineteen, he read Cicero's *Hortensius*. Like a James Joyce revelling in the "silver-lined" prose of Newman, Augustine had been spellbound by the style, though not by the moral insight, of his chosen author. The study of the *Hortensius* changed all that radically, "My heart began to throb with a bewildering passion for the wisdom of eternal truth."[100]

Still the throbbing for truth and wisdom were not enough, for he remained locked into an immoral life that had become habitual, "I was held fast, not in fetters clamped upon me by another, but by my own will, which had the strength of iron chains".[101] He struggled bravely to free himself from his moral enslavement to imperious habits only to find himself stuck fast in flesh and blood. He understood that it was one thing to know the goal, but another to reach it.[102] He found himself divided, "sick at heart and in torment." Eventually and in semi-despair he found the strength and energy he needed. On the bidding of the child's voice, *"Tolle, lege!"* he opened St Paul and read the first words he saw which were from Romans 13:13, "No revelling or drunkenness, no debauchery or vice, no quarrels or jealousies!". The impact was sudden and decisive, "for in an instant, as I came to the end of the sentence, it was as though the light of confidence flooded into my heart and all the darkness of doubt was dispelled".[103] The gift of God's grace, as a divine strengthener, had freed him from slavery and into the glorious freedom of the children of God. Christian conversion had sublimated both his early intellectual conversion and his despairing longing for moral goodness. He realized that he had been all along the subject of God's unmerited attention and now the recipient of the gracious favour of the Blessed Trinity. This experience of God's grace and love sets him on the way to becoming the *Doctor Gratiae atque Caritatis*. Over his life he will compose a psychology of grace in the individual (*Confessions*), a sociology of grace in human society (his many works on the Church), and a history of grace in time (*The City of God*), all works that still inspire as much for their theological insight as for their personal touching style.

As a young bishop Augustine wrote the *Confessions* as a work describing "a man turned towards the dark who was converted by grace to light and, therefore, professes the light in gratitude and reverence".[104] They are "a masterpiece of strictly intellectual autobiography",[105] a theology written in the I-Thou mode. As an old man of about seventy-four

---

100. *Confessions* III, 4, 7.
101. Ibid., VIII, 5, 10.
102. Ibid., VIII, 21, 27.
103. Ibid., VIII, 12, 29.
104. H. U. von Balthasar, *Man in History* (Sheed and Ward, London, 1967), p. 2.
105. P. Brown, *Augustine of Hippo*, p. 167.

he will look back upon them with considerable pleasure and tell us their precise purpose, "The thirteen books of my Confessions praise the just and good God both from my evil things and from my good things, and rouse up the human mind and affections to him".[106] This passage bears a striking resemblance to St Patrick's purpose in the *Confessio* 34, "Whatever happens to me, good or bad, I must accept with an even mind, and thank God always." After all, as Augustine explains elsewhere, "Confession comes not only from a sinner, but also and sometimes from someone praising. We confess therefore either by praising God or by accusing ourselves".[107] The Manichees avoided all confession and so refused to accept responsibility for the personality's involvement in sin.

　　　　Imagine, then, the reaction of Augustine upon hearing that human beings only need knowledge of the law in order to do good! Knowledge is already virtue. Imagine the great convert's thoughts upon seeing a host of ideas affirming human ability to do what is right from its native resources and without the help of the Mediator between God and humankind! And this is precisely what happened through the influence and writings of Pelagius and Julian of Eclanum. The resulting controversies were to occupy Augustine for the last decades of his life. He saw in his two adversaries "the enemies of the grace of God",[108] for they claimed that "grace is given to us according to our merits".[109] He wrote the final works of his life as refutations of these errors and expositions of the truth "The defence of the necessity of grace is, for Augustine, the defence of Christian freedom".[110] We have had occasion to see both the context and the argument of two of these works, the *De Dono Perseverantiae* and the *De Praedestinatione Sanctorum*, which were written for Christians in Gaul who were troubled by the advance of Pelagianism, and which have explicit resonance in St Patrick's *Confessio* 4, 33, 58.


### (v) Summary Conclusion

　　　　In the apparatus over twenty Fathers are linked textually with the pastorals of St Patrick and in the case of certain Fathers the linkage is with many of their works: this is so in the case, of, for example, Augustine, Ambrose and Jerome. Considering that we are dealing simply with two letters there is certainly a density of linkage, both linguistic and conceptual, between St Patrick's text and Patristic literature.

106. *Retractationes*, II, 32.
107. *Sermon*, 67, 1.
108. *Contre Duas Epistolas Pelagianorum*, I, 2.
109. Ibid., I, 2, 42.
110. Pope John Paul II, *Apostolic Letter on Augustine of Hippo*, p. 288.

Inevitably further questions arise. Did St Patrick delve into and study these Fathers independently? They certainly had an important presence in his theological education. Was there a compendium of texts available to the ordinary aspirant to the priesthood, identifying both theological authorities and sound doctrine? What country *could be* the intellectual milieu for such theological familiarity? Gaul? certainly. Britain? the positive evidence is simply not present. Answering such questions was not part of Fr Conneely's work, however. It had a distinct and definite goal: to consider whether on the foundation of textual enquiry one could observe a clear link between the writings of St Patrick and those of the Fathers. The results of his research puts such linkage beyond any reasonable doubt.

## 4. A note on excommunication in the Early Church

It is clear from the New Testament that from the beginning the Church had to deal with behaviour which was disruptive of the life of the Christian community. Jesus advised his disciples as follows:

> If your brother sins against you, go and tell him his fault, between you and him alone. If he listens to you, you have gained your brother. If he does not listen, take one or two others along with you, that every word may be confirmed by the evidence of two or three witnesses. If he refuses to listen to them, tell it to the church; and if he refuses to listen to the church, let him be to you as a Gentile and a tax collector (Mt 18:15-17).

With regard to those who are leading an immoral life, are usurers, idolatrous, slanderers, drunkards or dishonest, Paul asks Christians "not even to eat a meal with such a one" (1 Co 5:11). The penalty of exclusion from the community was prescribed for the immorality mentioned in 1 Co 5:1-2. Such a person is to be handed over to Satan "for the destruction of the flesh, that his spirit may be saved in the day of the Lord Jesus" (1 Co 5:5). In other words, punishment should be imposed on sinners to bring them to their senses so that they might repent and be saved.

For the first three centuries there are no collections of penal laws.[111] However the writings of the Fathers provide evidence that serious public offences such as idolatry, homicide and adultery merited severe punishment. Sinners could be reconciled to the Church after performing a public penance. Those who persisted in grave sin could be excluded from

111. (1) Cf. P. G. Michiels, *De Delictis et Poenis*, vol. 1: *De Delictis* (Universitas Catholica/Brasschaat-Belgium de Bievre, Lublin-Polonia, 1934), pp. 31-3.

the Christian community. The word "anathema" appears in the decrees of the Councils of Elvira (304), Nicea (325), and Arles (335). The word *excommunicatus* appears for the first time in a conciliar context in the decrees of the First Council of Toledo (400). Although its meaning is not always consistent, it implies some form of exclusion from the community, either from the Eucharist or from the social life of the community. This exclusion might be for a time or it might be perpetual. It could be imposed by the bishop as head of a local Church and it could be lifted by him.

We can now examine the letter of Patrick excommunicating Coroticus in the light of this tradition. The letter was provoked by a serious attack on the Christian community: the soldiers of Coroticus had "cruelly butchered and slaughtered by the sword" a number of Christians whom Patrick had just baptised and confirmed; they also abducted some of them and took some booty. Those captured were sold to "a foreign nation that does not know God". When, in accordance with the custom of Christian Roman Gaul, Patrick sent "a holy priest whom I had taught from his infancy, clerics accompanying him", (3) to redeem those who had been captured, the soldiers of Coroticus "made a mockery of the messengers" (3).

Patrick states plainly at the outset that this letter has his full personal authority:

> With my own hand I have written and composed these words, to be given, delivered and sent to the soldiers of Coroticus (2).

Then he solemnly announces this decree:

> Consequently, let every Godfearing person know that they [Coroticus and his soldiers] are excommunicate from me [*a me alieni sunt*], and from Christ my God for whom I am an ambassador (5).

The phrase translated above as "are excommunicate from me" can also be rendered as "are estranged from me". Patrick is indicating that Coroticus and his soldiers have revealed themselves to be "fellow citizens of the demons because of their evil deeds" (2). By their offences against the Church they have broken the bonds of ecclesiastical communion with their bishop. They are no longer brethren or fellow citizens, but strangers (alieni) "whom the devil has greviously ensnared" (4). Patrick does not use the word *excommunicati* but it is clear from the letter that this is indeed what is involved. The effects he desires are as follows:

> It is not lawful to pay court to such people, or to eat or drink with them; nor may their alms be accepted, until through rigorous

penance, unto the shedding of tears, they render satisfaction to God, and free the menservants and the baptised maidservants of Christ, for whom He died and was crucified (7).

This amounts to a form of social ostracism: Coroticus' social position is not to be acknowledged; hospitality, which was central to a chieftain's position in early Irish society, is not to be accepted from him. No one is to eat or drink with him or his men.

He begins his letter by stating: "I Patrick . . . declare myself to be a bishop. I believe with complete certainty that it is from God that I received what I am" (1). In this way he makes it clear that it is by virtue of his authority as a bishop that he is issuing this penal decree. He emphasises this point again:

> I am no maker of false claims. I have a share with those whom He called and predestined to preach the Gospel amid no small persectuions unto the farthest parts of the earth, even if the enemy gives vent to his malice through the tyranny of Coroticus, who has no reverence for God or for His bishops, whom He chose and to whom He granted the highest, divine, sublime power that those whom they should bind on earth would be bound also in heaven (6).

With an emphasis reminiscent of St Paul, Patrick insists that his power comes from God through his consecration as a bishop. It is a divine power, though some do not acknowledge it. It is a power which binds on earth and in heaven. Since Patrick has issued this condemnation in virtue of his authority as a bishop no one else can withdraw it:

> I request with the greatest gravity – whatever servant of God may be willing to be a bearer of this letter – that it shall on no account be withdrawn or hidden from anybody, but rather be read before all the communities, even in the presence of Coroticus himself (21).

Patrick's letter is not a stiff, impersonal decree. Rather it expresses the anguish of a shepherd whose flock has been ravished by "ravenous wolves" (12). The apostle is outraged at the treatment of his people. It is possible perhaps to sense in his outrage at the kidnap of his "sons and daughters" (15) the painful memory of his abduction as a child from his own home. The letter ends however with a promise of divine mercy:

> But if God inspires them to return, at some time or other, to a right mind towards God, so that even at a late hour they repent of such an impious deed – murder of the brethren of the Lord – and

so release the baptised women captives they previously seized: if God thus inspires them so that they deserve to live unto God and be made whole here and in eternity, peace be to them with the Father and the Son and the Holy Spirit. Amen (21).

This letter expresses in the clearest terms the heinous nature of the acts committed by Coroticus and his soldiers; murder and abduction are offenses against the Christian community and against God. Patrick imposes the penalty of excommunication on those responsible. His desire however is that the hurt inflicted on the Church be healed and that those who have inflicted it should return "to a right mind towards God" (21). It is the letter of a shepherd weeping with those who weep, suffering the agonies of his flock, pronouncing a severe sentence against those who have sinned against God and against the Church and, finally, calling them to repentance. Although the word is not used, all the elements of excommunication are present in this letter. Fr. D. S. Nerney S.J. studied the decree *Inter Ceteras* (ep 30) of Pope Innocent I (401-17) and concluded that Patrick "was conversant with the 'stylus curiae' in drafting a decree of excommunication"[112] (2). It is quite clear that Patrick's letter is in keeping with the tradition of the Church.

As a final point, one might note that the coercive power of the bishop over offending members of his flock – as illustrated by the action of Patrick – bears some resemblance to the coercive power of the poet in early Irish society. This relationship between poet and cleric is set down in a compilation of ancient Irish law known as the *Seanchas Mór*:

> Now until the coming of Patrick speech was not suffered to be given in Ireland but to three: to a historian for narration and the relating of tales; to a poet for eulogy and satire; to a brehon lawyer for giving judgement according to the old tradition and precedent. But after the coming of Patrick every speech of these men is under the yoke of the white [blessed] language, that is, the scriptures.[113]

Fear of the poet's power to satirise was used when necessary as a sanction against chieftains.[114] Patrick's use of episcopal power is entirely different, as can be seen from his desire for the reconciliation of those who had sinned against the Christian community. Nevertheless it is not unlikely that the power of the bishop carried an echo of the traditional power of the poet. Whether Patrick's action brought about the desired response on the part of Coroticus and his soldiers is however lost in the mists of history.

112. "A Study of St. Patrick's Sources II" in *Irish Ecclesiastical Record* 72 (1949), pp.14-26.
113. Quoted in R. Flower, *The Irish Tradition* (Clarendon Press, Oxford, 1949), p. 4.
114. V. Mercier, *The Irish Comic Tradition* (Clarendon Press, Oxford, 1962), p. 106.

## Chapter Three

# Faith-life and theology:
# St Patrick as a pastoral theologian of his time

1.  Introduction

2.  Faith and the whole economy of salvation
(a)  The divine economy of salvation
(b)  Faith-life in focus
(c)  Faith-life: reflection within it and fruitfulness of it
(d)  Faith-life and Patristic theology
(e)  Theology as an historical and multiform reality

3.  St Patrick as a Churchman in the Patristic era

# Chapter Three

# Faith-life and theology: St Patrick as a pastoral theologian of his time

## 1. Introduction

It was at the close of the Golden Age of the Fathers of the Church that St Patrick was educated for the priesthood, evangelized Ireland and wrote his two pastoral letters. This fact is of great significance for discerning the theological content and value of his writings and for measuring his own personal stature as a pastoral theologian of his time. His letters are the Irish contribution to Patristic literature. This value has been underestimated; indeed the only other contribution from the whole region of Ireland and Great Britain was that of Gildas in the sixth century.

The Fathers are those who, following the death of the Apostles, became leading figures in the life and thought of the Christian Church. Theirs are the earliest writings which are not in the canon of the New Testament as authoritative Scripture. They constitute the special formative stage of second generation life in the Church.

Since the entire Patristic period covers roughly the first eight centuries of our era, it is evident that assessing the Christian and theological content of the fifth century pastorals of St Patrick has a historical dimension which is specifically Patristic. This involves bringing into focus firstly the economy of salvation proclaimed in the Gospel message to all humankind; secondly, how the Gospel is to be lived in *faith-life*; thirdly, how faith-life is affirmed and protected in *faith-belief* and in doctrine. Doctrine of course is an historical reality, developing historically, sometimes in a context of profound reflection and Christian experience, at other times in a context of dangerously antagonistic controversy. It meets demands made on the communication of Gospel truth by particular cultures, times and places. In turn a sample of contemporary Christian writing can be expected to reflect both demand and response. Consequently, a spiritual grasp of the substance of the Gospel and of faith in it, an historical sense of the Age of the Fathers of the Church and of Patristic theology – these are all important for any theological appraisal of St Patrick's writings.

## 2. Faith and the whole economy of salvation

### (a) The Divine economy of salvation

Being made in the image of God, the human person is the ultimate subject both of faith-life on earth and vision-life in heaven. It is important then to be able to think, differentially, of life *in* the individual and of the whole divine providence for this life. The aim of this providence is the total, destined well-being (or salvation) of all individuals.

It has many aspects which together constitute the economy of our salvation. Thus nature is able to mediate a knowledge of God and of his omnipresence, to mediate also the belief that union with him will bring to rest every tendency and desire in us. Providence went further, historically, in covenanting, through the Jewish people, to be Emmanuel (God-with-us) in our journey through life. Finally, God became incarnate and salvation became an extending to us of the life of Jesus, true God and true man. Jesus has covenanted to be present to us (1) directly in a faith-life, i.e. in the medium of our own very minds and hearts; (2) through the medium of matter, in a sacramental life. He has also founded a Church to continuously presence, by proclamation and teaching, all that he has revealed of divine providence for us and to continuously dispense the sacraments.

Here we will devote our attention to the faith-life which, since the incarnation, God has covenanted to initiate. The Second Vatican Council describes how He becomes active in our interior life, making our very minds and hearts a medium of union with Him:

> The obedience of faith is to be given to God who reveals, an obedience by which man commits his whole self freely to God, offering the 'full submission of intellect and will to God who reveals' and freely assenting to the truth revealed by Him. To make this act of faith, the grace of God and the interior help of the Holy Spirit must precede and assist, moving the heart and turning it to God, opening the eyes of the mind and giving 'joy and ease to everyone in assenting to the truth and believing it'. To bring about an ever deeper understanding of revelation the same Holy Spirit constantly brings faith to completion by His gifts.[1]

This interior intercommunication between God and the human person fulfills the Old Testament prophecies of God writing his law, no longer on tables of stone (as with Moses) but, directly, on the very minds and hearts of his people:

1. *Dogmatic Constitution on Divine Revelation*, 5.

This is the covenant that I will make with the house of Israel after
  these days, says the Lord:
I will put my laws into their minds,
and write them on their hearts,
and I will be their God,
and they shall be my people.
And they shall not have to teach every one his fellow, or every one
  his brother, saying 'Know the Lord', for all shall know me.
(Jr 31:31 ff.)

It is important to spell out the reality of this faith-life. Of
course, it develops or remains undeveloped according to the response of
human freedom. We must become sensitive to the fact that the divine
invitation and initiative is a measure and testing of our love of God and
indeed of our general human excellence. And we must learn to think *differentially* of our *faith-life* and of the beliefs, personal and ecclesiastical,
which are also providential as formalizations of truth protecting our cor-
porate life together as Christians.

### (b) Faith-life in focus

It begins from a mysterious presencing of God in the medium
of the human mind and heart. Developing as a mutual presencing and
responsiveness, it is a life unique to each individual. And since God is
triune, the human individual has mysterious access through Jesus, in the
Spirit, to the Father.
Faith-life is a truth-giving, life-giving encounter but in the
darkness of a medium that has no proportion to the infinite reality of God.
"We see as in a glass, darkly" (1 Co 13:12). But endlessly we can enjoy
the influence of Jesus on our mind and heart; endlessly we can listen to
him as Master. Endlessly we can respond and love and know him better
as our new and true life and our salvation. Within his mysterious presencing, enjoying "the substance of things to be hoped for" (Heb 11:1), we are
in perennial hope and expectation of passing from darkness to light, from
faith to vision. In the meantime, once we do not fail, on our part, to live
with Christ, evidencing of a presencing of Christ and the Spirit of Christ
is not lacking in the form of living wisdom or peace or courage or love:
"the wind blows where it wills, and you hear the sound of it, but you do
not know whence it comes or whither it goes; so it is with everyone who
is born of the Spirit" (Jn 3:8).
Life with Christ is a life of heart as well as mind and it has a
transforming effect on our total humanness. The natural idiom and

content of communication is the rich human language of Scripture and Tradition which conserve Divine Revelation in the full reality of its historical context. Thus the interior life of faith is an arrival and development within the individual person of the divine economy of public revelation. St Vincent of Lerins puts it that the field in which divine seeds are sown is the field of the Church. Faith-life comes as such a truth-giving life to the human mind that it becomes a storehouse of scriptural images and thoughts and idioms. Early Christian writers speak of it as a lamp and move quickly, from description, to prayer for the kindling touch of Christ, our interior space being, as it were, the temple of his presence. Thus St Columban:

> Do you, Christ, deign to kindle our lamps, our Saviour most sweet to us, that they may shine continually in your temple, and receive perpetual light from you the light perpetual, so that our darkness may be enlightened, and the world's darkness may be driven from us. Thus do you enrich my lantern with your light, I pray you, Jesus mine, so that by its light there may be disclosed to me those holy places of the holy, which hold you eternal priest of the eternal things, entering there the courts of that great temple of yours, that constantly I may see, observe, desire you only, and loving you only may behold you, and before you my lamp may ever shine and burn.[2]

Since the Church is a community of faith, a person may grow up from childhood into adulthood without making any study of evidence for belief in the existence of God, revelation, etc. When one adverts to this he or she may not feel at all unreasonable, on the grounds that the key to the absence of doubt in his or her life is not credulity but an experience of presencing, and that an experiential life is above the need of "proof" by propositional evidence.

What is happening here is what happens in many contexts of natural faith. In our natural life we must and do assume many things without question, e.g., that the room in which I write will continue as it is, that the food I buy will nourish me. We act from countless fiduciary frameworks. They are the rule rather than the exception. In the human condition indeed we are alive and acting before we even have the ability to put anything we are doing in question. And every individual life must remain to a considerable extent fiduciary, not only because we live in the medium of matter already highly organised and working for us, but also because our life is embedded in the history of our countries, the cultural conventions of our time and our family rearing. The putting into words of this or that aspect of life and the investigative movement to reasoned belief about it can have great value but, humanly, this value has a limited

2. *Instruction* 12.

number of proper contexts and *per se* need never be given the appearance of competing with fiduciary life in general.

As a reality, indeed, *reasoned belief* looks quite weak beside the *zero unbelief* of faith-life, both the faith-life which permeates everyday natural activity and that which permeates the transcending life of the genuine Christian. If the word, faith, is used generically for both belief and life one might call the former, *belief-faith*. It can never of itself generate a *faith-life*. That is initiated in natural everyday life by our very nature when in every minute of every hour we are taking much for granted and exercising faith of some specific kind. In the context of union with God it is initiated in personal contact with God by God himself. What belief-faith in every context does is to bring to rest personal doubts or cultural demands for an enquiry of a certain kind. But it is not intrinsically necessary that the faith-life of everyone will be derailed by doubts or cultural demands. Human life is not constitutionally epistemological. Indeed the truth of the matter may be simply that modern thinking tends to produce an epistemological stammer in us.

### (c) Faith-life: reflection within it and fruitfulness of it

Faith-life is of its nature experiential: truth-giving and truth-developing. Reflection within it illuminates many matters concerning God, eternal life and this life. It generates wisdom that is consciously grounded in faith, learnt from the presencing of God incarnate. Further it disposes us to live in the way that conforms to the outlook of God.

Attention within, and to, faith-life leads naturally to the formation of what one might call a Scriptural consciousness. For Scripture is available, through the Church, as the natural source of language, truth and meaning in the interpresencing of God and human beings. And in the light of this inter-communication of disciple and Master, of creature and Creator, Scripture becomes an endless source of wisdom, contemplative and practical, other-worldly and worldly. Naturally so, for it is in the faith-life of the individual that salvation history is existentialized. In one of his discourses in St Peter's, Pope Paul VI imaged the presencing of Jesus in faith as providing a dual carriageway for our minds: "There starts from Jesus the way that reaches the true knowledge of the heavenly Father and of the intimate life of God, the Most Holy Trinity. And there starts from Jesus the way which descends to the true knowledge of humanity, to man's mystery, that of his nature and of his destiny".

Sacred Scripture is a book of God revealing himself and it is a book also of the human person as he or she really is with all his limitations and possibilities. In the Old Testament individuals appear and speak as we do, often hypocritical even in their dealings with God himself, selfish in their petitions to him for help; religious and political leaders are allowed to appear as they were, historically, prepared at times to mask ruthless decisions as the will of God. Scripture is the Word of God and the face of God is there, communicating wisdom and inspiration for living in truth; but the historic face of the human being is equally there, falsifying as well as transcending, dominating as well as struggling, exploiting as well as walking humbly and tenderly. Within faith-life with Christ, the two presences cease to be confused and confusing.

There is another reason why reflection within faith-life will tend to be Scriptural. Scripture itself is not, characteristically, either abstract or impersonal writing. Its wisdom is conveyed in much narrative and imagery, in listening to what "the Lord says" and in prayerful elevations of the mind to him. St Teresa of Avila, a Doctor of the Church, exemplifies the fact that faith-life tends to make us less desirous of explanations and less dependent on them in our eagerness to grow continuously in direct, concrete experience of truth. Quite humanly she remarked that she enjoyed the advantages of her outlook whenever explanations were particularly difficult to follow! In his letter to Proba (*Ep:* 130), St Augustine remarks:

> The nature of blessedness has been much discussed by many people; but why should we go to many people and much explanation? In the scripture of God it is put briefly and truly: 'Blessed is the people whose God is the Lord'.

The Scripture of God, when it is experienced within his presencing in faith-life brings to complete rest desires and worries about living in truth. But it leaves intact, too, whatever degree of natural curiosity and zeal for exploration and investigation we may have.

While nothing can be added to the fullness and perfection of God's gift of truth, which is given to us in Jesus Christ, man's receptivity and welcome for it can increase freely and indefinitely. Faith-life requires from our side a "yes" which enables divine thought to be received and to penetrate into our minds and enables the attitude of the crucified to plunge its roots into deeper levels of our heart. This twofold (divine and human) aspect of faith explains its transforming power and its fruitfulness in our lives. God does all, absolutely all; we are a new creation. But the new creation is a creation *of us*: it is a salvation that truly saves *us*. We say "yes" in it: "I live now, not I, but Christ lives in me" (Ga 2:20).

It has a fruitfulness of its own in everyday life when we do not sin against the light by following our own will. The person of faith becomes sensitive to the enormity of not being properly fruitful. Newman is a great example of this sensitivity. In his Sicilian illness he repeated often "I have not sinned against the light" and when he regained health his hymn "Lead kindly light" was his testimony to the presencing of God as the light of life. Coming as it did from intense suffering, it activated painful personal memories and it is said that Newman shuddered when he heard it sung.

There is an especial continuity between faith-life and sacramental life, between the presencing of God in faith and in sacrament. This continuity is clearly and tersely expressed by St Augustine: "How can we be said to eat the body and drink the blood of Our Lord if we do not receive him interiorly into our very minds and hearts?".

Obviously, faith-life is developmental. Possibly no beginning could be less manifest than its beginning. Certainly, no other form of life on earth could finally reach such astonishing excellence. The lives of saintly people, canonized and uncanonized, show that. Indeed the prophecies of the coming of the Kingdom of God and of the transformation of humankind are ultimately fulfilled and concretized in the coming of God to the minds and hearts of individual persons:

Your sun shall no more go down,
nor your moon withdraw itself;
for the Lord will be your everlasting light,
and your days of mourning shall be ended . . .
the earth shall be full of the knowledge of the Lord
as the waters cover the sea . . .
in the plains justice shall dwell
and righteousness shall abide in the gardens
(Is 6:20; 11:9; 32:16).

Transformed in attitudinal life, the person of faith-life becomes a continuing witness to Jesus Christ, for through him Jesus has a presence in the here and now. "I live now, not I, but Christ lives in me". The meaning of the moment is, on a last analysis, the martyrdom of the moment. For the formal principles which the person of faith invokes in judging a situation and deciding what to do are godly in character and emerge from his or her faith-life. Attitudinal vitality disposes one to gentleness with justice, to mildness with courage, to wisdom with temperance, to patience with understanding. This is the power of God at work in the human person, mediated as human virtue and excellence of conscience. The person is animated by the Spirit of God. In his or her own unique here and now the human person is a mediator of the very life of Christ.

"When the Son of Man comes, think you shall he find faith on the earth?" (Lk 18:8). Today he would certainly find a whole spectrum of belief-faith, much ecumenical activity there and much debate. But where and how often would he find faith-life? This life owed its first existence to direct encounters with Jesus in the flesh. After his death the proclamation of it became the responsibility of the Apostles and their successors and, through them, of the whole people of God. Is it vanishing from intellectual memory and education as the normal Christian life, and as providing our planet with the possibility of hosting a social personal development which would excel its evolutionary past?

### (d) Faith-life and Patristic theology

In the history of both faith-life and belief-faith the early centuries of our Christian era are seen, of course, as a most privileged period. The Apostles themselves are the authoritative witnesses to the life, death and resurrection of Jesus and to the Pentecostal coming of the Holy Spirit. Part of their mission is to begin a proclamation to the whole world that God has become incarnate to presence himself in the minds and hearts of all. This Good News is a call to respond to a new epoch of the presencing of God. They are sent and working for nothing less than implantation of faith-life. St Paul says to his Corinthian people:

> When I came to you, brethren, I did not come proclaiming to you the testimony of God in lofty words of wisdom. For I decided to know nothing among you except Jesus Christ and him crucified. And I was with you in weakness and in much fear and trembling; and my speech and my message were not in plausible words of wisdom, but in demonstration of the Spirit and power, that your faith might not rest in the wisdom of men but in the power of God (1 Co 2:1-5).

Patristic literature reflects Christianity as a phenomenon of both person and culture and it teaches us the difference. The Christian life came into existence first as a revolution within persons, as a radical change in the minds and hearts of individuals, so impressive to observers that it spread like a conflagration to them. In the apostolic age of eye-witness testimony to the life, death and resurrection of Jesus, Christians lived consciously and fruitfully from the mysterious, interior presencing of the Risen Lord and the Holy Spirit. A great deal of Patristic literature is written from within this faith-life, expressing and nourishing it meditatively, especially through the use of Sacred Scripture. The *presencing* of God and our *responsive acceptance* of it are seen as the primary or first-order Christian reality. And this is never really lost sight of.

But increasingly, as time went on, a great deal was written by the Fathers *from within the process of inculturation.* So much effort had to be made in the conquest of unbelief and the formalization of belief that gradually a gap was created between belief and actual living with Christ. The gap was not at all as wide as that which we experience today and it was always bridged in the writings of the Fathers. Nevertheless, it was there. On the one hand there was the Pentecostal coming of the Spirit and the Gospel call to respond to the presencing of Christ in the medium of our minds and hearts. On the other hand there was the harsh reality that again "He came to his own and his own received him not" (Jn 1:11): much of mankind was not disposed to accept the Gospel and the primary challenge seemed to be to generate belief-faith. Many people would not be convinced until the presentation of the Gospel was endowed with rational argumentative force.

Many Christians wanted to have at hand a philosophy that would enable them to defend themselves against intellectual accusations of all kinds, e.g., of atheism, idolatry. Converts like Clement of Alexandria, already trained in philosophy, wanted to transform the pagan philosophies into a Christian one. Tertullian spoke of the attempt to find support for Christian truth in "the writings of philosophers, or the poets, or other masters of this world's learning and wisdom . . . with the object of convicting the rivals and persecutors of Christian truth, from their own authorities, of the crime of at once being untrue to themselves and doing injustice to us" (*De Test. Animae*, 1).

Above all the Fathers were confronted with Gnosticism, a movement both religious and philosophical. If its challenge were not met intellectually and successfully, the whole of Christian faith-life would be undermined. Gnostics claimed to be an elite, recipients of absolute truth, with answers to the most fundamental questions about the world and man and eternity, and with a final solution to the problem of evil. However, while making unique claims to esoteric knowledge and certain salvation, it absorbed materials from philosophical schools of all kinds, from Greek and Oriental mystery religions and from astrological, alchemical and magical sources. Ideas, images and symbols were drawn from Sacred Scripture as well as from mythologies. In an arbitrary, irresponsible and even blasphemous manner, Gnostics adapted texts of both the Old and New Testament, claiming that their interpretations were guaranteed by esoteric traditions or special mystical experiences. Thus they portrayed the God of the Old Testament as evil, and they distinguished a Christ who only appeared in the semblance of a man from a real corporeal Christ, for they refused to accept that Christ could be born of a woman or that he suffered and died on Calvary. Expressing contempt for the law and the prophets of the Old Testament, and hostile to traditional morality and belief, they considered themselves as equal to Jesus himself.

The whole Gnostic movement over so many centuries has been so Protean, appearing at different times and in different places in so many forms that it is impossible to find a parallel for it. But in so far as it struck at the very heart of Christian faith-life and demanded an intellectual response from Christian leaders, one can point to the Liberalism which John Henry Newman opposed as being somewhat of a parallel to it. Paradoxically so, for in a sense this is an extreme opposite to elitism. Wishing to "track out the way which leads heavenwards", Newman found that he had to be tireless in his opposition to it:

> For thirty, forty, fifty years I have resisted to the best of my powers the spirit of liberalism in religion . . . Liberalism in religion is the doctrine that there is no positive truth in religion, but that one creed is as good as another, and this is the teaching which is gaining substance and force daily. It is inconsistent with any recognition of any religion, as true, it teaches that all are to be tolerated, for all are matters of opinion.[3]

The Fathers of the Church saw that the Christian life could never be inculturated in a milieu that was either grossly careless or grossly mistaken about truth. Doctrinal truth had to be worked out and developed. But they never lost sight of the fact that doctrine was there to protect, express, clarify, nourish and proclaim the presencing of God-Incarnate in the interpersonal intimacy of faith-life. Side by side, as parts of their total theology, there is both formal doctrine and reflection within faith-life. This differentiated blending of belief-faith and faith-life is uniquely powerful in Patristic literature.

The times might need to be pointed in the right direction by the formalization of sound doctrine but the individual needed to live, personally, within the actual presencing of God, mysteriously Triune and Incarnate also. This presencing is manifold: the omnipresencing of the Creator; the presencing of the Incarnate God and Holy Spirit in the faith-life of our minds and hearts; and the sacramental presencing of Jesus in the Eucharist. The writings of the Fathers testify to the amount of their reflection within faith-life and to their pastoral concern for the cultivation of this life in everyone as an ultimate existentialization of Christian tradition and Sacred Scripture. This attitude made for balanced thinking in matters of doctrine. Credal statements could not be disharmonious with faith-life or even ambivalent on crucial matters. In the event, the Church of the Fathers did achieve a sound judgement in its authoritative development of doctrine.

---

3. Speech on the occasion of becoming a Cardinal, 1879.

## (e) Theology as an historical and multiform reality

Theology is a science of God and of the divine economy for human salvation, with evidence provided by divine revelation and available in a continuous tradition from the Apostles, particularly in Sacred Scripture and authoritative teachings of the Church. Within this setting of evidence, theologizing is an activity of scholarship. The continuous thread running through it is the presence of Christian conscience, working academically in fidelity to revelation and in obedience to the obligations of furthering continuity in tradition, of inculturating the Christian life in every place and at every time, and of nourishing the faith-life within each individual also. Excellence in Christian theology is the excellence of an historical reality. It would be reductionist to identify it totally with the authoritative formalizations which are so important in it or not to hope for uncontentious variety in the theologies of different times and places. Indeed, field specialization which has become prominent gives rise to biblical theology, patristic theology, medieval theology, renaissance theology, modern theology; and to dogmatic theology, moral theology, pastoral theology, mystical theology and each of these is itself a set of theologies.

Innumerable Christian theologies are as possible and as normal as innumerable saints. Each of the latter is Christlike in his or her unique way, but there can be no finalized imitation of Christ although He is the source of holiness to each. Similarly, the definitive revelation of God, source of all true Christian theologies, is not a proposition or any theological system of propositions: it is the very person, Jesus Christ, in his historical reality and continued presence. The Congregation for the Doctrine of the Faith, in its *Instruction on The Ecclesial Vocation of the Theologian* says:

> Christ is the definitive Word of the Father in whom, as St John of the Cross observes, "God has told us everything all together and at one time" (*Ascent of Mount Carmel*, II, 22, 3) (41).

This is an all-important truth to bear in mind in modern times when theology forms itself in a culture that tends to be abstract and impersonal. It is all too easy to misinterpret the devotional quality of St Patrick's letters and fail to appreciate how much a part this quality was of a solid and authentic theology in the age of the Fathers.

Hans Urs von Balthasar is perhaps the theologian who, in recent years, has most distinctively elaborated the theme that each Christian theology has *per se* Christ as its formal object, and that there can be no end to the potential discernment by reason, in various theologies, of aspects of the wholeness of truth which is *real* in the being, life and presence of Christ. Further, he emphasizes that

> it belongs to the essence of this and *only* this science [i.e. theology] that its scientific objectivity rests on the decision to believe, and that there can be, therefore (theologically considered), no neutral objectivity, no consideration of the object of belief without belief, or apart from belief and unbelief. The theory which was favored at the beginning of our century – in which objective scientific method and subjective commitment were regarded as separable – even should it be applicable elsewhere, cannot be used here.[4]

The Incarnation is the redemptive mission of Christ to ourselves and the call for participation in it by ourselves: no *real* theology can develop in detachment. Oneness of subject and object that, however imperfect in degree, is essential for even abstract knowledge, must be perfect in degree for excellent, deep and intimate theology. A Christian theologian is *per se* one who believes and accepts Christ into mind and heart and his whole work is essentially a service to a believing community.

One of the most direct and dramatic communications of this truth to us is the life of St Paul. Religiously, from his youth he was a fervent believer and matured among the Chosen People as an excellent rabbinical theologian. The meeting with Jesus on the road to Damascus transformed his mind for ever: "I count everything as loss because of the surpassing worth of knowing Christ Jesus my Lord" (Ph 3:8), "For me to live is Christ, to die is gain" (Ph 1:21).

In *Method in Theology* Bernard Lonergan examines the complex activity of theologizing under eight specialties. There is first of all *research*, *interpretation* and *history*, culminating in historical judgments which depict the past. Then there is *dialectic*, *foundations* and *doctrines* which go to the root of conflicts, objectify the new horizon of Christian conversion, and express those judgements of Christian facts and values which are normative. Finally, there are *systematics* which tries to provide significant ways of relating, analogically, to the mysterious in Christian life, and *communications* which is the final stage of theology – the gaining "access into the minds and hearts of men of all cultures and classes" (p. 133).

When one relativizes these "functional specialties" to particular times, places, needs and to assisting varying inculturations and individual lives, one sees the community of theologians as generating a family of theologies rather than as constructing a single entity. The family likeness is manifest in continuous and explicit fidelity to tradition from the Apostles: every member of the family, past or present is a bearer of this tradition.

4. *Convergences* (Ignatius Press, San Francisco, 1983), p. 51.

At first, however, the differentiation between Christian religion and Christian theology, between Christian life and Christian dogma, did not exist. Christians were immediately and basically concerned with the transformation of human living through the faith, not with a development of doctrine. Lonergan speaks of a puzzling undertow to the current of early Church life and of the Patristic theology which mirrored it: "a concern for clarity and coherence, that was destined eventually to add to the ordinary language of the bazaars and to the religious language of the Gospels the incipient theological language of the Greek councils". Going forward but "without any explicit advertence on anyone's part" there began at Nicea, but continued down the centuries, the development of dogma. This was "the long-term outcome", an outcome that people like Tertullian or Origen or Athanasius "did not intend or desire".[5]

In this dogmatic development in the magisterium of the Church and in theology, there was a transition from a mode of writing, which sought to engage the whole person to one which kept attention focused on the aspect of truth alone, on its precise formulation and elaboration:

> The Gospels, and the apostolic writings generally, are not just a collection of true propositions, addressed only to the mind of the reader; they teach the truth, but in such a way that they penetrate the sensibility, fire the imagination, engage the affections, touch the heart, open the eyes, attract and impel the will of the reader. Conciliar decrees are totally different: so clearly and so accurately do they declare what is true that they seem to bypass the senses, the feelings and the will, to appeal only to the mind . . . (B)etween the scriptures and the councils there intervenes a process of synthesis, by which many sayings of scripture are reduced to a single fundamental proposition, frequently expressed in technical terms.[6]

The theological presentation and study of dogmas, then, has to tend towards a goal which is of the intellect alone. A special kind of clarity is produced and the nature, limits and value of dogmatic development is, itself, properly understood:

> (The) doctrine of the Christian Church concerning Jesus Christ advanced not from obscurity to clarity, but from one kind of clarity to another. What Mark, Paul and John thought about Christ was neither confused nor obscure, but quite clear and distinct; yet their

5. B. Lonergan, *The Way to Nicea* (Darton, Longman and Todd, London, 1977), Foreword, p. viii.
6. Ibid., p. 1.

teaching acquired a new kind of clarity and distinctness through the definition of Nicea. But further dogmas had to follow, and then the historical investigation of dogmas, before the fact and the nature of dogmatic development itself could be clearly established.[7]

The development of Christian dogmas and of dogmatic theology is really an aspect of Christian inculturation. The Western milieu is one which has sought to discover truth with intellectual precision and as true. It has organized every branch of its knowledge, too, on the basis of foundational truths from which one can deduce all the remaining ones. In this milieu, the dogmatic form of clarity, and with it a dogmatic theology, became historically mandatory for the Christian Church. Besides, particular religions and moral questions arose, over centuries, from time to time, in frameworks of current philosophies and scientific concepts. These demanded a Christian response, so precisely and prudently made that Christian belief would not be identified with the philosophic or scientific framework which, of course, could never be intrinsic to Christian truth and, culturally, might be later displaced.

Dogmatic theology is a special, valuable experiencing and presentation of what is in the Gospels and apostolic writings. We have seen that it exists by historical necessity as a response of Christian conscience to pressures from within Western culture.

However, it does not engage the whole person or easily nourish faith-life. And to be properly appreciated and used it requires a degree of intellectual development that simply cannot be expected of large numbers of people. The hazard is that with so much emphasis on beliefs, Christian faith will be identified with Christian *beliefs* rather than with *faith-life.*

This is what has actually happened (whatever be the full cause). And faith-life is too often, in otherwise educated circles, a forgotten possibility or marginalized as piety. People easily enquire: Are you Christian? Do you believe? There does not seem to be any comparable curiosity to prompt the question; do you have faith-life with Jesus Christ and the Holy Spirit?

Yet, for the Christian person, and of course for St Patrick in particular, faith-life and its nourishment must be the primary concern. Which theology, in the whole family of theologies, has served us best here? The truest answer is very possibly: Patristic theology and it is the theology of St Patrick's time.

7. Ibid., p. 13.

## 3. St Patrick as a Churchman in the Patristic era

There is of course much controversy about the life of Saint Patrick, for instance about the date, duration and detailed places of his missionary activity. Uncertainty in very many matters is inevitable because the tasks of scholarship are so formidable here, dealing as they are with writings of St Patrick himself and then with a gap of two hundred years before there are any written lives of him or other related records. Scholars are heavily involved in both textual criticism and historical criticism, i.e., in an analysis and comparison of diverse texts and in an investigation of sources (both of texts and traditions). Often uncertainty must be acknowledged and more than one competing conjecture be adjudged reasonably acceptable.

But concentrating on the direct evidence of St Patrick's own writing, what is put beyond doubt is the apostolic quality of his calling and the actuality of his stature as Apostle of Ireland. Further, considering the density of links that exist between his two pastoral letters and contemporary Patristic authors, there can be no doubt that these fifth century letters demand careful and detailed assessment as pastoral theology in the Patristic age. This is the subject matter of the next chapter.

*Chapter Four*

# The intellectual stature of St Patrick
## as apostle of faith-life

1. St Patrick's intellectual stature as pastoral theologian and Churchman

2. St Patrick's latinity

3. The pastoral relevance today of St Patrick's letters

# Chapter Four

# The intellectual stature of St Patrick
# as apostle of faith-life

## 1. St Patrick's intellectual stature as pastoral theologian and Churchman

The most important aspect of a balanced appraisal is taking into account how small in quantity are his writings and yet how relatively strong and positive is the evidence they provide. If one had to appraise a group of theologians on the basis, solely, of corresponding writings of theirs, there can be little doubt that St Patrick would not emerge unfavourably in any comparison. As we have seen, his *Confession of Grace* contains rich presentations of the economy of grace, of personal conversion, of merit, of mission and of faith-life as he experiences it. And his *Letter excommunicating Coroticus* is an authoritative document carefully written and structured in the curial style. The writer of these two pieces is manifestly a person of intellectual stature. He mediates deep insights into the nature of faith-life, of grace and its working within human limitations, of Christian authority and of a Christian responsibility which towers above class distinctions of any kind and takes under itself the uttermost parts of the earth. With the good sense of an honest witness, he communicates his own Christian love, feeling, grief and righteous indignation. Faced with the horrendous crime of Coroticus and his followers he writes his verdict of excommunication with judicial and decisive competence. And feeling hostility, coming from Britain, to his missionary work in Ireland, with all its unChristian implications of future isolation in store for his Irish flock, he can write an irenic pastoral on the theme of grace, with much self-revelation, in order to mediate better understanding and sympathy from senior clergy in Britain.

We find in his writing a process and form of theological thought which is typically Patristic, i.e. *reflexion within the presencing of God* in faith-life. Such reflexion is fully personal. It includes both discernment and responsiveness, both insight and affect, both light and warmth. It articulates itself both in doctrinal truths and in prayerful attitudes. Its idiom is predominantly that of Sacred Scripture which is quoted extensively and also echoed in it. All these qualities are present, to a remarkable degree, in St Patrick. Indeed, although his extant writings are no more than an open pastoral letter and a letter of excommunication, when one compares these texts with the Patristic literature of his time, one sees both how well versed he was in Patristic theology and how typical an exponent he was of it in content, style and method.

There can be no doubt that St Patrick's remarkable achievement as a Churchman lay in implanting, not only quickly and vigorously
but also interiorly, the *faith-life* in Ireland. The evidence is compelling.
The Irish Church took root strongly and flourished vigorously in numbers
and organization. Most remarkably, it developed monastically. Ludwig
Bieler remarks that, although Patrick did not organise the Church on
monastic lines (but in parishes and dioceses under priests and bishops,
respectively):

> [T]he growth of monasticism was counted by Patrick as one of the
> finest fruits of his missionary work . . . Twice in his writings he says,
> with almost the same words: "The sons of the Irish and the daughters
> of their kings are monks and brides of Christ".[1]

Such a rapid advance towards deep interior life and per-
manently intimate contact with God shows that Patrick implanted faith-
life as well as belief-faith, faith-life indeed with its natural priority. He
made the Irish people aware not simply of God but of Emmanuel (God-
with-us), not simply of Christ but of Christ-in-our-midst and with-us.

Monasticism in its primitive pre-Benedictine form, had
become familiar in the Western Christian world by the end of the fourth
century. A prominent fifth century form of spirituality was Augustinian
monasticism. Very possibly, St Patrick experienced the monastic environment of Gaul:

> [There] St Martin had founded Ligugé and then Marmoutier. The
> latter had developed with hitherto unprecedented speed. Cassianus
> had gathered round him a group of contemplative spirits in the abbey
> of St Victor, in Marseilles. At Saint-Claude, St Romanus and St
> Lupicinus were soon to found the abbey of Condat. But the most
> brilliant and most efficacious of these centres of Christian influence
> was *Lerins*. Founded towards the close of the fourth century by St
> Honoratus, a young Gallic patrician, inspired by the example of the
> Eastern monks, on the island which today bears his name, the Lerins
> community quickly attracted Christians by the hundred – perhaps by
> the thousand. Soon the uninhabited islands were filled with colonies
> of hermits and with the cells of the contemplatives – the "seekers of
> God" as St Hilary of Arles, one of them himself, described them.[2]

In chapters 40-43 of the *Confession of Grace*, St Patrick
expresses his wonder and joy at the conversion of the Irish people and at

1.  *Ireland: Harbinger of the Middle Ages*, p. 9.
2.  H. Daniel-Rops, *The Church in the Dark Ages*, p. 84.

the simultaneous espousal by many women and men of the virginal state. He certainly promoted the consecrated life among his converts. However, little is known of that life as transplanted by him. We tend to identify it with distinct buildings, a formal rule and community organisation. He never speaks in those terms. We may surmise that, for example, some monks functioned, individually as clergy, that some lived as hermits; we may surmise that, for example, some women ministered to the needs of the clergy in St Patrick's churches, that some lived at home. What alone is clear about the Patrician Church is that the spiritual ideal of a consecrated life, with celibacy as a component, was there for both women and men.

As Bieler points out (p. 26) it was in the following century that "the great wave of monastic foundations in Ireland" occurred. But this and other aspects of the development of the early medieval Irish Church bear the stamp of the completely Christian personality of the founder. It was no accident that in Irish missionary activity of the early middle ages there was a remarkable union of monastic and missionary understanding of the Gospel.

The whole-heartedness and single-mindedness of St Patrick are evidently a key aspect of his intellectual stature both as a person and as the apostle of Ireland. In his life the single principle of order was Christ. One might say that his integrity, like St Paul's, shone with this principle. And since beauty is the splendour of order, one might add that herein lies the magnetic intelligence of his person, his life and his writings.

Dr. R. P. C. Hanson gives a memorable description of this attraction, observing how "transparently honest" and "unexpectedly effective" his writing is, conveying not only his meaning but his feelings. He does not employ rhetoric; he had missed a higher education and so had missed his training in it. But "no rhetoric stands in the way" of opening his soul to the reader – "he does not write a line simply for effect"; nothing "tempts him to say what he does not mean". He is a man of flesh and blood whose piety "is not a piety nourished with miracles but rather fed on faith in God's love", grown from the intense religious experience of turning to God, as a slave, for help and receiving it. "But he is no mere pietist obsessed with his own religious experience. He knows that behind all God's mercies to him there lies His greater mercy to the whole human race". In piety warm, deep, living and never insincere, the authentic Patrick of the pastoral letters "is as far as possible from the menacing, ever-successful, omniscient, bloodless, superman of the later Lives".

Dr. Hanson concludes with what he conceives to be the secret of the attractiveness of the Apostle of Ireland – the fact that from the time of his slavery, he had never stopped seeing his real helplessness and realizing that he had found a helper and friend in God:

He could never quite lose this image of himself as utterly helpless, utterly defenceless, and abandoned. This is why we feel an inextinguishable sympathy with Patrick. He has managed to convey to us so movingly his own feeling about himself, not what he would like us to feel or to think, but what he really felt himself. But we never imagine that he is indulging in futile self-pity. Patrick does not pity himself, because, as he himself tells us, in his moment of helplessness and extreme need he found a helper and a friend in God. He could never forget his terrible experience as an impressionable boy, but neither could he forget that through this experience he had met "him who is powerful", who drew him out of the deep mud and set him on top of the wall.[3]

## 2. St Patrick's Latinity[4]

Specialists in Patristic theology have not yet turned their attention to the study of the theological content of St Patrick's writings. On the other hand his latinity has been carefully examined and found to be wanting in correspondence to traditional rules of cultivated language. Since, throughout the Roman Empire, Latin was at least the second language of higher culture, education and ecclesiastical life, there was a traditional term for this deficiency – rusticity (*rusticitas*). One might expect that these two facts together would have resulted in an adverse judgment on St Patrick as a writer. Yet all are agreed on the powerful impact he makes on the intelligence and feeling of the reader. It follows that no appraisal of him, intellectually, can be complete without examining this phenomenon.

The medium in which he wrote was Latin as spoken in everyday life, and this vulgar or colloquial Latin varied from region to region

3.  *Saint Patrick: His Origins and Career* (Clarendon Press, Oxford, 1968), pp. 208-209.
4.  Basic examinations of this subject are as follows: Ludwig Bieler, *Libri Epistolarum Sancti Patricii Episcopi* (Stationary Office, Dublin, 1952), Part II: Commentary ("aims at nothing more than a study of St Patrick's Latin against the background of his time and his models"); id., "The Place of St Patrick in Latin Language and Literature" in *Vigiliae Christianae* VI (1952), pp. 65-98; Christine Mohrmann, *The Latin of St Patrick: Four Lectures* (Institute for Advanced Studies, Dublin, 1961); ead., "The Earliest Irish Continental Latin", in *Vigiliae Christianae* XVI (1962), pp. 216-233. For the uninitiated it may be well to indicate that the study of Patrick's Latin is but a local area of a vast field with two aspects: late Latin in general, in its evolution towards the Romance languages, and the "special" Latin (*Sondersprache*) of early Christian writers. On the former one may mention (out of many) Einar Löfstedt, *Late Latin* (Oslo and Harvard University Press, 1959); on the latter the late Christine Mohrmann was the international expert, and the author of several volumes of *études sur le Latin des Chrétiens*.

in the Roman Empire: it would not have been the same in Britain as in Gaul. In the fifth century it was a Christian or Church Latin also. It was free of the standardizations which later developed into the Romance languages of different countries – French, Spanish, Portuguese and Italian. St Patrick used this colloquial medium to such effect that his writing is transparently personal and the reader is moved by the direct and felt impact of a totally sincere bearer of the Christian tradition. This literary excellence has been appreciated by scholars but it has puzzled them also because the poor academic quality of Patrick's Latin is evident to them, and the serious gaps in his Latin education are well known to them also.

His own perception of his limitations may guide us as we try to form a linguistic picture, however schematic, of that long period between his escape from captivity in his early twenties and his return as bishop in his forties or early fifties. He does not tell us of this period, possibly because it had not been a subject of attack from his critics. But it was a long period of years, including some years at home in Britain, an indefinite period of education for the priesthood (most probably in Gaul), and in Ireland possibly some missionary years as a deacon. Looking back, as he neared the end of his "laborious episcopate", and appraising his ability for the task of writing in Latin, he saw himself as disadvantaged in two ways:

> I was not a student as others were, who thus thoroughly drank in the law and the holy Scriptures, the two in equal measure, and never changed their language from childhood but rather were always engaged in perfecting it. Whereas I have had to change my language and speak that of a foreign people (*Conf.*, 9).

Thus, his first big limitation was that, through being taken captive and enslaved, he had never been educated in literary Latin. The middle stage of his education had been interrupted and he had completely missed his third level studies at the school of the *rhetor*. With this teacher he would have learnt the art of speaking and writing effectively and with rhetorical skill, studying literary texts and Roman law also. It was nothing less than realism on his part to feel the distance between himself and readers (especially critics) who would be qualified in literary Latin, have a knowledge of classical literature, and be skilled in rhetoric.

His second big limitation, as he perceived it, was that not only had he not been able to develop, continuously, in fluent spoken Latin and to move from it into a higher literary Latin, but he had not the benefit of continuous development from childhood in any particular spoken language. The background of spoken language in his life was varying and had been subject to big and sudden changes:

(i) In his native Britain there was British Celtic (of which Welsh is our direct descendent) and colloquial Latin. Because of the wealth and public position of Patrick's family, it is not absolutely clear how each would have entered into his daily life. Many scholars, such as Bieler, Jackson and Mohrmann, are convinced that Latin was not his first language.

(ii) Suddenly as a slave, of fifteen or sixteen years, he had to learn Old Irish, weakening whatever command of Latin he had acquired.

(iii) Later, for some years he studied for the priesthood in Gaul, most probably, and he had to learn the colloquial Latin there. He then encountered biblical and patristic Latin also.

(iv) Back in Ireland (including, possibly, a missionary period before he returned as bishop) his speech had to be in Old Irish again. His use and practice of Latin was confined to his prayer-life, to reading his Latin Bible, and to beginning a Latin liturgy for his new Christians who knew no Latin at all.

Always in his life there was some other language competing with Latin. Also, the conditions for learning and practising Latin itself were never, in their different ways, good. And so, as an elderly bishop, with many years of preaching and teaching in Old Irish behind him, he found the task of writing in Latin, for a reading public, daunting. Bieler makes his summary appraisal of St Patrick's Latin as follows:

> The Latin Patrick knew best was the language of his ecclesiastical surroundings. It was a society without literary ambitions. The lowest vulgarisms would be avoided under the influence of the Bible, and out of a sense of ecclesiastical dignity, but apart from strictly theological language one would without scruples commit oneself to a certain carelessness as regards word-forms, idiom, and the finer distinctions of grammatical categories. Certain spellings (*tegoriolum* C 18, *pos tergum* C 46, *zabulus* E 4) as well as grammatical peculiarities (sense constructions, avoidance of counting by deduction, vague use of conjunctions, absolute nominative in apposition, parataxis, syntactical contamination) and even the obscurity of allusions and the loose connection of ideas might reflect colloquial habits which Patrick acquired among those "brethren in Gaul".
>
> The influence of the spoken language would be counteracted not only by grammatical instruction, but even more so by reading. The nature of Patrick's stylistic imitation can be studied in his borrowings from the Bible. Patrick not only adapts his models freely to his needs, but also tends to use biblical phrases with a new meaning.[5]

5. "The Place of Saint Patrick in Latin Language and Literature", *Vigiliae Christianae* VI (1952), pp. 75-76.

Observing that his Latin is not bookish although he is frequently drawing from the Bible, Dr. Mohrmann writes:

It was only while preparing for his ordination, when he made the acquaintance of biblical Latin and at the same time got into contact with the living Latin of Gaul, that his language took the definite form we know from his writings: a very elementary colloquial Christian Latin interspersed with many biblical elements. In its structure this language is based on the living language of the fifth century and it is free from the standardization of early medieval Latin.[6]

How did St Patrick surmount his linguistic handicaps as he dictated, in Latin, his *Confession of Grace* and his *Letter excommunicating Coroticus*, to be read by the well-educated and, in the case of the excommunication, to be also proclaimed aloud?

A proper answer must surely focus, primarily, on the fact that these pieces of writing, so well thought out in structure and detail, expressed aspects and segments of his apostolic life. Accordingly, he was drawing on the Christian language of his faith-life both for what he wrote and for the way he wrote it. Words, images, idioms and inspiration were forthcoming as models from Sacred Scripture especially, and from Patristic texts, the teaching Church and the liturgy. Bieler observes (with perhaps too much emphasis on St Patrick having to labour in his writing and not enough weight given to how much the habitual in his life helped him to be fluently expressive):

Conscious of his shortcomings, he is anxiously looking for models; what comes most readily to his mind is the Scriptures and – within a limited range – the Fathers of the Church. He builds up his text like a mosaic from reminiscences of his reading, pressing phrases and idioms into a service for which they were not always intended. Hardly ever does he make an attempt at periodizing; and when he tries, he fails. If in spite of all this his language has a strange appeal, the reason is that behind the words we feel a great personality.[7]

What has been said so far about Patrick's latinity has been in the nature of generalised statements and overall judgements. and they add up, more or less, to an acceptance, with due *apologia*, of Patrick's own estimate and our own first impression of his *rusticitas*. But of course such self-deprecatory qualifications of their own stylistic capacity were a

6. "The Earliest Continental Irish Latin", *Vigiliae Christianae* XVI (1962), p. 218.
7. *The Life and Legend of St Patrick: Problems of Modern Scholarship* (Clonmore & Reynolds, Dublin, 1949), p. 56.

commonplace of early Christian writers. It will not be surprising therefore if when we look at some details of Patrick's style we can to some degree qualify the qualifications. His prose is not entirely without art. And where there is syntactical obscurity it is not necessarily to be explained in every case by a weak control of the language.

To take the point about syntax first, the example of St Paul comes to mind. Paul was hardly a *rusticus* in Greek, yet the difficulty of his syntactical joinery is well known, in, for example 2 Corinthians. Now it is significant for an understanding of St Patrick that St Paul was of central importance to him, both as a model of the ideal missionary Apostle and as a source of the ideas and the language in which to express that ideal. The stylistic relevance of that connection between Paul and Patrick is not that the latter learned his syntax from the former. The point is rather that the broken arches of the syntax have the same explanation in both men. And that explanation lies in their dynamic burning temperaments. Christine Mohrmann writes at one point: "There is, obviously, a sort of tension between what Patrick, a dynamic man with rhetorical talents, wishes to say and what he is able to say".[8] That comes close to the point, but does not quite touch it. The real point is that in those two dynamic and fiery temperaments thought and feeling are racing ahead of expression, so that inevitably the syntax finishes up "out of sync" with the intended meaning. We get good illustrations of this in the occasional passages where Patrick is clearly attempting a more conscious eloquence and a more elaborate structure, e.g. *Conf.* 34, 41.

This explanation of Patrick's syntax is all the more intelligible when we remember that Patrick (like St Paul) probably dictated his story, orally and spontaneously, that is, without much literary premeditation. This results in the oral style briefly discussed by Christine Mohrmann.[9] Its characteristics are those of a man thinking aloud . . ., sometimes hesitating, and therefore at times unclear in his *syntax* – but for all that clear enough in the sequence of his *thought*. And there are few passages in Patrick that are not clear enough when read that way. We are reinforced in this way of reading the *Confessio* when we examine the *Letter excommunicating Coroticus*. There we see that Patrick was capable of composing in a much tighter and more ordered syntax – when required by such a formal, even juridical, document.

But we have not said everything when we have suggested those explanations of Patrick's apparent *rusticitas*. There are more positive things to be said about his latinity. When we look closely at his style we notice many details which are too frequent to be accidental, and must therefore be interpreted as validating what we said earlier – that Patrick's

8.  *The Latin of St Patrick*, p. 33.
9.  Ibid., p. 12ff.

prose is not without positive elements of deliberate art. Those are elements which in their ultimate origin are from the stylistics of the classical world, but were put to new use, and often more effective use, in the new context of the new "rhetoric" required by the new subject-matter of early Christian writing and homiletics.[10]

Here we can do little more than list some of those features, with only a minimum of analysis and illustration – enough to indicate Patrick's acquaintance with them, and the consequent necessity of considerably qualifying his designation as a *rusticissimus*.

We might first mention a more global or inclusive feature of his style, his tendency to paratactic sentence structure. It is usual to explain this as due either to the influence of the Bible or to the naïveté of the unsophisticated narrator who has only an unsophisticated common language. But when we notice other features contained within this structure it becomes less easy to attribute it to either the Bible or literary naïveté. For those other features are not all of them biblical, and certainly not naïve. I refer to *parallelism* and *balanced length* of clauses within the paratactic structure. Add to that the further balance of frequent antithesis of clauses, the force and emphasis achieved by such artistic devices as the carrying on of a word from clause to clause (*anaphora*) or the rhythmical elaboration of an idea by synonyms. Add further the linking symmetries of alliteration, assonance, and similarity of sound at the end of clauses (*homoioteleutaion*).[11]

See, for example. *Conf.* 13: ammir*amini . . . magni . . .* et domin*icati* re*thorici . . .* scrut*amini*; *Conf.* 16: et fides *augebatur* et spiritus *agebatur*; *Conf.* 54: honor qui nondum *videtur* sed *corde creditur*: *Conf.* 55: melius convenit *paupertas* et *calamitas* quam *divitiae* et *diliciae*; *Conf.* 37: ut *darem* ingenui*tatem* meam pro utili*tate* aliorum (cf. *Letter*, 10); *Letter*, 15: qua*propter, ecclesia pl*orat et *pl*angit *filios* et *filias* suas quas adhuc *gl*adius nondum interfecit, sed *prolongati* et ex*portati . . .* ibi ve*nundati . . .* Add finally Patrick's vivid art of suddenly stepping out of such subtleties into a classical, clinching, summary statement (*sententia*, e.g. *Conf.* 5, 23, 26, 46, 47; *Letter*, 3, 16, 20), or into the punches of a passionate sequence of vivid conjunctionless statements of brute fact (*asyndeton*, e.g. *Letter*, 13), or into the poignant spiritual intensity of direct address in apostrophe (e.g. *Conf.* 48, 51, 53; *Letter*, 16, 17, 18).

To point to those elements of art in Patrick's prose is not to deny the general truth that his Latin is the "vulgar" Latin of late antiquity,

---

10. Cf. e.g. A. N. Wilder, *Early Christian Rhetoric: The Language of the Gospel* (SCM Press, London, 1964).
11. Bieler considers those stylistic elements only briefly (*The Place of St Patrick . . .*, pp. 94-5), and not very positively; Patrick employs them ". . . naïvely to be sure, but not without effect".

"the living language of the fifth century", as Christine Mohrmann has said. And yet the *paradox* is that (as Bieler has expressed it) in spite of all this his language "has a strong appeal . . .". And he goes on to give the reason – "the reason is that behind the words we feel a great personality". That reason is true, but it is not the whole of the reason. Behind – or rather through – the words, and through the great personality, we feel the grandeur of a great theme. The theme of a man's "confession" before his God, the theme of a life's great call from lowly origins to a great mission, and the retrospective realisation of its great fulfilment. "I cannot stay silent . . . What shall I give back to the Lord for all he has given to me?". The paradox to which I have referred consists in the fact that Patrick's style, despite his own *rusticitas* and the *vulgare* of his Latin, becomes an adequate medium for the grandeur of his theme, rises to the height of his great argument.

It would take us too long here to deal *in extenso* with this paradox. But it is so central to Christian Latin stylistics, and Patrick is such a striking – and so unnoticed – illustration of it that even a brief survey of his latinity should not end without pointing to that overall aspect of Patrick's stylistic achievement. The more detailed analysis of the stylistic principles involved, and their far-reaching implications, may be read in the seminal chapter on *Sermo Humilis* by Erich Auerbach, in his volume on *Literary Language and its Public in Late Latin Antiquity and the Middle Ages*.[12] He does not refer to St Patrick but St Patrick's writings provide prime material to illustrate the new Christian stylistic principles which Auerbach's analysis elucidates. (The elucidation will be given greater depth by reading the first two chapters of his *Mimesis*[13] for the excerpts in which he compares and contrasts the stylistic principles of the Old and New Testaments with those of classical Greek and Roman literature).

Those new Christian principles turned a central principle of Greco-Roman stylistics upside down. The classical exposition of why and how they did so is contained in St Augustine's treatise on style in Book Four of his *De Doctrina Christiana*. The problem of style comes into that work as an aspect of the general problem with which that work deals – how the Christian should evaluate and what use he should make of the rich culture and educational ideals of Greece and Rome. On style the sum of St Augustine's answer is that all the good tunes should not be left to the Devil – least of all by a "new people" whose very mission was "communication", to "go and teach all nations . . .". And of good tunes in the art and craft of language Greco-Roman civilization had a repertory developed over a thousand years.

12. (Routledge & Kegan Paul, London, 1965).
13. *Mimesis: The Representation of Reality in Western Literature* (Princeton University Press, Princeton, 1974).

At the heart of Greco-Roman stylistic theory was a triple classification of literary "matter" into the lowly or ordinary, the intermediate, and the high or grand. From the stylistic principle of decorum, according to which the "form" should be fitted to the "matter", there followed the consequence of a triple classification of style also into the lowly or plain (*humilis*), the intermediate, and the high or grand. St Augustine sums it up in a sentence from Cicero. "He, therefore, will be eloquent who can speak of small subjects simply, of intermediate subjects restrainedly, of great subjects grandly" (*De Doct. Chr.*, IV 17,34).

The very nature and implications of Christianity, and the very style of its Scriptures, overturned this principle. The Incarnation was a *kenosis*, an emptying of the very Godhead into the figure of the lowly and ordinary. Conversely that figure contained, veiled, the sublime mystery of divinity. And not only that, *everything* ordinary was now seen to be weighty with consequences for eternity. *Everything* is now a "great" thing. "Unless, perhaps, because a cup of cold water is a small and most insignificant thing, we should also regard as small and most insignificant the promise of the Lord that he who gives such a cup to one of His disciples 'shall not lose his reward'" (*De Doct. Chr.*, IV 18,37).

Does this mean then that the Christian must always write in the grand style? Not at all. For decorum here too is to fit form to matter. And so, just as the matter of Christianity can reveal – and conceal – the sublime in the lowly, so can, and should, the form of its expression. For the true feature of the grand style is "not so much that it is adorned with verbal ornaments as that it is charged with emotions of the spirit . . . It is enough for the matter being discussed that the appropriateness of the words be determined by the ardour of the heart rather than by care in the choosing of words" (*De Doct. Chr.*, IV 20,42). And for this principle Augustine had the example of Scripture itself – "a book that all could read, and read easily, and yet preserved the majesty of its mystery in the deepest parts of its meaning: for it offers itself to all in the plainest words and the simplest expressions, yet demands the closest attention of the most serious minds" (*Confessions* VI 5,8).

It is otiose to say anything more about Patrick's stylistic *rusticitas*. And yet if there is one quality that it expresses it is his sense of the grandeur of his call and his mission, expressed not by "verbal ornaments" but by that Augustinian "charge" of those "emotions of the spirit" and that "ardour of the heart". Let us quote just one sample, a sample in which, had the passage not become a cliché, we would feel, as in the Gospels, the most ordinary events and the simplest words charged with the power of the numinous. The passage is from chapter 23 of the *Confessio*, which recounts the "vision of the night" in which "a man coming as it were from Ireland" gives Patrick a letter.

> ... And I read the beginning of the letter, which ran: 'The Voice of the Irish'; and as I was reading the beginning of the letter aloud I thought I heard at that very moment the voice of those who lived beside the wood of Voclut, which is near the Western sea, and thus they cried out as with one voice: 'We beg you, holy youth, to come and walk once more among us'. And I was greatly troubled in heart and could read no further ...

Beside that description the vision that invited St Paul to Macedonia lacks both the charge of the numinous and the concrete circumstantiality of the "minute particulars" (Ac 16:9-10).

There is one last feature of Patrick's literary capacity that should be noted. However we estimate his qualities they inhere not just in the details of his style but also in his sense of structure in the composition of his story. Sparse though his *Confessio* be in autobiographical facts it moves through well-marked stages, from birth and youth to "before I die". And those last words are beautifully prepared for in a cadenza, a dying fall, that begins in chapter 56: "Behold then, I now commend my soul to my most faithful God . . .". A cadenza that also gives the work a cyclical structure by returning to the theme that compelled the writing of this *Confessio* from the beginning: "Let me make return to the Lord then for all His bounty to me" (*Conf.* 57; cf.3).

And finally a coda in two short chapters. "Here then, one more time, let me briefly set down the theme of my confession . . . And that is my confession before I die" (*Conf.* 61-62).

The author of that conclusion had the sense of an ending – even if he did not know it, and thought he was a *rusticus*.

### 3. The pastoral relevance today of St Patrick's letters

Many inspirational benefits are associated with St Patrick's pastoral letters but their crucial relevance today lies
(i) in their communication of faith as *life with Christ*;
(ii) in their proclamation of the *absolute value to Christ* of every single human being everywhere; and
(iii) in the way in which, while being supremely active and practical, St Patrick always kept in sight, like an horizon, that his pastoral objective was transforming minds and hearts.

In these three aspects the Western world has become seriously flawed as a witness to Christian life.

Firstly, it is so abstract in its general pursuit of knowledge that while it cannot be said not to "know" Christianity, neither can it be said to have much "sense" of the presencing of Christ among us. The ancient Greeks differentiated two kinds of knowledge: *techné* and *phronésis*. The *technai* are the whole range of subjects which one can expect to find in a centre of universal learning, a university. Each subject is the kind of explanatory knowledge that can be formulated and learnt; it is justified by being grounded in principles; it provides methods for various forms of expert making, ordering or organisation. One can acquire *technai*, possess them as expertise, apply them and explain with them. And we can determine how and where they will be applied; Aristotle indeed described them as "powers of opposites": even the *techné*, medicine, can be used at will to bring about not only life but death. Today there are many critics of our Western ethos as one in which almost complete ascendancy is given to the value of technical knowledge, and in which there is forgetfulness of the kind of knowledge necessary in concrete life for individual development in intellectual excellence, personal judgment, personal responsibility.

Aristotle used the word, *phronésis*, for this kind of knowledge, a living wisdom. In its reality it is as much a power (virtue) for good as an ability to experience a concrete situation with insight as to what is the wise and valuable thing to do, the good decision to take and implement. The *phronimos* (our word, *prudent* person, falls very short of the Greek term in meaning) is committed to pursuits of real value and, as a person with responsible autonomy, to not becoming blind to the challenges of excellence. The striving of such a person gradually develops a *phronetic* quality, i.e., it developes as an activity of experiencing with perceptiveness, with human affectivity and with true discernment. Such mental resourcefulness of the person in concrete life integrates his or her whole history, dispositions, attitudes. It cannot be reduced to methods or universal knowledge provided antecedently by *technai*. It is completely bound up with the kind of person one is.

In our day, knowledge is largely identified with *techné*. The ancient Greek differentiation is almost lost. The knowledge people seek as indispensable is learnable expertise; the education in schools is technical, not at all finalised towards personal excellence in judgment. Are even universities more than universal resource centres for *techné* in all its forms? Education has little to do with *phronésis*, personal wisdom, light for concrete life. Public debate is concerned with, for example, Christianity as a body of formulated doctrine, a "technical" reality (in the eyes of some: another ideology), not as a particular personal, moral, phronetic way of life: faith-life with the Messiah.

It is not surprising that as a witness to Christian life, the Western world gives testimony that is flawed by, among other things, this mistaken identity. Doctrine indeed may be importantly true, protecting faith-life or defending it, historically, against some exercise of intellectual power endangering it. A belief too may be an unconditional certitude, a strong personal interfacing with conventional society. But the *presence* of Christ cannot be *there*, in either doctrine or belief, but in the persons themselves, and faith at its foundations is nothing less than the life of a person with Christ. Such a life is not just a pious or devotional structure on the foundation of faith: it is faith-life itself.

The second aspect of the Western world challenging pastoral attention is that, while not at all lacking in theoretical formulation of individual rights and of structures of injustice, it tolerates actual widespread inhumanity in forms of de-humanizing oppressions, degrading addictions and destructive mismanagement of our human environment. It is a world that needs to re-establish itself in elementary truth and in natural human goodness.

St Patrick's pastorals present the Christian vision of individual worth. As a slave St Patrick discovered and never forgot that he was a "thou" to God. He understood then and responded then to the Good News of faith-life with God incarnate; and he did so in the profound, responsible and unswerving way that is the essence of a saint. He preached this as the supreme truth to be delivered to all peoples and every individual – the timeless essence of every Christian apostolate.

Within faith-life both the central importance and responsibility of the individual are secure. As an aspect of *sensus fidelium*, the Church today is seeing that the defence and development in responsibility of the individual is the supreme pastoral work. And here its courage and wisdom and solidarity are being put to the test. Everywhere, every hour, Christian feeling and Christian conscience is being challenged to defend fellow humans of all ages who are being killed, left destitute and uneducated, or exploited. Christians are being pressurized, in educated circles, to reason themselves into discriminating against some individuals on the basis of the rights of others who are sometimes specially privileged by human law itself. The "folly of the Cross" – that each and every individual *needs to be* and can be redeemed and saved as the unique person they are; that there is no one who is not of absolute value to Christ; that Christ seeks to and can transform all, even those who, like Coroticus, kill and exploit and whose misdeeds cry for vengeance to the Father of all – all this is being dismissed and forgotten as a utopian absolute.

The final aspect of St Patrick's writings for consideration is the way they witness to profound Christian truth in their theology of grace and of divine love. They must seem strange to modern eyes as pastorals where they devote room in a credal statement to affirming: God can make us obedient to His love in and by the grace of His presencing. But for St Patrick evangelization was, in its reality, God-with-us, transforming minds and hearts by the grace and love which constitute His presencing to us. Supremely active for Christ, St Patrick nevertheless saw spiritual development as a growing from within, mind and heart being the medium of faith-life with Christ whose God-filled humanity is "for us and for our salvation". Thus the encounter of divine love with human nature and with human freedom is an all-important aspect of his pastoral vision. Of course the vision developed through the quality of his own *evangelization*, of his fidelity to the *magisterial teaching* of the Church, and through his accept-ance of the mind of St Augustine as the truest leader in the *theological debating* of his time. But the outcome was a pastoral vision that was sim-ple, direct and personal in quality and yet brought to his labours the horizon of deep spiritual truth.

In modern secular times pastoral communication has its own particular difficulties, emphases and possibilities. However, the special spiritual quality of St Patrick's vision and work is something we must respect and learn from. The history of evangelization has of course its con-tinuity of essence. St Patrick himself was Pauline and Patristic. The medievals were uniquely comprehensive, conceptually. Some of the greatest modern and contemporary minds have a spiritual kinship with St Patrick. The call, "back to the Fathers" was of supreme significance in the life of John Henry Newman and reminds us that the *Confession of Grace* and the *Letter excommunicating Coroticus* are the contribution of Ireland to Patristic literature, and the sole contribution from all these islands until that of Gildas a century later, unless we include a series of Pseudo-Pelagian (British) treatises and letters purportedly written in early fifth-century Britain and Sicily.[14]

The fullest and clearest contemporary expression of continuity with the spirit of St Augustine (accepted and echoed in St Patrick) is that of the great Patristic theologians, Henri de Lubac and Hans Urs von Balthasar. Their context like Augustine's is that of human nature in its ultimate well-being: are we characterised by a natural desire for God in the metaphysical sense of a capacity, in some form, for union with God? St Augustine had communicated the Christian response in simple human terms: "you have made us for yourself, O Lord, and our heart knows no rest until it finds rest in you". To the Christian mind it is clear that, per-sonal being as well as bodily being that we are, we are uniquely compatible with a life of union with God. And indeed this is our actual destiny. It is equally clear that we have no permanent natural disposition or capacity which we can exercise to achieve union with God. Medieval theologians coined the term "obediential capacity" (*potentia obedientialis*) indicating that our capacity is precisely a capacity for obedience to grace: we become actually capable of union with God and of Beatific Vision only when we are given the grace to become so and respond obedientially to that grace.

14. Cf. E. Dekkers, *Clavis Patrum Latinorum* (Steenbrugge 2, 1961) 730, 731-6, 763.

Hans Urs von Balthasar used the idiom, obediential capacity, with an increased extension and explanatory power. Ultimately what is true of a *free* creature is a mysterious personal openness. But the capacity to respond to a call for union with God must come with that call: the grace must be a grace to listen and hear and then to respond. Thus obediential capacity becomes now a composite term combining in its total meaning a reference to a mysterious openness in us along with a reference to the power of divine love. In developing the medieval idiom in this way, von Balthasar re-expressed St Augustine's view that in the most profound context of the dynamism of the human person, i.e., when God presences Himself in grace, divine love has the power of making us obedient. (To quote from the credal statement in St Patrick's *Confession of Grace* (4) "he *makes* believers and listeners *in order that* they shall be sons of God and fellow heirs with Christ"; earlier, in c.2, he had said: "The Lord opened my unbelieving mind".) Von Balthasar puts it:

> We can . . . speak of *obediential potency*, but we must remain conscious that the transnatural potency to which we refer in the word *potentia* is absolutely not the creature's own potency (if so, the potency would be a form of natural potency), but rather a potency belonging solely to the Creator. The power of God is so great that his creature will obey him even when it finds in its own being neither the disposition, nor the tendency, nor the possibility of such obedience.[15]

We cannot but admire the fact that this, one of the deepest points in Christian spiritual exploration over centuries, finds an echo in the pastoral letters of St Patrick. However, it is not really so surprising. We know that the fruit of his labours was remarkably spiritual in character:

> Consequently, then, in Ireland, they who never had knowledge of God, but up till now always worshipped only idols and abominations – how they have lately been made a people of the Lord and are called children of God; sons of the Scotti and daughters of chieftains are monks and virgins of Christ! (*Conf.* 41).

Further, his pastoral vision was uniquely powerful in its awareness of the grace of God. Like St Paul, he came to Ireland in his own weakness, without plausible words of wisdom, but with the power of God, with pastoral principles nourished from his faith-life:

15. *Mysterium Salutis* V, "L'Accès à Dieu" (French ed.), p. 48.

And now, to all who believe and hold God in reverence, should one of them condescend to inspect and accept this writing put together in Ireland by Patrick, a mere unlettered sinner, this is my prayer: that if I have accomplished or brought to light any small part of God's purpose, none shall ever assert that the credit is due to my own uneducated self, but regard it rather as a true fact to be firmly believed that it was all the gift of God. And that is my confession before I die (*Conf.*, 62).

# Selected Bibliography

A  The Writings of St Patrick

B  The Biblical and Theological Dimension of the Two Pastoral Letters

C  The Fathers and St Patrick

D  The Life and Chronology of St Patrick

# Selected Bibliography

## A  The Writings of St Patrick

BIELER, L. (ed), *Libri Epistolarum Sancti Patricii Episcopi:* Part I — Introduction and Text; Part II: Commentary (Dublin: 1952). A critical edition of the latin text of St Patrick's *Confession* and *Letter*.
—— *The Works of St Patrick. St Secundinus: Hymn on St Patrick.* (Maryland and London: 1953) (Ancient Christian Writers, Vol. XVII). English translation with notes.
—— "The Place of St Patrick in Latin Language and Literature": *Vigiliae Christianae*, Vol. VI, 1952.
GROSJEAN, P., "Notes D'Hagiographie Celtique": *Analecta Bollandiana*, 61 (1943); and 63 (1945).
HANSON, R. P. C., *Saint Patrick: His Origins and Career* (Oxford: 1968).
—— and BLANC, C., *Saint Patrick: Confession et Lettre à Coroticus* (Paris: 1978).
—— *The Life and Writings of the Historical Saint Patrick* (New York: 1983).
MALASPINA, E., *Gli Scritti di San Patrizio*, Coll. cultura christ.ant. (Roma: 1985).
MOHRMANN, C., *The Latin of Saint Patrick* (Dublin: 1961).
MacPHILBIN, L., *Mise Pádraig* (Baile Átha Cliath: F.Á.S.: 1960). A translation into Irish of the *Confession* and *Letter*.
WHITE, N. J. D., *Libri Sancti Patricii: The Latin Writings of St Patrick.* Reprinted from the Proceedings of the Royal Irish Academy, 25C (1904-5) (Dublin: 1905).

## B  The Biblical and Theological Dimension of the Two Pastoral Letters

BIELER, L., "Der Bibeltext des Heiligen Patrick", *Biblica* 28 (1947), pp. 31-58; 236-263.
BROWN, R. E., FITZMEYER, J. A., MURPHY, R. E. (eds), *The New Jerome Biblical Commentary* (London: 1990). There are extensive bibliographies to the relevant sections and topics.
DEVINE, K., *A computer-generated Concordance to the Libri Epistolarum of Saint Patrick* (Dublin: 1989).
DRONKE, P., "St Patrick's Reading", *Cambridge Medieval Celtic Studies* 1 (1981), pp. 31-38.
HANSON, R. P. C., "Witness from St Patrick to the Creed of 381", *A.B.*, 101 (1983), pp. 297-299.

—— "The Mission of St Patrick", *An Introduction to Celtic Christianity* (Edinburgh: 1989), pp. 22-44.

HITCHCOCK, F. R. M., "The *Confessio* and *Epistola* of Patrick of Ireland and their Literary Affinities in Irenaeus, Cyprian and Orientius", *Hermathena* no. 47 (1932), pp. 202-38.

HERREN, M., "Mission and Monasticism in the 'Confessio' of Patrick" in *Sages, Saints and Storytellers. Celtic Studies in Honour of Professor James Carney.* Donnchadh Ó Corráin et al. eds. (Maynooth: 1989), pp. 76-85.

*Holy Bible*, The. R.S.V. Catholic Edition.

HOWLETT, D., "Ex Saliva Scripturae Meae", in *Sages, Saints and Storeytellers* (supra), pp. 86-101.

KITTEL, R. (ed.), *Biblia Hebraica*, 15th edition (Stuttgart: 1969).

LÖFSTEDT, E., *Late Latin* (London: 1959).

MARSH, T., "St Patrick's Terminology for Confirmation" in *Irish Ecclesiastical Record* (March 1960), pp. 145-154.

MERK, A., *Novum Testamentum graece et latine*. 9th edition (Rome: 1964).

NERNEY, D. S., "A Study of St Patrick's Sources", *Irish Ecclesiastical Record,* 5th ser. 71 (1949), pp. 497-505 and 72 (1950), pp. 14-26, 97-110, and 265-280.

*Nova Vulgata bibliorum sacrorum editio* (Vatican City: 1979).

O'DONOGHUE, N. D., "The Spirituality of St Patrick", *Studies* 50 (Summer 1961), pp. 152-164.

—— *Aristocracy of Soul. Patrick of Ireland* (London: 1987).

Ó RAIFEARTAIGH, T., "The Enigma of St Patrick", *Seanchas Ard Mhacha* 13, No. 2 (1989) pp. 1-60.

—— " 'Silva Focluti, Quae est Prope Mare Occidentale'. (Saint Patrick's Confession, 23). A New Approach", *The Maynooth Review* 4, No. 1 (1978), pp. 25-27.

OULTON, J. E. L., *The Credal Statements of St Patrick as Contained in the Fourth Chapter of his* Confession: *A Study of their Sources* (Dublin and London: 1940).

RAHLFS, A., *Septuaginta.* 8th edition, 2 vols (Stuttgart: 1965).

RATZINGER, J., "Originalität und Ueberlieferung in Augustins Begriff der 'Confessio' ", *Revue des études augustiniennes* 3 (1957), pp. 375-392.

VOEGELIN, E., *Order and History.* Vol. 1: *Israel and Revelation* (Baton Rouge: 1957).

WEBER, R. (ed.), *Biblia sacra iuxta vulgatam versionem.* 2 vols. (Stuttgart: 1969).

## C. The Fathers and St Patrick

### *(a) Texts of the Latin Fathers*

DE LUBAC, H., DANIELOU, J. (eds.), *Sources chrétiennes* (Paris: 1942 ff.).
MIGNE, J. P., *Patrologia cursus completus*, Series latina (Paris 1844-), 1-221.
—— *Corpus Christianorum* (Turnhout, 1953- ).

### *(b) Collections offering English translations*

DAVIES, O. (ed.), *The Spirituality of the Fathers* (London, Dublin, Edinburgh: 1991 ff.).
QUASTEN, J., PLUMPE, J. (eds.), *Ancient Christian Writers* (Westminster: 1946 ff.).
SCHAFF, P., WACE, H. (eds.), *A Select Library of Nicene and Post-Nicene Fathers of the Christian Church* (New York: 1886-1900). Reprinted by Wm. Eerdmans, Grand Rapids, Michigan.

### *(c) One volume anthologies*

BETTENSON, H. (ed.), *The Early Christian Fathers* (London: 1978).
—— *The Later Christian Fathers* (London: 1977).
HOARE, F. H. (ed.), *The Western Fathers* (London: 1980).

### *(d) Standard English manuals*

DI BERARDINO, A., QUASTEN, J. (eds.), *Patrology*, Vol. 4 (Westminster: 1986).
QUASTEN, J. (ed.). Patrology, 3 vols. (Utrecht-Antwerp: 1983).

### *(e) Histories of the Church*

DANIELOU, J., MARROU, H. I., *The Christian Centuries*, Vol. 1 (London: 1984).
FREND, W. H. C., *The Rise of Christianity* (London: 1984).

## D. The Life and Chronology of St Patrick

BIELER, L., *The Life and Legend of Saint Patrick* (Dublin: 1949).
—— *St Patrick and the Coming of Christianity* (Dublin: 1967).

BINCHY, D. A., "Patrick and His Biographers, Ancient and Modern", *Studia Hibernica* (1962), pp. 7-173.

BURY, J. B., *The Life of St Patrick and His Place in History* (London: 1905).

BYRNE, F., *Irish Kings and High Kings* (London: 1973).

CARNEY, J., *Studies in Irish Literature and History* (Dublin: 1955).

DUFFY, J., *Patrick in his own Words* (Dublin: 1975).

MacNEILL, E., *St Patrick Apostle of Ireland* (London: 1935).

O'RAHILLY, T. F., *The Two Patricks* (Dublin: 1942).

RYAN, J. (ed), *Saint Patrick*. Radio talks (Dublin: 1958).

SHAW, F., "Post-Mortem on the Second Patrick", *Studies* 51 (1963), pp. 237-67.

# Appendices

I.   The actual writings of Fr Conneely concerning St. Patrick

II.  Fr Conneely's notebooks

III. Various other Patristic authors cited in the notebooks to whom a special place is not assigned in the Indices

# Appendices

## I. The actual writings of Fr Conneely concerning St Patrick

They are as follows:
1. Seventy-three notebooks
2. A typescript of his final translation of the *Confession*.
3. A typescript of his final translation of the *Letter*.
4. Miscellaneous jottings on loose leaves concerning Patristic texts.
5. Hand-written material in which he formulated some of his conclusions and textual interpretations.
6. Letters of Fr Conneely in which he set out his general framework and general conclusions. (Relevant excerpts).
7. *Far East* (1961): March issue in the Patrician Year, edited by Fr Conneely.

## II. Fr Connelly's notebooks

There are seventy-three notebooks in all. They are divided into three categories:
(1) Notebooks dealing directly with Patristic authors (1-41);
(2) Notebooks dealing with various topics to which Patristic authors contribute (42-53);
(3) Notebooks dealing directly with Saint Patrick (54-73).

| Note-book: No. | Category: Patristic Authors | Specific Titles |
|---|---|---|
| 1 | Ambrose | |
| 2 | Augustine | A: *Propositiones ex Ep. ad Romanos* (1) |
| 3 | | B: *Propositiones ex Ep. ad Romanos* (2) |
| 4 | | *Magni et Pusilii* (cf *Contra Julianum* at back) |
| 5 | | *Contra Julianum:* A: Books I, II, III, IV, V, VI |
| 6 | | *Contra Julianum:* B: Books III, V. IV, II, VI, II |
| 7 | | *Contra Julianum:* C: Books III, IV, V, VI |
| 8 | | *De Praedestinatione Sanctorum* |
| 9 | | *Exposito Ep. ad Galatas* |

| No. | Patristic Authors | Specific Titles |
|---|---|---|
| 10 | | *Epistola ad Sixtum* |
| 11 | | On Grace |
| 12 | | *Credentes, Obedientes* |
| 13 | Cassian | |
| 14 | Cyprian | *Testimonia* |
| 15 | Cyprian (2) | |
| 16 | Eusebius of Vercelli | *De Trinitate* (cf also of Gregory of Elvira, Ambrose and Novatian) |
| 17 | Hilary of Poitiers | *De Trin.* I, II, III. Also Penance, Repentence, Confession |
| 18 | | P.C.4. Also Phil. 2:6-10. |
| 19 | | The Son. Born when? |
| 20 | | *De Trin.* II, III, VI. |
| 21 | | *Clarificatio Filii. De Trin.,* I, III |
| 22 | | *De Trinitate* III. Important for C.4. |
| 23 | | *Libri De Trinitate:* Analyses I, II, III |
| 24 | | *De Trin., IV.* Important for C.4. |
| 25 | | *De Trin:* The Holy Spirit |
| 26 | | *Dedit illi omnem potestatem* |
| 27 | | *Omnia tenentem* |
| 28 | | *De Trinitate* IV, VII, VIII. (cf also Phoebadius) |
| 29 | | Trinity: IX, X, XI, XII |
| 30 | | Christ in Two Natures: *De Trin.,* IX, III |
| 31 | | Main argument of *De Trinitate* I and P.C.4 |
| 32 | | *Spiritaliter, Duo dii.* |
| 33 | | *De Trin.:* The Father: 1) source of all things; 2) Himself Unoriginate. Also Nicetas of Remesiana |
| 34 | | *Tractatus super Psalmos* I. cf also Ambrose, Nicetas of Remesiana |
| 35 | | *Tractatus super Psalmos* II |
| 36 | | "A" Notebook. cf also Basil, Ambrose, Cassian, Rufinus, Chromatius |
| 37 | | Varia. cf also Chromatius, Augustine, Jerome |
| 38 | Jerome | |
| 39 | Maximus of Turin, Hilary of Arles, Paulinus of Nola. | |
| 40 | Pelagius | |
| 41 | Prosper | |

| No. | Various Topics | Patristic Authors |
|-----|----------------|-------------------|
| 42 | *Caritas* | cf Patrick, Augustine, Prosper |
| 43 | *Conversio* | cf Augustine, Prosper |
| 44 | Divinity of Christ | cf Ambrose, Origen, Palladius, Jerome, Pelagius, Augustine, Gregory Naz., Peter Chrys., Basil, Victorinus of Pettau |
| 45 | *Omnitenens* | cf Prosper, Gregory Illib., Augustine, Origen, Ambrosiaster, Irenaeus, Novatian, Theophilus of Antioch, Eusebius of Vercelli |
| 46 | *Pater sine Principio* | cf Hilary, Arius, Arnobius, Phoebadius, Gregory Illiberitanus |
| 47 | *Principium* | cf Augustine, Prosper |
| 48 | *Fidem servare; piscatores; convertimini.* | cf Hilary, Ambrose, Jerome, Cyprian, Pacian, Councils |
| 49 | *Commemoratio delictorum* | cf Ambrose, Jerome, Cassian, Origen, Sulpicius Severus, Pelagius, Paulinus of Nola |
| 50 | *Qui reddet unicuique (1)* | cf Pelagius, Pseudo-Augustine, Augustine, |
| 51 | *Qui reddet unicuique (2)* | Prosper, Jerome, Cassian |
| 52 | *Corripere, castigare, emendare;* | Daniel and the three youths. cf Biblical references, Cyprian, Jerome, Augustine, Ambrose |
| 53 | *Itaque, caro, fortissime* | General Notebook. Cf. Ambrose, Jerome, Rufinus, Origen, Eusebius of Caesarea |

| No. | St Patrick | Specific Topics |
|-----|------------|-----------------|
| 54 | | Councils on *crimina* as barring ordination. cf also Jerome, Augustine, Origen. |
| 55 | | *Consolatio, humiliasti.* cf Augustine, Jerome, Hilary, Cassian, Ambrose, Eusebius Gallicanus, Pacian, Paulinus of Nola, Chromatius, Caesarius of Arles, Pelagius, Cyprian |
| 56 | | Confession 12 and 13. *Quis me stultum excitavit.* cf Augustine, Hilary |
| 57 | | Confession 40. *Indigentem, Desiderantem.* cf Augustine, Prosper |
| 58 | | Confession 56, Letter 5: *pro quo legationem fungor. Donavit me. Transtulit. Aptare.* cf Augustine, Prosper, John Chrysostom |
| 59 | | *Quod Deus promittit, Ipse facit:* Confession 38-41, Letter 11. cf Prosper, Augustine, Paulinus |

| No. | St Patrick | Specific Topics |
|-----|-----------|-----------------|
| 60 | | *Sapientia,* obedience, continence. cf Augustine, Prosper, Pelagius, Jerome |
| 61 | | Scripture in Patrick: I |
| 62 | | II |
| 63 | | III |
| 64 | | IV |
| 65 | | re Confession: Patrick's Credal Statement (A) |
| 66 | | re Confession: Patrick's Credal Statement (B) |
| 67 | | Letter excommunicating Coroticus I |
| 68 | | Letter excommunicating Coroticus II |
| 69 | | Translation of Confession and Letter (i) |
| 70 | | Translation of Confession and Letter (ii) |
| 71 | | Varia on a theme of *indoctus, sapientia, ignorantia, didici* |
| 72 | | Varia re God's protection of him and grace; his relation to his homeland and to Gaul |
| 73 | | Varia on his personality and spirituality |

NOTE: Notebooks Nos. 61-73 do not come under the card index of references.


### III. Various other Patristic authors cited in the notebooks to whom a special place is not assigned in the Indices

| | |
|---|---|
| Ambrosiaster | Notebook No. 45 |
| Eusebius of Caesaria | Notebook No. 53 |
| Eusebius Gallicanus | Notebook No. 55 |
| Gregory Illiberitanus | Notebooks Nos. 45, 46 |
| Irenaeus | Notebook No. 45 |
| Palladius | Notebook No. 44 |
| Theophilus of Antioch | Notebook No. 45 |

# Indices

# I *Index Locorum Sacrae Scripturae*

**V.T.** Genesis (Gn)

| | Patricius |
|---|---|
| cf 3:5 | 236:1-2 |
| 12:1 | 256:8-9 |
| 12:10; 14:54 | 240:19 |
| cf 26:5 | 235:9-10 |
| 37:21 | 242:6-7 |
| cf 41:34 | 251:8 |

Exodus (Ex)

| | |
|---|---|
| 3:11 | 245:16-17 |
| 4:10 | 238:8 |
| cf 20:6 | 235:9-10 |
| | 249:21-22 |
| 20:17, 13 | 256:1 |

Deuteronomy (Dt)

| | |
|---|---|
| cf 5:10; 7:9-10 | 249:21-22 |
| 5:21, 17 | 256:1 |
| 10:17 | 252:1 |
| | cf 240:21 |
| 23:21; 24:15 | 243:22 |
| cf 28:26 | 252:14-16 |
| 28:48 | 244:6 |
| cf 32:15 | 235:9 |

Ruth (Rt)

| | |
|---|---|
| 3:13 | 252:18 |

1 Samuel (1 S)

| | |
|---|---|
| cf 3:7 | 235:17– 236:1 |
| 12:2 | 250:3-4 |
| | 250:23-24 |
| cf 12:3 (VL) | 250:20-21 |
| | 250:23-24 |

2 Samuel

| | |
|---|---|
| 7:18 | 245:16-17 |

1 Kings (1K)

| | |
|---|---|
| cf 3:9 ff | 236:1-2 |
| 14:11; 16:4 | 252:16 |

2 Kings

| | |
|---|---|
| 17:12 | 248:7 |
| 17:18 | 249:19 |

1 Chronicles (Ch)

| | |
|---|---|
| cf 17:16, 26 | 236:3-5 |
| cf 21:3 | 243:22 |
| cf 29:12 | 251:27-28 |

2 Chronicles

| | |
|---|---|
| 6:37 | 236:5 |
| | 245:8 |
| cf 20:6 | 251:27-28 |
| cf 29:10 (LXX) | 235:11-12 |
| cf 36:15-16 | 248:12 |

Nehemiah (Ne=2 Ezra)

| | |
|---|---|
| cf 11:25 | 251:8 |

Tobit (Tb)

| | |
|---|---|
| 4:20 | 240:2 |
| cf 8:5 (13:4.7) | 235:7 |
| 12:7 | 236:24-5 |
| 13:4 | 235:12 |
| cf 13:6 | 237:9 |
| 13:7 | 236:5 |
| | 245:8 |

Job (Jb)

| | |
|---|---|
| cf 2:10 | 245:20-21 |
| cf 4:3-4 | 249:31-32 |
| cf 4:13 | 242:16 |
| 18:21 | 235:7 |
| 20:15.16.26 | 255:20-22 |
| cf 27:6 | 244:23-24 |
| 38:21 | 246:8-9 |

| | | |
|---|---|---|
| | 3:13 | 247:3 |
| | 3:16 | 238:15 |
| | | |
| | 1 John (1 Jn) | |
| | 2:1 | 243:16 |
| | 2:17 | 253:1-2 |
| | 3:14 | 256:3 |
| | 3:15 | 256:2 |
| | 3:16 | 243.6 |
| cf | 3:20 | 245:5-6 |
| | | |
| | Revelations (Rv) | |
| | 2:23 | 252:5 |
| | 5:11 | 249:21-22 |
| | 6:15-16 | 237:10-11 |
| cf | 11:5 | 253:4 |
| | 19:5 | 238:23 |
| | 20:10 | 258:29 |
| | 21:4 | 258:19-20 |
| | 21:8 | 258:19-20 |
| | 22:5 (21:4) | cf 252:21-22 |
| | | 258-12-13 |
| | 22:15 | 258:19 |

# II *Index Auctorum*

**AM** Ambrosius      Patricius
Dav *De apologia prophetae*
    *David*

| | |
|---|---|
| 1, 9, 48: 47 | 235, 14-15 |

  fi *De fide ad Gratianum*

| | |
|---|---|
| 1, 1, 8 | 236, 22b |
| 1, 67 | 236, 12-13b |
| 2, 85; 34 | 236, 10b |

 inc *De incarnationis*
    *dominicae sacramento*

| | |
|---|---|
| 1, 89f | 236, 9 |

  Lc *Expositio Evangelii*
    *Secundum Lucam*

| | |
|---|---|
| 5, 55 | 235, 14-15 |

 off *De officiis*
    *ministrorum*

| | |
|---|---|
| cf 1, 140; 2, 144; | |
| 3, 65 | 249, 5-6 |

 pae *De Paenitentia*

| | |
|---|---|
| 2, 38; ibid. 28; 40; | |
| 41; 53 | 235, 14-15 |
| 2, 73 | 254, 2 |
| 2, 92 (cf 73: 91) | 257, 21 |

  Ps *Explanatio super*
    *Psalmos XII*

| | |
|---|---|
| Ps 37, 2; 31 | 235, 14-15 |
| Ps 37, 10 | 257, 21 |
| Ps 39, 23 | 249, 5-6 |

118 Ps *Expositio de Psalmo*
    *CXVIII*

| | |
|---|---|
| 118, 4, 11 | 235, 9 |
| cf 118, 5, 17 | 235, 14-15 |
| 118, 9, 14 | 244, 8-9 |
| cf 118, 10, 34 | 239, 6 |
| 118, 15, 20 | 253, 5-6 |
| cf 118, 17, 35 | 236, 2 |

 sa *De sacramentis*

| | |
|---|---|
| 1, 2, 8 | 249, 5-6 |

 sp *De Spiritu Sancto*

| | |
|---|---|
| 2, 4 | 236, 22b |

**AN**
Bob *Fragmenta theologica*
    *Arriana e codice*
    *Bobiensi rescripto*

| | |
|---|---|
| 17 (CC87, 256 (*V197*) | |
| =PL13, 104B) | 236, 9.10 |

**AR** Arnobius
 cfl *Conflictus Arnobii*
    *catholici cum Sera-*
    *pione Aegyptio*

| | |
|---|---|
| 1, 11 | 236, 9 |

**AU** Augustinus

| | |
|---|---|
| cf *Confessiones* | 243, 24– |
| cf 2, 3 | 244, 2 |
| 4, 16-31 | 249, 9-10 |
| 7, 10 (cf 10, 6-8) | 243, 6-9 |
| 7, 11; 11, 13 | 236, 10 |
| 10, 27; 37 | 235, 14-15 |
| 10, 29 | 239, 2-3 |
| | 239, 15-16 |

Chr *De gratia Christi et*
    *de peccato originali*

| | |
|---|---|
| cf 26; 45 | 238, 23 |
| 31 | 236, 3-4 |
| | 245, 13 |
| | 247, 3-4 |
| cf 31 | 256, 7-8 |
| | 256, 21-3 |

---

*NOTE: The patristic sigla for authors and titles (extreme left margin) are taken from H. J. Frede, *Kirchenschriftsteller. Verzeichnis and Sigel.* Beuron 1981 (Vetus Latina. Die Reste der altlateinischen Bibel 1, 1), and the *Aktualisierungshefte* thereto, 1984 (Band 1/1A) and 1988 (1/1B). The patristic citations are taken from the most recently available critical editions, or otherwise from J. P. Migne, *Patrologia Latina* (1844-1855). Biblical references with an asterisk denote 'an exegesis of this text'.

# III *Index Conciliorum*